Citizenship and Moral E(

Citizenship offers young people opportunities to engage both actively and critically with a wide range of fascinating, provocative and controversial issues. Preparing young people for life in a liberal democracy and equipping them to deal in the marketplace of ideas can be a much more challenging and rewarding task than simply preparing them for a life in work.

Citizenship and Moral Education aims to give teachers the concepts and strategies they need to contribute to children's moral, ethical and political development, and the resources required to reflect in depth on values education. Clearly written, concise and informative, the book is divided into three sections:

- Part One brings to the surface a number of fundamental questions about Citizenship and Moral Education: why are these subjects important? What values are they based on and what do they seek to achieve in the context of the school?
- Part Two examines the place of Citizenship and Moral Education in the curriculum. In particular, the links with critical literacy, the Arts, the Humanities and RE/PSHE are explored as ways of developing empathy, imagination, social engagement, personal identity and values.
- Part Three addresses issues of pedagogy and practice: how should these subjects be taught and assessed?

This timely, stimulating and thought-provoking book will be valuable reading for teachers, student-teachers and other classroom professionals.

J. Mark Halstead is Professor of Education and Head of the Department of Community and International Education, University of Huddersfield, UK.

Mark A. Pike is a Senior Lecturer in the School of Education, University of Leeds, UK, and a member of the Centre for Citizenship and Human Rights in Education.

Citizenship and Moral Education

Values in action

J. Mark Halstead and
Mark A. Pike

Routledge
Taylor & Francis Group

LONDON AND NEW YORK

First published 2006
by Routledge
2 Park Square, Milton Park, Abingdon, Oxon OX14 4RN

Simultaneously published in the USA and Canada
by Routledge
270 Madison Ave, New York, NY 10016

Routledge is an imprint of the Taylor & Francis Group, an informa business

© 2006 J. Mark Halstead & Mark A. Pike

Typeset in Times New Roman by
Keystroke, Jacaranda Lodge, Wolverhampton
Printed and bound in Great Britain by
MPG Books Ltd, Bodmin, Cornwall

British Library Cataloguing in Publication Data
A catalogue record for this book is available from the British Library

Library of Congress Cataloging in Publication Data
A catalog record for this book has been requested

ISBN10: 0–415–23242–2 (hbk)
ISBN10: 0–415–23243–0 (pbk)
ISBN10: 0–203–08859–x (ebk)

ISBN13: 978–0–415–23242–5 (hbk)
ISBN13: 978–0–415–23243–2 (pbk)
ISBN13: 978–0–203–08859–3 (ebk)

Contents

Abbreviations

AGC	Advisory Group on Citizenship
DfEE	Department for Education and Employment
DfES	Department for Education and Skills
EAL	English as an Additional Language
ICT	Information and Communication Technology
LEA	Local Education Authority
Ofsted	Office for Standards in Education
PSHE	Personal, Social and Health Education
QCA	Qualifications and Curriculum Authority
RE	Religious Education
SCAA	School Curriculum and Assessment Authority

Introduction

It is an especially exciting and challenging time to be involved in the teaching of Citizenship and Moral Education in schools. Children and young people have opportunities to engage with a range of fascinating, complex, provocative and controversial moral and political issues which concern the ways in which they live and the society they live in. In the UK, the introduction of Citizenship as a new subject on the curriculum has prompted considerable debate about what schools should teach. What *should* children and young people learn at school? There is a growing recognition that schools should prepare children for *life* and not simply *work*. Preparing someone for *living* rather than *working* is a weighty responsibility; it is, perhaps, a simpler task to consider the level of numeracy or literacy a person may require in order to perform certain forms of employment. But how should children live? How should they be prepared to live? Which values should children have? How should they be taught to behave? Preparing children for life in a liberal democracy and equipping them to deal wisely in the marketplace of ideas may be a rather more challenging task than that of preparing them for work within a capitalist economy. After all, an astonishing variety of goods is currently on offer.

Moral Education is a vital and unavoidable aspect of Citizenship because dispositions and values, as well as skills and knowledge, are to be fostered. Understanding the values of a liberal democracy or how the electoral system works is one thing but teaching children to 'believe in' these ways of living is another matter and raises a number of questions. Moral ambiguity certainly surrounds the requirement to assess active citizenship. Does the State have the right to be involved in the lives of its citizens in such a way? And what role does the State have in the promotion and inculcation of certain values or dispositions? If these are different to those of the child's family what happens then? Should schools teach children values, and if so which values should be taught and how should they be taught? We argue here that schools and teachers cannot help teaching children about how to live and that there are certain values which schools have the obligation to teach children as they contribute to the well-being of all. We examine where these values come from, how they can be taught and where they can be integrated into the curriculum.

Citizenship and Moral Education are areas where many teachers may experience fairly high levels of anxiety and there may be several reasons for this. Perhaps above all there is a feeling that in approaching these topics teachers are treading on dangerous ground. They do not want to give offence, and are aware that the values of the home may not be the values of the school. Indeed, there may be widely divergent expectations relating to moral and civic education on the part of all those with a legitimate interest in what goes on in schools. But teachers also realise that they cannot wash their hands of these matters either. Society expects schools to contribute to the moral and civic education of the young, and the teaching of Citizenship is now a legal requirement. Teaching Citizenship entails the promotion of values as well as specific forms of activity and deals with highly sensitive and deeply provocative issues. It addresses the very heart of what education is about and how it should be accomplished.

This book is designed to support educational decision-makers, school managers, teacher trainers, new and experienced teachers, researchers, student teachers, inspectors, school governors and general readers as they wrestle with these issues. In particular, the book offers a distinctive contribution to debates about Citizenship and Moral Education by paying close attention to underlying principles and values, by emphasising the links between citizenship and education in morality, by stressing the contribution of the Arts and Humanities in particular, and by drawing attention throughout the book to the need for critical reflection. Topics which have already been covered effectively elsewhere (including the links between Citizenship and Special Needs, Science and Environmental Education and ICT) are only touched on lightly as this has allowed us to concentrate more fully on what we perceive to be the key issues. The book is designed for all those with an interest in children's moral and political development and in the way that moral and civic values are passed on from one generation to the next. Although most of the examples are drawn from British secondary education, the emphasis on theory and underlying principles means that the book will be of interest and practical use to a much wider audience, including international readers with an interest in comparative approaches.

At the risk of some oversimplification but in order to aid readers, we might indicate that the first part of this book (Chapters 1–3) concerns the *why* and the *what*, the second part (Chapters 4–7) is about the *where* and the third (Chapters 8–11) is about the *how*. Firstly, in addressing the *why* and the *what* we consider the specific values to be taught and why they should be taught. We seek to answer questions such as: What is 'Citizenship'? What is 'Moral Education'? Why should these subjects be taught? Why has Citizenship been introduced as a compulsory subject at this time? What are the philosophical roots which underpin the current formulation and teaching of Citizenship? The context is provided and concepts are explained which underpin the teaching of Citizenship and Moral Education in schools. Secondly, we evaluate the curriculum or *where* Citizenship and Moral Education should be taught with special reference to the Arts and the Humanities. Thirdly, we address the *how* and turn to matters of pedagogy: How should one teach? How should learning in this area be achieved? How can it be assessed? How should it be 'delivered' in school?

In Chapter 1 we explore the concepts of citizenship and morality, and outline their recent historical development in the English school curriculum. We argue that citizenship provides the unifying force that enables people from different beliefs and backgrounds to live together co-operatively in spite of differing allegiances, opinions, priorities and tastes. Living together as citizens requires a framework of shared political and civic values, and we argue in Chapter 2 that political liberalism provides this framework without impinging unduly on the freedom of citizens to pursue their own vision of the good. However, children need opportunities to learn not only political and civic values but also personal moral values if they are to become mature moral citizens, capable of meeting the moral challenges they face in their ordinary lives. Moral Education is therefore a necessary supplement and counterbalance to Citizenship Education, and indeed it provides a basis from which the ethical appropriateness of laws and political decisions can be judged. Chapter 3 discusses the aims of Citizenship Education, which are analysed under three headings: to help children to understand their role as citizens, to develop a commitment to this role in practice, and ultimately to engage in critical reflection on the rights and responsibilities associated with this role. The aims of Moral Education similarly involve the development of moral understanding, moral commitment and action, and moral autonomy and critical reflection.

In Chapter 4 we look at the contribution of critical literacy to Citizenship, including the development of the skills of communication and discernment, and also examine the relationship between language, identity and values. In Chapters 5 and 6 we argue that it is in the Arts and the Humanities that students are most likely to encounter issues relating to their own role as citizens and moral agents, and also that these two domains develop empathy, imagination, social engagement and a broad understanding of moral and civic issues. In Chapter 7 we show that Citizenship and PSHE have much in common in both content and approach, but we argue that it is justifiable to keep a form of Moral Education outside these subjects (perhaps within Religious Education, for example) since Moral Education provides the resources for identifying and critiquing unjust laws or oppressive political action.

In Chapter 8 we sketch seven models of Citizenship provision in schools and argue that a combination of discrete and integrated provision is most likely to be successful, so long as decisions about integration are based not on convenience but on which subjects have the greatest capacity to provide good citizenship lessons. We also look at communication and ICT skills in Citizenship, and the teaching of controversial issues. The different ways that children learn values are explored in Chapter 9, including direct instruction, observation, participation and guided action, and reflection; the parts played by teacher example, the hidden curriculum, the ethos of the school, school rituals and the school environment must not be underestimated. In Chapter 10, we consider the morality of assessing citizenship, and warn of the danger that assessment might lead to an overemphasis on the aim of producing informed citizens at the expense of the aim of producing committed, autonomous citizens who play an active part in their communities. Finally, in Chapter 11 we set out some of the contemporary challenges facing Citizenship and Moral Education: the need for teachers and other adults to demonstrate respect in their dealings with school children; the challenges of implementing social justice in school policy and practice; and the need to prepare children for an uncertain future.

Any book like this is inevitably the product of conversations, discussions and interaction over many years with more people than we can name individually, but we would like to thank all friends and colleagues who have offered both moral encouragement and practical help. In particular, we would like to thank Dr Monica Taylor, who was involved in the early planning of the project and without whom the volume would never have got off the ground; Jenny Lowe, who took on the unenviable task of preparing the Bibliography; Bill Leedham and Dr Jenny Lewis for advice on Humanities and Science Education respectively; Mark Cottingham and John Kershaw for consulting on the manuscript; and our families, whose love, support and intellectual stimulation sustained us through the pressures of writing. The birth of Jeremy Pike while writing provided an important incentive to complete the manuscript. The book is a genuinely co-operative effort, but for those who are interested, primary responsibility for Chapters 1, 2, 3, 7, 9 and 11 lies with Mark Halstead, and for Chapters 4, 5, 6, 8 and 10 with Mark Pike.

Part I

Why Citizenship?
Why Moral Education?

Chapter 1

Concepts and contexts in Citizenship and Moral Education

The concept of citizenship

The concept of citizenship has not always occupied as central a place in life in the United Kingdom as it has in other countries, such as France and the United States. David Miller goes so far as to say that 'citizenship – except in the formal passport-holding sense – is not a widely understood idea in Britain' (2000a, p. 26). However, the coincidence of a number of factors over the last ten years or so has served to raise awareness of the concept of citizenship significantly within the UK. The first of these is the extensive debate among journalists, politicians and academics about the nature of Britishness (see, for example, Crick, 1998a; King, 2005; Modood, 1992; Parekh, 1991), supported by a growing list of publications on citizenship (Callan, 1997; Crick, 2000a, 2001; Demaine, 2004; Lister, 1997; Miller, 2000b). The second factor is a number of recent initiatives for existing and prospective British citizens, including the publication of *Life in the United Kingdom: a journey to citizenship* (Life in the UK Advisory Group, 2004) and proposals such as citizenship classes and tests for immigrants, formal citizenship ceremonies and identity cards. The third is the introduction of Citizenship as a core subject in the National Curriculum in secondary schools, with which the present chapter is centrally concerned.

But what exactly is citizenship and how should the concept be interpreted? At its most basic level, 'citizenship' refers to membership of a state or country or similar settled political community. However, there are layers of complexity even within this ostensibly simple definition. First, we need to clarify precisely what community or communities are referred to in the definition: in other words, what are we citizens of? Secondly, we need to clarify what benefits citizenship offers and what rights and duties the term 'membership' implies. What does a country expect of its citizens? Is it this membership that gives citizens their primary identity? How far does the loyalty demanded of citizens extend? Let us look more closely at these two issues.

With regard to the first point, citizenship since the late eighteenth century has been associated particularly with the nation-state. It is almost universally the nation-state that identifies individuals as citizens, usually on the basis of parentage or place of birth; that produces documents confirming citizenship; that regulates whether and how immigrants, refugees and other 'aliens' may be granted citizenship; and that defines the rights to which citizens are entitled. However, the sovereignty of the nation-state is gradually being eroded and challenged: externally, by economic, political, military and environmental factors which are global or at least international; and internally, by regional and local nationalisms and the increasing ethnic diversity of most modern states. It is probably going too far to extend the concept of citizenship, as do Engle and Ochoa, to the relationship of individuals to 'their families, their religious institutions, the workplace [and] the school' (1988, p. 17), though it is true that each of these institutions can make substantial demands on individuals' loyalty and can be organized more or less democratically. But it is the use of the language of citizenship to refer to loyalties that cross the boundaries of nation-states that is becoming increasingly common nowadays. 'European citizenship' was recognized as a legally meaningful concept in the Maastricht Treaty of 1993, though we are told EU citizenship is not intended to replace national citizenship (cf. Davies and Sobisch, 1997; Hoffmeister, 2004). Many Muslims consider themselves to be citizens primarily of the *umma*, the worldwide community of believers, and many Christians believe themselves to be citizens first and foremost of God's Kingdom (see Chapter 6); in such cases loyalty to a *political* entity is secondary. 'Global citizenship' is more of a rhetorical term that draws attention to human interrelatedness and interdependence as well as to universal rights and responsibilities (Demaine, 2004; Ibrahim, 2005; Lynch, 1992; Oxfam, 1997). The claims made on a citizen's loyalty by both international and devolved communities may certainly lead to a more multilayered understanding of political identity, as each adds a further layer of civil, political and social dimensions. At best, such multiple citizenship may provide an enriched understanding of what citizenship is. However, there are also a number of problems: loyalties may be in conflict, especially where the different groups to which the citizen is attached have divergent purposes; loyalties may be diluted, when there are different communities making equal claims on the individual citizen; and in particular, the citizen's primary loyalty may no longer be towards the nation-state.

With regard to the 'membership' sense of citizenship, citizenship is normally thought of as providing a unifying force that enables people from different beliefs and backgrounds to live together. Beiner, for example, presents the problem of defining citizenship as a matter of identifying what exactly it is that 'draws a body of citizens together into a coherent and stably organised political community, and keeps that allegiance durable' (1995, p. 1). In the annual British Council lecture for 2004, Gordon Brown spoke of British citizenship in terms of 'rediscovering the shared values that bind us together' – values such as liberty, civic duty, public service, fair play, local democracy – and 'creating a shared national purpose' (Brown, 2004). Miller sees citizenship as providing the 'reference point from which [different citizens'] claims on the state can be judged' (2000b, p. 41). For Isin and Wood, there are two things that together make up citizenship: a set of shared cultural, symbolic and economic practices, and a set of civil, political and social rights and duties (1999, p. 4). These two dimensions of citizenship merit closer investigation.

The first dimension, the shared cultural and other practices, draws attention to the fact that citizenship in the nation-state is inevitably tinged with the national culture, whether this finds expression in language, religion, history or tradition, or indeed all four (Kymlicka, 1999, pp. 94–7; Miller, 2000a, pp. 31–3). Others have suggested that citizenship may also involve issues to do with the arts, sports, leisure, the environment and technology. However, too strong an emphasis on national culture may lead to something like the 'Tebbit cricket test', according to which people have the right to full citizenship only if they conform to cultural preconditions (cf. Andrews, 1991, p. 13). This narrow view of citizenship is increasingly problematic in a multicultural society, especially when it is assumed that one's primary identity is derived from one's citizenship. In a society where Christians, Muslims, Sikhs, Hindus, Jews, Buddhists, non-believers and others live side by side, it is likely that the number of cultural practices that they have in common will be limited. Hirsch's notion of 'cultural literacy' (Hirsch, 1987) may be perceived as culturally oppressive, at least if it is understood crudely as an argument that minority groups should conform more closely to the culture of the majority for the sake of social cohesion (see Chapter 5 below). Certainly some minority groups in the UK are feeling this oppression in the debates about the failings of multiculturalism following the London bombings of 2005. There are many potential problems for minority groups if citizenship is tied too closely to particular forms of culture (cf. Halstead 1995a, 1995b, 2003). Some minority groups do not even share the economic assumptions of the majority (for Muslim attitudes to charging and paying interest, for example, see Fahim Khan, 1995; Mannan, 1986). It is for these reasons that the British citizenship tests are considered by some Muslims to be an attempt 'to impose western values on Muslims' (Jassat, 2003, p. 1) and that Muslims are campaigning for their primary identity to be defined in religious terms rather than in terms of their citizenship or their place of origin (Halstead, 2005b, pp. 145–6).

The second dimension of citizenship, the rights and duties of citizens, is in many ways less controversial. Conover *et al.* (1999) report from a focus-group based study some fifteen years ago that British people tend to think of citizenship in these terms anyway. In 1950, T. H. Marshall classified the rights of citizens into three categories, the civil, the political and the social, and his discussion has formed the backbone of much thinking about citizenship for over half a century (see, for example, Bulmer and Rees, 1996; Crick, 2000a, pp. 7–8; Davies *et al.*, 1999, pp. 2–3; Miller, 2000b, p. 44). By 'civil rights', he means those rights that are necessary to individual freedom (including the right to property, to trial by jury and so on), by 'political rights' he means the right to participate in political power by voting and in other ways, and by 'social rights' he means welfare rights, health care and education and the right to share in the social heritage, the economic structures and the civilized life of society. Corresponding to the rights is a set of duties that are incumbent on all citizens. Thus civil rights are balanced by the obligation to keep the law and more generally to demonstrate a set of civil virtues in one's life, such as honesty, decency and self-respect (White, 1996). Political rights are balanced by the duties one has to one's country. Michael Walzer includes the following in his list of the things a country can legitimately expect of its citizens: commitment or loyalty; defence in time of war; civility and obedience to the law; tolerance; and active participation in political life (1980, pp. 54–67). Social rights are balanced by the duty to help others in society through voluntary activity, community service and other forms of active citizenship (cf. Crick, 2000a, p. 7; Twine, 1994). But the citizen's duties may in turn be counterbalanced by the right to protest (if one considers taxation unjust, for example) or the (limited) right to be a conscientious objector (if a war offends one's most fundamental beliefs).

The concept of 'active citizenship', which is integral to the Citizenship curriculum in schools, is itself a complex one (Linsley and Rayment, 2004; Potter, 2002). It may imply that the citizen is actively involved in 'shaping the way his or her community functions' (Miller, 2000a, p. 28), but it may also conjure up caricatures of the 'good-hearted, property-owning patriot who serves as an unpaid JP if asked' (Ignatieff, 1991, p. 26) or of the bicycle-riding anti-foxhunting campaigner who is 'a bit of a busybody keeping the neighbours in line' (Phillips, 1991, p. 77). More seriously, active citizens may be people who try 'to change unjust laws, . . . to democratise voluntary bodies, even [to participate in] the occasional demo and aggressive non-violent protest' (Crick, 2000b, p. 78). Their central concern is active participation in the political, civil and social life of the community, and their actions are based on a sense of their obligations and responsibilities as citizens as well as a commitment to values such as fraternity and the common good. Citizens are equal with respect to these rights and duties, and it is the emphasis on individual freedom, rights and equality that makes this a liberal understanding of citizenship. The underlying values and justification of this approach are explored more fully in Chapter 2 of this volume. However it is recognised that not everyone shares these assumptions, and not everyone chooses to be an active citizen in this sense. People can legitimately choose to find their fulfilment in other directions.

Beyond this broadly liberal conception of citizenship lies a whole range of different perspectives and theoretical approaches to the topic. Many have argued that in a postmodern, global age, Marshall's vision of liberal citizenship is no longer adequate. Isin and Wood (1999), for example, discuss the relationship between citizenship and identity, and argue that our understanding of citizenship has been transformed by recent work on ethnic, sexual, cosmopolitan, technological and other rights and identities. Others have explored the concept of citizenship from the perspective of disability (Marks, 2001), sexuality (Richardson, 2001), youth culture (Blackman and France, 2001), ecology (Clark, 2004) and particularly feminism (Dillabough and Arnot, 2004; Lister, 1997; Yeatman, 2001). It could be argued, however, that what these new approaches provide is not so much a dramatic reconceptualization of citizenship as differing perspectives on its core values, including rights, justice, equality, interdependence, participation and belonging.

It has already been suggested that citizenship provides a unifying force enabling people from different beliefs and backgrounds to live together in spite of widely differing allegiances, opinions and tastes. If citizenship is to achieve this goal, it is clear that some systematic attempt must be made to help the next generation to understand and develop a commitment to their role as citizens. This is what the present volume is all about.

The context of Citizenship Education in England

Although no consistent tradition of education for citizenship in English schools existed in the twentieth century, the initiative to launch Citizenship as a new core subject in the National Curriculum in 2002 with five per cent of secondary schools' curriculum time (and to include Citizenship within PSHE in primary schools) was not without roots. Prior to 1970, political education had been discussed by educational philosophers (Dewey, 1916/2002; Oakeshott, 1956), mentioned in official publications (Ministry of Education, 1949) and sometimes studied at school under the heading of 'Civics' or the 'British Constitution', but there was a general assumption that students would learn about politics mainly through subjects like History (Department of Education and Science, 1967). In 1970, however, the lowering of the voting age to 18 was a significant turning point, for it would seem irresponsible for schools not to prepare children to exercise this new right. But what form should this preparation take? Davies *et al.* (1999, pp. 16–22) identify three main trends in such preparation for citizenship over the next thirty years:

- Political literacy, which was the goal of the Programme for Political Education (supported by the Hansard Society and the Politics Association). The underlying philosophy was to develop political understanding and the skills needed for active citizenship (Crick and Porter, 1978).
- Radical approaches and the conservative backlash. A number of initiatives came to the fore in the 1980s, including Peace Education (Hicks, 1988), World Studies (Heater, 1980), Global Education (Pike and Selby, 1988), environmental education, anti-racist and anti-sexist education and other approaches based on social justice. The backlash against these initiatives, although spearheaded by a very small number of activists (Cox and Scruton, 1984; Marks, 1984; Scruton, 1985) was well placed to influence government policy against them on the grounds that they lacked balance and were politically biased.
- Education for Citizenship, which was the subject of a report by the Speaker's Commission on Citizenship (1990) and was included as one of five cross-curricular themes in the National Curriculum (National Curriculum Council, 1990a). The guidelines issued for Citizenship in 1990 included eight components: community; pluralism; rights and responsibilities of citizens; specific explorations of the family; democracy in action; the citizen and the law; work and employment; and leisure and public services (National Curriculum

Council, 1990b). Though the guidelines have been criticized as ineffective (Beck, 1998, pp. 97–102; Potter, 2002, pp. 18–23), the main reason in our view why they were largely ignored was the pressure on teachers to deliver the newly defined core and foundation subjects of the National Curriculum. However, one outcome was a dramatic increase in the number of publications devoted to citizenship education.

These developments have been well documented elsewhere (Batho, 1990; Davies *et al.*, 1999; Frazer, 2000; Heater, 2001; Kerr, 1999) and will not be explored in more detail here.

The establishment of the Advisory Group on Education for Citizenship and the Teaching of Democracy under the chairmanship of Professor Bernard Crick in 1997 and the publication of that group's report a year later (AGC, 1998) mark an important turning point in the history of Citizenship Education in England. The Advisory Group set out a clear definition of 'effective education for citizenship' consisting of three elements – social and moral responsibility, community involvement and political literacy – each of which involves knowledge, skills and values. It also set out a flexible framework for the effective delivery of Citizenship Education, which it recommended should be made statutory. A further report (Advisory Group for Education, 2000) made similar recommendations for sixteen- to nineteen-year-olds in education and training.

The Advisory Group's work led directly to a revision of the National Curriculum to incorporate Citizenship Education explicitly for the first time. In primary schools, Citizenship became part of a non-statutory framework for Personal, Social and Health Education (PSHE) from August 2000, and in secondary schools it became a new statutory foundation subject for students aged eleven to sixteen from September 2002. Guidance at primary level sets out four components for PSHE and Citizenship, one of which is 'preparing to play an active role as citizens'. Many examples and suggestions are given of ways to take citizenship work forward, and a whole-school approach is recommended (QCA, 2000a). At secondary level, National Curriculum documentation sets out programmes of study and attainment targets for Key Stages 3 and 4, based on three aspects of citizenship:

- becoming informed citizens;
- developing skills of enquiry and communication;
- developing skills of participation and responsible action.

(QCA/DfEE, 1999a, pp. 6, 14–15, 31)

By the end of Key Stage 4 (i.e. age sixteen), the anticipated attainment levels for the majority of students are described as follows:

Pupils have a comprehensive knowledge and understanding of: the topical events they study; the rights, responsibilities and duties of citizens; the role of the voluntary sector; forms of government; provision of public services;

and the criminal and legal systems. They obtain and use different kinds of information, including the media, to form and express an opinion. They evaluate the effectiveness of different ways of bringing about change at different levels of society. Pupils take part effectively in school and community-based activities, showing a willingness and commitment to evaluate such activities critically. They demonstrate personal and group responsibility in their attitudes to themselves and others.

(QCA/DfEE, 1999a, p. 31)

A detailed curriculum model for Citizenship has not been prescribed, and many decisions about the delivery of the subject have been left to the professional judgement of schools. Different models are described in Chapter 8. However, non-statutory guidance emphasizes links with other subjects while also recognizing that discrete provision for citizenship and/or whole-school or suspended-timetable activities will be needed in order to ensure coverage of topics (like political literacy) not found elsewhere in the school's curriculum. It is clearly recognized that Citizenship involves experiences in both formal and hidden curriculum, and emphasis is placed on students' active involvement in the life of the school and the local community (QCA, 2001a). Sample schemes of work have been drawn up with suggested learning activities, ideas for developing active student participation and a Teacher's Guide for a series of topics (QCA, 2001b, 2002a, 2002b; see also www.standards.dfes.gov.uk/schemes). The Department for Education and Skills (DfES) has also set up a Citizenship website, with details of resources, school case studies and curriculum development projects carried out by the Citizenship Foundation, CSV and other voluntary organizations working in Citizenship education (www.dfes.gov.uk/citizenship). The Qualifications and Curriculum Authority has produced exemplification of assessment issues in Citizenship (www.qca.org.uk), and the Office for Standards in Education has produced a framework for the inspection of Citizenship, which clarifies the standards that are expected in the subject (www.ofsted.gov.uk).

A number of other initiatives have been launched to support the work of Citizenship in schools. New PGCE programmes in Citizenship have been set up by the Teacher Training Agency (TTA) in some university education departments. A subject organisation, the Association for Citizenship Teaching (ACT) has been established, with its own journal and annual conference. Voluntary sector organizations have been funded to provide additional resources where a need has been identified; for example, the Institute for Citizenship has produced a teaching resource in Citizenship Education for young people with special educational needs. Funds have also been allocated to support medium- and long-term research into the impact of Citizenship Education. The Department for Education and Skills commissioned the National Foundation for Educational Research (NFER) to undertake an eight-year longitudinal study of students who began secondary school in 2002 (and who were thus the first students to receive the full statutory provision of Citizenship Education) (Kerr et al., 2003). In 2005 the NFER completed an evaluation of the Post-16 Citizenship Development Programme, run by the Learning and Skills Development Agency as a pilot scheme to find out the best ways of delivering Citizenship Education at 16 plus. A Citizenship Research Synthesis Group was set up in 2002 (based at Bristol), with the initial aim of reviewing the impact of Citizenship Education on the provision of schooling, and the implications for teacher education (Deakin Crick *et al.*, 2004, 2005). International comparisons have also made a significant contribution to the development of Citizenship in the UK (Hahn, 1998; Ichilov, 1998; Smith and Print, 2003). Perhaps the most important international research project in this area has been the International Association for the Evaluation of Educational Achievement (IEA) Civic Education Study, which looked at ways in which young people are prepared for their role as citizens in democracies (Torney-Purta *et al.*, 1999, 2001). The English data included, for phase one, a qualitative case study of developments in Citizenship Education in England (Kerr, 1999) and, for phase two, a survey of the civic knowledge, understanding, attitudes, engagement and participation of a sample of 14-year-old students (Kerr, 2003).

There have inevitably been various critiques of the report of the Advisory Group on Education for Citizenship and of the subsequent introduction of Citizenship into the National Curriculum. Some are broadly sympathetic to the underlying liberal values (see Chapter 2 for a discussion of these), but question whether adequate recognition has been given to human rights (cf. Osler, 2000), to the complexity of values like tolerance and respect (McLaughlin, 2000), to the need to meet the challenges of social change (Elliott, 2000) or to the conflicting interests and concerns of the various groups currently supporting Citizenship Education (Frazer, 2000, pp. 99–100). Other critiques may be divided into 'conservative' and 'radical' ones (Kristjansson, 2004, pp. 211–12). On the 'conservative' side, critics like James Tooley have argued that the report of the Advisory Group is politically skewed towards a left-wing agenda by failing to problematize terms like 'ethical trading', 'peace-making' and 'sustainable development' (2000, p. 145), and that since there are many resources for developing citizenship outside the school, there is no justification for taking valuable time away from core subjects. He is in any case opposed to 'any attempt to bring higher-order values into the curriculum through government edict' (2000, p. 147). On the 'radical' side are critics who object from a variety of perspectives to the liberal values which we argue in Chapter 2 of this volume underpin current approaches to Citizenship Education in England as in other western countries. Some feminists criticize the way that Citizenship reinforces male dominance (Pateman, 1989, p. 14; cf. Okin, 1992; Phillips, 1991), while postmodernists may argue that since societies are now fragmented and individual identity diffused, the 'individual–society contractual relation (on which citizenship has been said to depend) no longer exists' (Gilbert, 1992, p. 59; cf. Wexler, 1990). We prefer to view Citizenship Education as an opportunity for children and young people to reflect on local, national and global issues, on their own beliefs and values as young citizens, and on the kind of society in which they wish to live.

The concept of morality

There are two main ways of thinking about morality. The first is in response to the question: what kind of person should I be? The second is in response to the question: how should I behave? Of course, the two are linked, and the questions may be rephrased using religious language, but in the first view morality consists of possessing a set of virtues or personal qualities, whereas in the second view morality is a shared set of rules or principles for personal and social behaviour. Both approaches need to be explored if we are to arrive at a rounded view of the concept of morality.

With regard to the question 'What kind of person should I be?' some people may respond that it is best to be oneself, to be true to one's own nature. However, there are three problems with this response. First, there is no agreement over whether human nature is good or bad. Hobbes (1651/1996) maintained that human beings are innately bad, that human nature is nasty and brutish, whereas Rousseau (1762/1911) believed in the innate goodness and innocence of human nature. Christians who accept the doctrine of original sin believe that human nature is in need of redemption. Secondly, the uniqueness of human beings, compared to other forms of life, is related to their ability to make conscious choices (rather than merely following instinct), and they are, in some sense, responsible for their own choices and actions. Existentialists take this to an extreme, arguing that it is impossible to make generalizations about human nature since all individuals are unique and are free to make themselves as they choose; each individual must take responsibility for the kind of person he or she is, and it is inauthentic to look to others for advice or to allow society to seek to shape us into 'good citizens' (cf. Sartre, 1948/1971; cf. Cooper, 1999). Thirdly, most human beings live in groups and therefore need some rules or customs in order to avoid conflict. Hobbes, for example, argues that when human beings live in society, a 'social contract' is needed to restrain their natural tendency to wickedness, and such an agreement is in the best interests of society as a whole (1651/1996). To extend Hobbes' argument, our sense of virtue is constructed by the community in which we live, that community reinforces virtuous behaviour in various ways, and children are encouraged to internalize the virtues by family, school and community. Those who refuse to act co-operatively with the rest of the group probably have less chance of leading a rewarding life. It is easy to see in these circumstances how virtues like loyalty, friendliness, courage, generosity and compassion may come to be valued.

The nature of virtue has been a topic of discussion at least since the time of the ancient Greeks. Aristotle, for example, relates virtue to appropriate forms of reasoning when he says, 'Virtue is a character state concerned with choice, lying in the mean relative to us, being determined by reason and the way the person of practical wisdom would determine it' (Aristotle, 1962, 1107a1). A virtue is an entrenched personal quality that has some significance for human flourishing or well-being. There is no shortage of lists or ways of classifying virtues. Christ's

Sermon on the Mount provides one such list in the Beatitudes (which commend the peacemakers, the merciful, the pure of heart, those of a gentle spirit, and so on; see Matthew 5: 3–12, *New English Bible*), and St Paul provides another in his list of the fruits of the Spirit (love, joy, peace, patience, kindness, goodness, fidelity, gentleness and self-control; see Galatians 5: 22, *New English Bible*). Many religions not only provide lists of virtues and corresponding vices (e.g. Catholicism's four cardinal virtues – prudence, justice, fortitude and temperance – and seven capital vices or 'deadly sins' – pride, avarice, lust, envy, gluttony, anger and sloth), but also offer role models of virtuous behaviour. Of course, the way virtue is understood may vary over time and depending on context, and MacIntyre (1984) argues that it is vital to take account of the cultural context and social tradition within which specific understandings of the virtues have developed. With this in mind, Ungoed-Thomas argues that it is important to identify what he calls 'the first virtues of education' (1996, pp. 151–3): he claims that the first virtue for persons (especially in the context of education) is respect; for the curriculum, truth; for the community, fairness; and for citizenship, responsibility. Others may disagree with the prioritization: some make 'caring' the most important virtue (Gilligan, 1982; Noddings, 1984), some 'love' (Halstead, 2005c; Wilson, 1995). However we rank the virtues, Hume wisely reminds us that 'it is one thing to know virtue, another to conform the will to it' (1739/2000, Book 3, Part 1, section 1). The term 'character', which has become increasingly popular in American approaches to moral education, combines the sum total and distinctive pattern of a person's virtues and enduring traits with the sense that he or she can be counted upon to act in accordance with those traits. In other words, it includes a sense of personal integrity, consistency and steadfastness of purpose (McLaughlin and Halstead, 1999, pp. 134–5; cf. Peters, 1974, pp. 245–51).

The question 'What kind of person should I be?' is essentially about human goodness, whereas the question 'How should I behave?' is at core a matter of knowing right and wrong. Of course, an Aristotelian answer to the second question would be to exercise good sense and do what a virtuous person would do. But for many people, this answer does not provide sufficient guidance; they look for a shared set of rules as guides to moral behaviour. But what rules? How do we know what is right? In our search for an answer, we can distinguish between externally imposed rules, internally imposed rules and rationally determined rules.

Externally imposed rules may come from different sources:

- Religion: All religions have a lot to say about morality, and many provide rules to live by (such as the Ten Commandments or the *shari'ah* or the Golden Rule). However, the moral rules of religions are not in agreement over every particular, and it is clear in any case that morality can stand alone, without the support of religion.
- Law: A growing number of people in the West appear to be taking their perspective on right and wrong from the law, on the assumption that if something is not illegal it is not immoral either. But the relationship between the

law and morality is a controversial one (see Devlin, 1965; Hart, 1963); the legalization of homosexual acts between consenting adults in England in 1967 did simultaneously change the underlying *moral* issues. Evidently the legalization of an action is not the end of the matter morally speaking, and there are differing views about the role of the law in the West in relation to the upholding of moral values.

- Socialization: As has already been seen, children are often expected to conform to community norms and to internalize the rules that older community members agree on or simply take for granted.
- The dominant social class: Marxist ideology argues that the interests of the ruling classes are presented as universal morality, and that those who accept such universal morality are victims of 'false consciousness'.

The problem with having different sets of rules from different sources is that they can't all be right in an absolute sense. So can there be any universal moral rules that are always true? Moral absolutists believe that there are, though they may disagree as to what they are. Moral relativists argue that all moral systems may be equally valid within their own context (Harman and Jarvis-Thomson, 1996). Against absolutism, it is claimed that moral values clearly change over time; slavery, which is morally abhorrent to us, was once almost universally accepted. Against relativism, it is claimed that it is inadequate to say that actions like torturing children may be acceptable in some cultural contexts. There are two possible routes out of this impasse. One is the subjective (or perhaps faith-based) route, which leads one to say something like, 'I don't know whether or not these rules have universal validity, but I know they're right for me'. The other is the rational route, which leads one to say, 'I don't believe we can ever attain absolute certainty in moral matters, but we need to ensure that our moral judgements are as rational as possible'.

Subjectivism covers a range of views. Some people ('emotivists') claim that the basis of moral obligation is to be found in radical personal feelings of approval or disapproval. Hume (1739/2000), for example, argues that moral statements like 'Murder is wrong' are simply a way of reporting one's feeling of disapproval of murder, though he does accept that the similarity of our feelings makes it possible in practice to organize society in line with what makes people happy. Ayer (1936) extends Hume's ideas by arguing that moral statements are simply expressions of happiness or disgust, and that moral debate is futile and meaningless. Others like Moore (1903) have suggested that we intuit certain moral principles and base our moral judgements on them; or that individuals base their moral judgements on the core moral principle of love, asking in any given circumstances what love requires them to do; or that it is the fact that an action is based on a personal code of values that makes it moral. Interestingly, a version of moral subjectivism has underpinned official statements about citizenship and moral education in England. The curriculum guidance document *Education for Citizenship* states that 'pupils should be helped to develop a personal moral code' (National Curriculum Council,

1990b, p. 4), and the discussion document *Spiritual and Moral Development* says that morally educated school leavers should be able to 'articulate their own attitudes and values; . . . develop for themselves a set of socially acceptable values and principles, and set guidelines to cover their own behaviour' (SCAA, 1995, p. 6). A similar philosophy lies behind the Values Clarification approach to moral education that was popular in the US in the 1960s and 1970s (see below; Raths *et al.*, 1966).

Moral reasoning involves the application of rationally justifiable moral principles in a rational way to the specific circumstances of any case where a moral judgement or decision is called for. There are four main moral theories which generate moral principles as part of a rationally structured system. The first is Natural Law, a Christian moral tradition formalized by Thomas Aquinas in the thirteenth century, but based on the philosophy of Aristotle (cf. Finnis, 1980). According to this theory, everything in the world was created with a natural purpose (which is clear from its design), and fulfilling that purpose is the 'good' that we should aim for. For example, since it is natural to want to stay alive, the preservation of life becomes a valid moral principle. The second is Utilitarianism, a theory developed by Bentham (1799/1948) and elaborated by Mill (1863/1970) that maintained that the goodness or badness of an action should be judged on the outcomes: the right thing to do in any situation is the thing that gives the greatest happiness to the greatest number of people. Apart from this general rule, some utilitarians believe that it is possible to construct a system of rules on the basis of the collective experience of happiness or pain in a whole society (Smart and Williams, 1973). The third is Deontology (the science of duty or moral obligation). Kant believed that a moral action is one that is done from a sense of duty (which means being motivated to obey a set of compulsory rules), and that one's moral life is a struggle between one's sense of duty and one's natural inclinations (Kant, 1785/1948). The compulsory rules (or 'categorical imperatives') can be discovered rationally by the universalizability principle: one should only do something if one is prepared for everyone else to do it as well, and for it to be a universal law. For example, one should never lie unless one is prepared to accept that everyone should be free to lie whenever they choose. Kant also stresses the importance of moral imagination, the capacity to imagine oneself on the receiving end of one's own moral decisions. The fourth is Social Justice, and draws on the work of John Rawls in particular. He argued that a just and humane society could best be determined by a group of equal, rational and self-interested individuals making their choice behind a veil of ignorance about their own place in that society; he believed that this situation would generate an appropriate balance between individual freedom on the one hand and justice for the least privileged members of society on the other, because everyone would want some protection against a possible future life of poverty.

There are a number of problems with this heavy dependence on rationality in the moral domain. The first is that moral virtues like altruism, which provide a motivation for some people's moral decisions, don't easily fit into a rational framework. The second is the fact that being in a position to work out the right thing to do does not guarantee that it will actually be done; in other words, without moral motivation and will, moral reasoning may have limited benefits (Haydon, 1999; Straughan, 1999). The third is that 'reason' itself may not be a source of moral wisdom but may in fact be morally neutral: it can be used to plan human suffering (as in the Holocaust) just as much as to promote human well-being. Postmodernist thinkers like Foucault argue that rationality itself has been colonized by the powerful to strengthen their own position and oppress the underclasses. For some, postmodernism has shattered many taken-for-granted 'grand narratives' about shared moral values and universal moral truths. Replacing these 'foundational philosophies' are: a moral domain without signposts; a greater plurality of moral beliefs and practices; an increase in moral uncertainty and scepticism; an ironic, almost playful detachment on the part of some moral thinkers; an increase in single-issue moral campaigns; and a general increase in tolerance of diversity (cf. Bauman, 1993, 1994). MacIntyre (1984) shares many of the postmodernists' misgivings about the way reason has been used by ethical theorists, and sees hope for the future in the moral traditions in the life of communities. Central to the success of local communities are the dispositions or virtues of their members, and so we return to something like the 'virtue theory' of Aristotle, with its emphasis on imitation, habituation and the development of moral sensitivity through guidance and experience rather than training in rational decision-making.

The context of Moral Education in England

For as long as there has been education there has been moral education, and indeed the formation of character and the development of virtue have for many centuries been seen as the very core of the educational endeavour. However, the early history of moral education need not concern us here. As with Citizenship Education, a major turning point in the history of Moral Education in England occurred in (or just a few years before) 1970. Prior to that time, moral education in England, as in many other countries, was tied closely to religious education. Around that time, however, a number of initiatives coincided to set Moral Education on a new path. The Farmington Trust Research Unit was established in 1965 to carry out research into Moral Education (Wilson *et al.*, 1967; Wilson, 1973). The Schools Council Project in Moral Education was set up in 1967, producing both theoretical work and new teaching materials including the *Lifeline* series (McPhail *et al.*, 1972). The *Journal of Moral Education* was founded in 1971, under the sponsorship of the Social Morality Council (later the Norham Foundation). A wide range of approaches to moral education were adopted in schools over the coming years, though it was rarely a timetabled subject (as it became in countries like Canada and Malaysia) on the assumption that good morals were more often 'caught than taught', and it was often seen as primarily the domain of Religious Education (Halstead, 1996, p. 9). Research continued into some of the fundamental problems of moral education, such as moral motivation and whether you can teach children to be good at all (Straughan, 1982, 1988).

This was also a period of intense international interest in moral education, particularly in the US, where two key strategies were developed that were to have a major impact on thinking in England. The first of these was Values Clarification (Raths *et al.*, 1966; Simon *et al.*, 1972), which put forward the view that values must be chosen freely from alternatives after consideration of the consequences and that an individual must cherish, publicly affirm and act on the value, and do so repeatedly. The theory was based on the assumption that it is wrong, particularly in a pluralist society, to seek to impose values on children, and on the belief that children will care more about values which they have thought through and made their own. It has been criticized widely for being rooted in a spurious relativism and for failing to recognize that it is possible to make mistakes in matters of value (Kilpatrick, 1992, ch. 4). Nevertheless, its influence can be seen in England in the Humanities Curriculum Project (Schools Council, 1970), and it may in fact under-lie the approaches of many texts and materials in use in schools (see Chapter 6). The second strategy is the Moral Reasoning approach developed by Kohlberg (1971). Central to this approach is the belief that children should be presented with moral dilemmas and be encouraged to discuss them in a way that helps them to see the inadequacies of their current moral thinking and move them to a higher level (Blatt and Kohlberg, 1975). This approach has dominated research into moral development since the 1970s, but it has been criticized for playing down the social, cultural and religious influences on people's moral values; for underestimating the need to learn basic values before tackling controversies; and for failing to take adequate account of a more feminine ethic of care, responsibility and love (Gilligan, 1982; Noddings, 1984).

Current approaches in England take their rationale from the 1988 Education Reform Act, which requires state schools to provide a balanced and broadly based curriculum, paying attention to the 'spiritual, moral, cultural, mental and physical development of pupils at the school and of society', in order to prepare young people for 'the opportunities, responsibilities and experiences of adult life' (Great Britain Statutes, 1988, p. 1). What really put Moral Education on the official agenda, however, was the statutory requirement in the 1992 Education (Schools) Act that school inspections had to cover the same five areas of pupils' development. Since then, the Office for Standards in Education (Ofsted) has progressively refined its view of what moral development means and in 2004 issued guidelines entitled *Promoting and Evaluating Pupils' Spiritual, Moral, Social and Cultural Development* (Ofsted, 2004b). Official guidance was also forthcoming in a discussion document first issued by the National Curriculum Council in 1993 entitled *Spiritual and Moral Development* (SCAA, 1995), which set out an explicit list of the moral values schools should promote but offered little in the way of concrete guidance on how the values should be taught or what resources were available. In 1996, the National Forum on Values in Education and the Community was set up, which produced a statement of agreed values relating to the self, relationships, society and the environment. A Mori poll confirmed that there was general agreement in society on these values, and they are included in the current National Curriculum handbooks (QCA/DfEE, 1999b, pp. 147–9). These developments clearly have implications for teacher training, but anecdotal evidence (in the absence of research) suggests that training in Moral Education within initial teacher education remains patchy. However, Ofsted reports that pupils' moral development is 'generally good', that schools adopt a 'co-ordinated and consistent approach' and that teachers 'provide for pupils, whether consciously or unconsciously, a moral framework of values' (Ofsted, 2004b, p. 15).

Despite this confidence, many crucial questions remain unanswered. What is distinctive about Moral Education? What do we know for sure about it? What can teachers and what can parents do in the moral domain? What resources and support do they need in order to do it? What constitutes success and failure in Moral Education? What can Moral Education realistically hope to achieve? What is its relation to Citizenship Education? In what areas is further research most urgently needed? (Cf. Taylor, 1996, pp. 9–19.)

Since 1997, there appears to have been a gradual merging of Moral Education with Citizenship, at least in the minds of some government leaders and some academics. Perhaps this is because of a realization that both are concerned with developing pupils' understanding of society's shared and agreed values. Perhaps it is because Moral Education has had to adapt to perceived rapid changes in society (in family life, work patterns, cultural diversity, media power, the rise of terrorism, antisocial behaviour, and so on), and these have been linked with a growing disillusionment among young people with current political processes. Perhaps it is to do with a realization that citizens have moral obligations, that moral virtues and civic virtues are not unconnected, that literacy has both moral and political dimensions (see Chapter 4). For whatever reason, however, the National Curriculum for Citizenship seeks to incorporate Moral Education. Citizenship, we are told, helps pupils to become

> thoughtful and responsible citizens who are aware of their duties and rights. It promotes their spiritual, moral, social and cultural development, making them more self-confident and responsible both in and beyond the classroom. It encourages pupils to play a helpful part in the life of their schools, neighbourhoods, communities and the wider world.
>
> (DfEE/QCA, 1999c, p. 183)

Let us conclude with a note of warning, however. The strong emphasis on moral responsibility here may well be part of the government's political agenda, but if that is to be the extent of Moral Education in the future, it is a very impoverished form of moral education that we are left with. Halstead (2006) argues that morality is a broad concept which would be distorted if taught only or mainly through Citizenship Education. Students need to learn empathy, moral imagination and moral judgement, as well as concepts like love, justice and fairness, and Moral

Education provides the main principles and skills needed if students are to be able to respond critically to the values underpinning Citizenship. If moral values are an essential part of being a person, they should be central to the whole of education, not confined to one small part of the curriculum – and this of course is one reason why we are advocating Citizenship across the curriculum.

Chapter 2

Underlying values in Citizenship and Moral Education

This chapter is written to highlight the fact that values are as central to Citizenship as to Moral Education and to emphasize the need for teachers to become confident in discussing values openly. There is no escaping from values. The decision to provide Citizenship Education in the first place is based on the assumption that it will be valuable for children (and for society as a whole). As we shall see in the next chapter, the selection of aims involves explicit or implicit value judgements, and values permeate every aspect of the planning and the teaching of Citizenship Education. Above all, the subject involves the transmission of values. But what values? It is suggested in this chapter that liberalism provides the most influential framework of fundamental values in the UK, with its focus on freedom, equality and rationality, and that liberal values permeate the curriculum of the common school generally, and the subject of Citizenship in particular. This being so, we shall argue that it is essential for teachers to be aware of core liberal values, to have thought them through, to have debated them with colleagues, to understand their implications for practice, and ultimately to be in a position to justify the values which underpin their work and which they pass on to children and young people.

Before explaining in more detail what we mean by 'liberalism' in the context of Citizenship Education, however, we need to be clear about the term 'values'. This chapter falls into six sections. In the first, we examine the concept of 'values' and argue that the term refers to the principles by which we judge things to be good, right, desirable or worthy of respect. The second examines the role of the school in values development and the complexity of this role in view of the diversity of values in contemporary society. The third section suggests that the best way to understand the values that underpin programmes of Citizenship or Moral Education in any society is to start with an examination of the framework of shared values that holds that society together; in the UK as in other western societies this function is performed by liberal values. The fourth section examines the relationship between liberal values and Citizenship Education, particularly from the perspective of the political, legal and economic dimensions of life. The fifth section examines the relationship between liberal values and Moral Education, particularly with reference to moral reasoning. The final section considers some of the main challenges to liberal theory and argues for a tolerant approach to alternative ideologies in the liberal society.

What are values?

There have been numerous surveys of values over the last twenty years (see, for example, Abrams *et al.*, 1985; Barker *et al.*, 1992; Francis and Kay, 1995), but there is still a lot of disagreement over the concept of 'values' itself. Mary Warnock defines values as 'shared preferences'; she writes: 'What we value is what we either like or dislike . . . The crucial word in this definition is *we*. In speaking of values, there is a presumption that humans . . . *share* the preferences so designated' (1996, p. 46, original emphases).

However, we find Warnock's definition unsatisfactory in two ways. First, it confuses, or at least does not distinguish between, private and public values (we recognize the complexities in this distinction, but it has its uses; cf. Pike 2004d). Private values may be preferences, but are not shared. Raths *et al.* emphasize this personal dimension in their definition of values: 'beliefs, attitudes or feelings that an individual is proud of [and] is willing to publicly affirm' (1966, p. 28); of course, such a definition suits their purposes in arguing for a values clarification approach to moral education. Public values, on the other hand, are shared, but are more fundamental than mere 'preferences', as many writers have recognized. Shaver and Strong, for example, consider values to be 'our standards and principles for judging . . . things to be good, worthwhile or desirable' (1976, p. 15). No community can exist without some shared values in this strong sense, and no community activity (such as teaching or running a school) is possible either. Secondly, Warnock's definition confuses 'values' with 'valuing something'. I may value the comforting presence of my cat on my knee, but this does not make it one of my values. It is true that to talk of the *value* of something (as in the phrase 'value-added') has always been to talk of its worth, and that when we *value* something we are making a high estimate of its worth. However, the term *values* (in the plural) nowadays seems to be used to refer to the criteria by which we make such value judgements, that is, to the principles on which the value judgements are based.

For the purposes of the present volume, we have adapted the following definition from Halstead and Taylor (2000a, p. 3). Values are *principles and fundamental convictions which act as justifications for activity in the public domain and as general guides to private behaviour; they are enduring beliefs about what is worthwhile, ideals for which people strive and broad standards by which particular practices are judged to be good, right, desirable or worthy of respect.* Examples of values are justice, equality, freedom, fairness, happiness, security, truth. Values can therefore be distinguished from related and sometimes overlapping terms like 'virtues' (which are personal qualities or dispositions like truthfulness, generosity, courage, loyalty or kindness) and 'attitudes' (which are acquired tendencies or predispositions to behave in a predictable manner, such as openness, tolerance, respect and freedom from prejudice).

This definition is appropriate for most teachers as a basis for the teaching of Citizenship in the common (state) school, and occupies the middle ground in the debate about whether values are subjective or objective. At one extreme is the view of values as a set of subjective criteria for making judgements. This may be linked to a postmodern, relativist view that no set of values can be shown to be objectively better than another. This view has sometimes been claimed to provide a useful way of resolving disputes over values in culturally plural societies: 'You have your values and I have mine'. At the other extreme is the view of values as absolute, that is, applying everywhere and at all times. In this view, certain human actions are always right or always wrong, irrespective of circumstance. Between the two extremes is the view that certain values, such as human rights or equal opportunities, have some kind of objectivized quality, perhaps because 'some social arrangements and patterns of behaviour promote well-being more than others' (Beck, 1990, p. 3). These values may therefore be explored in a systematic and objective fashion, though it is also acknowledged that they are socially constructed and that the extent to which they are recognized may vary over time and from one group or society to another.

It is important to note that there are different types of values. They are often categorized either on the basis of the ideology which gives rise to them (e.g. liberal, Catholic, Marxist, feminist, evangelical Christian, Islamic or humanist) or on the basis of the different disciplines or departments of life to which they belong (e.g. political, civic, economic, legal, cultural, social, moral, spiritual, artistic, scientific, religious, environmental or health-related). Citizenship is most frequently associated with political, civic, economic and legal values, but we argue in Part Two of this volume that the inclusion of a wider range of values results in an enriched understanding of the possibilities of Citizenship.

The role of the school in values development

Values are woven into the content of Citizenship as much as they are into Moral Education. For example, equal opportunities, democracy, tolerance, fair competition and the rule of law are all values, and those responsible for the teaching of Citizenship want their students to do more than simply understand these values and the part they play in the institutions of our society. They want them in some way to make them their own and to develop a commitment to them in practice. In just the same way, we would be reluctant to call people morally educated if they understood a wide range of ethical theories and understood the need for moral behaviour in society but did not actually behave morally themselves. To be a morally educated citizen, a person must (a) understand key moral principles and their importance, (b) have arrived at that understanding through a process of reflection, rather than being simply indoctrinated, and (c) behave morally in practice. The role of the teacher in both Citizenship and Moral Education therefore involves the transmission of values.

Some teachers may initially feel uncomfortable with this. They may object to any expectation that they will transmit values to students for two reasons: first, that values are an individual's private concern, and the imposition of values on anyone is wrong in principle (this argument is the main justification for the *values clarification* approach to moral education; see Raths *et al.*, 1966); and second, that there is such a diversity of values in contemporary society that it is impossible to find consensus on any particular framework. Warnock, for example, warns of the danger of making sex education 'moralistic in tone' (1979, p. 89). Of course in using the word 'moralistic' here, Warnock is begging the question, because it implies an over-dogmatic approach to morality which is by definition anti-educational. But we believe that it is impossible in practice to impart knowledge about citizenship or morality without some kind of values framework, and that this is not a matter of 'imposition' of values on students. Indeed, there are strong arguments to support the view that learning values (and not just learning *about* values) must be considered an essential part of any programme of Citizenship or Moral Education:

- Some values are essential to any civilized society (such as human rights, tolerance, respect for persons or anti-racism), and students need to learn these.
- However culturally diverse a society is, it cannot be considered a society at all unless its citizens have some values in common. These values are likely to be those that are central to the political institutions of the society (such as democracy and equality before the law), and students need to share these values if they are to have full citizenship and participate in the institutions.
- Some personal qualities are so highly valued in society as a whole that teachers are expected not to be neutral about them. For example, it is not a matter of indifference to most parents whether their children grow up caring or uncaring, responsible or irresponsible, honest or dishonest. These are moral values, but they also form part of a broader understanding of what it is to be a citizen.
- In studying Citizenship, students will inevitably be exposed to a wide range of values, but if there are no opportunities for systematic reflection on and discussion of the values involved, students are more likely to develop their values haphazardly rather than in a rational way.
- If students are not given direct help and guidance in school, but are left to pick up their values as and when they can, this may leave them open to influence or manipulation at the hands of those less concerned for their well-being than the school is. This suggests that the values underpinning Citizenship should be explored and articulated openly, so that teachers may have more confidence in offering guidance to students.

Though the processes of understanding citizenship and morality, and of values development more generally, begin in earliest childhood and go on throughout life, the school is uniquely placed to influence these processes by providing opportunities for discussion, reflection and increasing understanding. The common school has three distinct (and perhaps not always compatible) roles to play in values development. The first is that as a public institution it should reflect the values on which the society of which it is a part is based. This does not mean that it should present these values uncritically, for developing critical understanding is central to the mission of all schools. But the school has the responsibility to ensure that the influence it exerts is balanced, partly at least because it represents the official view of society. The school's influence may thus help to counterbalance any extreme opinions and values which the student has picked up elsewhere. The more this influence is the result of reflection, open debate and the democratic search for shared values, the more justifiable it is in seeking to shape children's developing values. The second role is to fill in gaps in students' knowledge and understanding, including knowledge of the importance of values. Schools are in a strong position to assess students' existing understanding and to adapt their provision in the light of emerging needs. The concept of 'needs' brings us back to the question of values again, because to describe something as a need is to make a positive value judgement about it, and we make such judgements on the basis of our values. The third role of the school, and perhaps the most important, is to help students to choose a rational path through the variety of influences that impinge on their developing values. The voice of the school enters the students' consciousness alongside all the other influences which together form the raw material from which the individual student constructs his or her own civic and moral values; but students need help with sifting, evaluating, synthesizing, appraising and judging the different influences on their values development, and schools are uniquely placed to develop these essential skills. Students are likely to make sense of civic and moral values in different ways (at one extreme, for example, some groups may eschew all political activity including voting on the grounds that 'the powers that be are ordained by God' and in any case they are not citizens of this world), but this need not be a problem from a liberal perspective so long as their decisions are the outcome of rational reflection rather than indoctrination and so long as the public interest is not harmed.

If teachers are to help students to become critically reflective adults with a thought-through commitment to civic and moral values, this implies not only that teachers themselves must have a clear sense of what it is to be critically reflective in the domain of values, but also that they must have a good knowledge of the values that underpin Citizenship and Moral Education, experience of critical discussions of such values, and the ability to relate such values to the differing needs and experiences of children. The remainder of the present chapter is an attempt to aid such reflection.

Core liberal values

If it is part of the role of Citizenship and Moral Education to encourage reflection on and commitment to society's core values, the first step is to identify what those core values are. One way of doing this is through questioning things we normally take for granted in our society, for example:

- Why are people allowed to do things that are generally considered irritating, like telephoning us about double glazing, or trying to make converts on the doorstep?
- When electing members of Parliament, why do we follow the principle of 'one person, one vote' rather than giving more weight to the vote of someone who is very knowledgeable about politics?
- Why are people taxed according to the level of their income rather than, say, the colour of their eyes?

We may answer these questions in various ways, but ultimately the answer to the first question has something to do with freedom, the answer to the second something to do with equality and the answer to the third something to do with rationality. Even if we broaden the range of questions, the same three values of freedom, equality and rationality seem to underpin the answers.

It has been argued elsewhere (see, for example, Halstead, 2005a) that these represent the three fundamental liberal values. Liberalism of course is hard to define because it exists in many different versions; it is perhaps best understood by contrasting it with non-liberal worldviews such as totalitarianism. We adopt a broad understanding of liberalism here, one which encompasses a wide range of political perspectives from conservatism (*pace* Scruton, 1984, pp. 192ff) to certain forms of socialism (cf. Freeden, 1978, pp. 25ff), but at its core is the work of contemporary philosophers like Rawls, Dworkin, Hart, Berlin, Raz, Gutmann, Macedo and Kymlicka. Historically, liberalism has its roots in Protestantism, with which it still has much in common, but philosophically, liberalism may be said to have its origin in the conflict between two core values or principles.

The first of these is individual liberty – freedom from arbitrary external restraints in the pursuit of one's own interests and desires and in the fulfilment of one's potential. The second is the equal right of all individuals to such liberty, which implies an equality of respect for all individuals within the structures and practices of society and a rejection of arbitrary discrimination against any individuals. It rules out the hierarchical ranking of individuals according to which some have a greater claim to freedom than others (as in slavery), and its strongest forms can be seen in attempts to equalize life prospects or distribute wealth and power more equitably. These two values, freedom and equality, exist in a state of tension; the more freedom people have, the less they end up equal, and vice versa. Some liberals have argued that freedom is the more important value (Hayek, 1960; Berlin, 1969), others that equality is (Dworkin, 1978; Gutmann, 1980; Hart, 1984). It is partly this tension which gives rise to the need for a third core liberal value, that of consistent rationality, which ensures that all decisions and actions are based on logically consistent rational justifications, and which rules out the uncritical acceptance of dogma (whether based on authority or revelation).

Taken together, these three values provide the basis for a liberal worldview. Certain forms of human behaviour are ruled out in principle on this worldview, including prejudice, intolerance, injustice and repression. Other forms of human behaviour are considered essential, though ways of putting them into practice may still be hotly debated. The principle of personal autonomy – the freedom to work out a course of action for oneself – depends on the core values of freedom and rationality. The principles of state impartiality and individual tolerance and respect combine the core values of rationality and the equal right of all individuals to liberty; thus the liberal state is expected to show official neutrality on religious matters, together with a respect for the equal freedom of conscience of all individuals unless their religious beliefs are harmful to other individuals or against the public interest. The principle of the just resolution of conflict relates equally to freedom, equality and rationality.

On the basis of these values and principles, it is possible to construct liberal theories of politics, of law, of economics and of ethics. The first three lie at the heart of Citizenship and the last at the heart of Moral Education. Let us look at each a bit more closely.

Liberal values and citizenship

The political and legal domains have always been the most central arenas for liberal debate. Democracy is seen by liberals as the most rational safeguard against tyranny and the best way of guaranteeing the equal right of citizens to determine for themselves what is in their own best interests. Pluralism is seen as the most rational response to diversity within the state. The state is not an end in itself, but 'exists to regulate the competition among individuals for their private ends' (Strike, 1982, p. 5). It provides the means of protecting the public interest and ensuring social justice. Liberalism upholds the rule of law, which exists to prevent harm and to maintain order in society by protecting persons and property. Key liberal causes that are often enshrined in law are human rights (including the rights of women, children and minorities), free speech, opposition to censorship, racial equality, and opposition to the enforcement of private moral values through the criminal law (Hart, 1963).

Rights are central to liberalism. Some rights are fundamental (such as the right to life itself and the right not to be enslaved) in the sense that without them the three core liberal values cannot be achieved. Other rights are established by rational debate as the most appropriate means of ensuring the just resolution of conflict and general human well-being. These rights are open to negotiation even among liberals, and may have to be fought for, even though they involve claims based on liberal ethics. They are often enshrined in, and defined by, law; examples include the right to education, the right to low-cost housing, the right to free medical care and the right to a minimum wage. Often these rights are to do with the definition of roles and relationships and the distribution of power (for example, women's rights, parents' rights). Sometimes the rights are little more than a rhetorical expression of desires and needs, or a preference for particular social goals, such as students' rights and animal rights. A right is only a claim or a demand unless it is built into the social or institutional structure and there is an apparatus for implementing it. It will not usually be invoked except to redress injustice.

Typically, no one conception of the good life is favoured in liberalism, and a vast range of lifestyles, commitments, priorities, occupational roles and life-plans form a marketplace of ideas within the liberal society. Liberalism makes an important distinction between the private and public domains. Religion, for example, is seen as a private and voluntary matter for the individual (though the practice of religion is a moral right based on the core liberal value of individual liberty). Thus the liberal state is expected to show official neutrality on religious matters, together with a respect for individual freedom of conscience; some people have called this 'liberal silence' (cf. Costa, 2004, p. 8). To do otherwise would leave the state open to the charge that it was 'biasing the marketplace of ideas by giving certain metaphysical and religious claims, certain ultimate convictions, the stamp of state authority and legitimacy' (Fishkin, 1984, p. 154). But in the public domain, the liberal state has the responsibility to promote the political values outlined above.

Some major debates within liberal political theory include the extent to which democracy should entail representation (which may satisfy the protection of interests) or participation (which may also contribute to human development); the extent to which political liberalism is necessarily part of a comprehensive liberal worldview, as opposed to an 'overlapping consensus' among different comprehensive worldviews (Rawls, 1993); the compatibility of nationalism with liberal values (cf. Miller, 2000b); the way that civil liberties and state power should be balanced; and the tensions between the right-wing emphasis on stability, non-interference, free enterprise, initiative and merit, and the left-wing emphasis on egalitarianism and the fight against social injustice – in other words the tensions between those who believe people should be rewarded according to their work and their merit and those who believe they should be rewarded according to their need.

Liberal economic theory accepts the holding of private property as legitimate and supports the notion of the free market economy, though the state may intervene to regulate the economy if necessary, to ensure free and fair competition and to prevent harm to others through gross inequalities of wealth and welfare. Liberalism does not, however, require a particular stance with regard to any of the following debates: the debate between those like Hayek (1960) who continue to support the old liberal principle of laissez-faire and more modern liberals who emphasize the need for tighter government control, for example in monetary policy or welfare distribution; the debate between supporters of capitalist free enterprise and those who wish to see a significant redistribution of wealth and income, for example by providing a minimum wage or by progressive taxes; and the debate between those who emphasize the need for free enterprise and efficiency, and those who argue for an increase in industrial democracy.

The relevance of the values and the debates set out in this section to Citizenship in schools is not open to question, and many of the issues touched on here will occupy a central place in any course offered to students.

Liberal values and Moral Education

Liberalism is just as much concerned with ethics as it is with politics and economics, and as such it provides an important basis for Moral Education in schools. However, it does not provide a single unified view of ethical theory. As we noted in Chapter 1, the major division in liberal moral theory comes between those like Bentham and Mill who believe that *good* is of prior importance and who therefore judge the morality of actions and decisions in terms of their consequences, and those like Kant who believe that *right* is of prior importance and who therefore judge the morality of actions and decisions in terms of a set of moral duties. The dominant view in the former category is utilitarianism, which maintains that the justice of institutional and individual action may be measured by its capacity to promote the greatest happiness of the greatest number. The latter category has produced a range of different views, depending on how the moral duties are conceived. These include intuitionism (which involves the attempt to fit a set of unrelated low-level maxims of conduct together into a consistent whole, and thus may be considered the nearest philosophically respectable approximation to 'common sense'), and distributive justice (which itself, as we have seen, may be understood in different ways, from simply giving people equality of opportunity at one extreme to meeting the needs of the least advantaged first at the other). Liberal moral theory may be seen as an alternative to religious morality, with rules of conduct based on rational principles rather than on prescriptions deriving from religious authority or revelation (though in practice there may be a significant overlap between religious and liberal moral rules).

At a personal level, certain forms of human behaviour based on the three core liberal values are essential from a liberal perspective. These include truth-telling, promise keeping, treating others justly, respecting self and others, avoiding harm to others, being in control of one's own life and body, tolerating diversity, exercising responsibility, supporting the rational resolution of conflict, and accepting the general rule of law, and accepting constraints on one's own actions in order to protect the interests of others. Morality according to this view is seen as a set of norms or rules for behaviour that are rationally justifiable through their connection with core liberal values. Morally educated citizens are those who have thought through and internalized these norms. And moral behaviour in practice is also a rational activity, in that decisions on how to behave in any given situation are reached after careful reflection, paying due attention both to the principles involved and to the likely consequences of the actions taken. Laurence Kohlberg's approach to moral education (discussed in Chapter 1) is specifically directed towards the development of moral reasoning.

What is also missing from the liberal account of morality is any sense of how one should live one's life or what sort of person one should be. An alternative approach to liberalism's rational morality makes the 'virtues' central (Carr, 1991). Moral Education according to this view seeks to develop desirable personal qualities, and to make students into certain kinds of people. One version of this approach is 'character education' which seeks to introduce students to certain approved virtues and through a range of classroom and extra-curricular activities ensure that the students start to reflect these virtues in their lives (Lickona, 1991). Apart from practical difficulties with this approach, however, there are difficulties in identifying what qualities are virtues (how should we rank patriotism? humility? ambition?), and sometimes apparently good qualities may lead to unfortunate outcomes. It seems hard to dispense with the core liberal value of rationality.

Challenges to the liberal framework of values

Of course, liberal values are not universally shared, even in western countries. Fundamental challenges come in particular from Marxism (cf. Harris, 1979; Matthews, 1980), from existentialism (cf. Cooper, 1999), from radical feminism (cf. Graham, 1994), from postmodernism (cf. Hutcheon, 2003), and from various religious worldviews including the Catholic (cf. Arthur, 1994; Burns, 1992), the evangelical Christian (Pike, 2004d, 2005a) and the Islamic (Halstead, 2004). To those committed to such worldviews, liberalism may be seen as just one more challengeable version of the good. Jean Baudrillard's version of postmodernism, for example, offers a serious challenge to the core liberal value of rationality (1983, 1992). The Islamic worldview, on the other hand, is based on values drawn from divine revelation, and produces an approach to education which is at odds at several crucial points with liberalism. In Islam, the ultimate goal of education is to nurture children in the faith – to make them good Muslims – and children are not encouraged to question the fundamentals of their faith but to accept them on the authority of their elders. How are liberals to respond to such views? Some consider them intolerable, and suggest that the state should intervene to protect the rights of the children to be liberated from the constraints of their cultural environment and to grow up into personally autonomous adults (Raz, 1986, p. 424). The moral justification of such intervention according to liberal principles, however, needs to be tempered by considerations of the social disunity and conflict it would cause. The best hope for a way forward in our view lies with a more tolerant and culturally sensitive approach based on such liberal values as freedom of conscience, respect for diversity and the search for shared civic values. Such an approach would allow non-liberal forms of life (i.e. communities, traditions, cultures) to pursue their own vision of the good as they choose, so long as they do not harm others or act against the public interest.

Chapter 3

The aims of Citizenship and Moral Education

It is sometimes claimed that we have reached an all time low in interest in politics among the British public, and particularly among young people. It is by no means clear that this claim is historically accurate, but the perception of political disengagement and cynicism among young people was a major factor behind the introduction of Citizenship as a compulsory subject in English secondary schools in 2002. Giddens tells us modestly that 'citizenship education can improve the lives and school experiences of young people' (2000, p. 14). But many more extravagant claims have also been made for what the subject would achieve. The Advisory Group on Citizenship suggests that it would tackle young people's boredom with politics and their sense of disempowerment, counter their suspicion of institutionalized authority, reduce crime, and even change the political culture of the country (AGG, 1998, pp. 7, 14–16; cf. Crick, 2000b, p. 80). Hargreaves claims that the subject will provide the cement to hold a pluralist society together (1994, p. 37). There is also a widespread assumption that Citizenship provides an important and widely acceptable way of delivering moral education and values education more generally (Crick, 1998a; Halstead and Taylor, 2000b, p. 170).

There is clearly a potential conflict between the goal of improving the lives of young people and the goal of improving the political culture of the country, though the two may go together. But how appropriate and how realistic are these as aims for Citizenship? In Chapter 1 we briefly considered what a country may legitimately expect of its citizens. The present chapter explores the issue of aims in more detail (cf. Rowe and Newton, 1997). The first section examines the aims of Citizenship Education under three headings: the informed citizen, the active citizen and the critically reflective citizen. For ease of comparison, the second section uses a similar structure to examine the aims of Moral Education. The third section considers strategies for implementing these aims, particularly contrasting the closed approaches of civic conformity and character education with more open approaches. In conclusion, the implications of open approaches for schools, teachers and the curriculum are explored.

Aims of Citizenship Education

Citizenship Education may be narrowly or broadly conceived. In its narrow sense, citizenship education aims to produce 'citizens capable of addressing in the ballot box political arguments posed by democratic debate', whereas in the broader sense its aim is to create 'citizens who share in a common social endeavour' (Pearce and Hallgarten, 2000, p. 7). The narrow conception is education *about* citizenship, which is designed to produce informed or politically literate citizens. The broader conception is education *for* citizenship, in other words, education which is intended to produce active citizens with a commitment to certain public values and practices. Citizenship education on this view includes not only political literacy but also moral and social responsibility and community involvement. There is a third set of aims for citizenship education – to produce autonomous, critically reflective citizens who participate in political debate and discussion and campaign actively for change where they consider it appropriate. These three ways in which the aims of Citizenship Education can be characterized will now be examined more fully.

To produce informed citizens

No one could deny the importance of this aim, but for some people it is the only legitimate aim for Citizenship Education. On this view, the subject is a value-free activity that stands back from the aim of producing active, committed citizens and aims simply at providing information about citizenship. The task is a cognitive one, of extending children's knowledge and understanding of political ideas, institutions and issues. Citizenship thus becomes a subject with its own body of knowledge, understanding and skills; for example, students learn about what they are entitled to from public agencies, about the rights which the state guarantees to its citizens, and about the corresponding obligations which it demands. The aim of fostering citizens who are well informed or politically literate (cf. Beck, 1998, p. 108; Davies *et al.*, 1999, p. 17) has little overlap with the aims of moral education.

The emphasis on political literacy makes it comparatively easy to draft a list of appropriate subject matter which will achieve this aim:

- local and national government, elections and political institutions;
- the legal system, courts, police, crime and punishment;
- education;
- democracy and participation;
- citizens' rights and responsibilities;
- pluralism, multiculturalism, diversity and social cohesion;
- social institutions, health and social welfare;
- international organizations;
- national identity and patriotism;
- multiple citizenships: local, national, European and global/international;

- equal opportunities and race relations;
- liberal values, civic virtue and the principles underpinning one's society;
- alternative ideologies;
- economics, including inflation, free market economies, stock markets, taxation systems, mortgages, insurance;
- war;
- current events and the role of the media;
- responsibilities to the planet;
- controversial issues – understanding both sides;
- preparing for an unknown future.

There are strong arguments for making this the main aim of Citizenship Education. First, it may be more important for children to leave school politically literate than with experience of voluntary activities and other forms of participatory experience in the school context (Davies *et al.*, 1999, p. 21). Indeed, Engle and Ochoa argue that it is a responsibility of citizens to be informed, for 'participation in a democracy is irresponsible if it is not informed' (1988, p. 16), and in any case knowledge itself is empowering (AGC, 1998, p. 20). Secondly, an approach based on knowledge and understanding avoids many of the difficulties encountered in a value-laden approach (Beck, 1998, pp. 103–8), including the problem of the lack of agreement over the values which Citizenship Education should promote and the problem of whether the inculcation of beliefs, attitudes and values has any place in a liberal education anyway. A comparison may be made with Religious Education, which used to encourage acceptance of Christian beliefs but now aims to produce people who have knowledge and a sympathetic understanding of religion(s). Thirdly, this model avoids the problems that arise in trying to assess values education (Halstead and Taylor, 2000a, pp. 55–7), and makes monitoring and assessment much more straightforward. The knowledge and understanding students have gained can be tested easily through GCSE and other forms of assessment and examination (Cross, 2000). Fourthly, in view of the fact mentioned in the previous chapter that many teachers appear to be hesitant about their role in values education and prefer not to engage in it (cf. Halstead and Taylor, 2000b, p. 170; Passy, 2003), a value-free knowledge-based approach to Citizenship Education may have a better chance of long-term success.

This aim is uncontroversial; the question is whether it goes far enough. For many people, it does not.

To produce committed, active citizens

If the aim of Citizenship Education is not only to develop political literacy but also to encourage moral and social responsibility and community involvement, it must include the development of values, dispositions, skills, aptitudes and commitments as well as knowledge and concepts (AGC, 1998, pp. 11–13, 44–5). However, as soon as any kind of link is acknowledged between Citizenship Education, values education and commitment, a number of complexities arise relating to the aims of the subject. The first involves the kind of loyalties and commitments that Citizenship Education can legitimately encourage in view of the lack of agreement about the public virtues and shared values that form the basis for the subject (cf. McLaughlin, 1992, pp. 242–3). What does the term 'commitment' imply in the context of citizenship? How are we to define committed citizens? What virtues would we expect committed citizens to possess, and can such virtues be taught? The second set of complexities relates to the role of schools in developing students' values. Are schools primarily agents of socialization? Should they simply reflect society's current values? Or should schools adopt a more active and critical role in leading social change (cf. Halstead and Taylor, 2000a, pp. 15–16)? We must now turn to these topics in more detail.

With regard to the loyalties and commitments that are developed in Citizenship Education, some are uncontroversial. We would expect all students to learn to obey the law, to pay their taxes, to fulfil their other legal obligations as citizens, and to develop a commitment to those shared values without which society cannot operate; these are discussed more fully below. Beyond that, there may be a legitimate diversity of response. It is clear that not everyone wants to participate actively in the political, civil and social life of the community, and not everyone wants to organize a neighbourhood watch scheme or engage in campaigns against fox-hunting or in support of car-sharing. Some people may choose simply to live helpful and neighbourly lives without questioning the political and economic status quo. But in relation to these non-obligatory values, Citizenship Education should at least introduce students to a wide variety of possible ways of being an active citizen, and encourage serious reflection on the implications of different approaches to living in the world.

With regard to the role of the school in developing students' values, most proponents of Citizenship Education agree that this involves a range of democratic values, including a sense of public responsibility, an ability to see beyond one's own interests and commitments to a wider view, and a willingness to identify with the broader political community (Miller, 2000, pp. 28–9). Without common values, ideals and procedures such as these, a democratic society 'would lack not only coherence and stability, but also freedom, equality, tolerance and many other features of a moral and civilised life' (McLaughlin and Halstead, 1999, p. 148). White (1996) argues that democracy is distinguished by its values – justice, freedom and respect for personal autonomy – more than by specific institutions and procedures, but that for democracy to work citizens need to be *disposed* to use their knowledge and skills democratically. If education is to prepare students for citizenship, she argues that it must help them to acquire the civic virtues or dispositions that citizens require for democratic institutions to flourish (cf. Callan, 1997; Kymlicka, 1999, pp. 79–84; McLaughlin and Halstead, 1999, pp. 146–55).

The distinction between public and private values has been touched on earlier, but if education in public values is central to Citizenship Education, it is worth looking at the distinction more closely. McLaughlin offers the following summary of the concept of 'public values':

> Public values are those which, in virtue of their fundamentality or inescapability, are seen as binding on all persons. Frequently embodied in law, or expressed in terms of rights, they include such matters as basic social morality and . . . a range of fundamental democratic principles such as freedom of speech and justice. Public values in [liberal] societies also include ideals such as personal autonomy and the maximisation of the freedom of individuals to pursue their fuller conception of the good within a framework of justice through the distribution of 'primary goods' (basic rights, liberties and opportunities). The liberal project is to specify a range of public values, free of significantly controversial assumptions and judgments, which can generate principles for the conduct of relations between people who disagree.
>
> (1995, pp. 26–7)

From a liberal perspective, private values are more substantial views of human good which go beyond the public framework. They may be more or less reasonable, and more or less controversial, but what distinguishes them from public values is that there are no conclusive objective grounds which everyone will accept as appropriate for selecting one set of private values over another. The liberal state will therefore tolerate a wide range of differing private values and adopt a neutral stance between them, so long as they operate within a framework of justice, and it is respect for difference and diversity of this kind that contributes to making a liberal state pluralist.

The educational task of preparing students for citizenship of such a state thus involves encouraging them to develop a substantive commitment to the public values and the civic virtues or dispositions which allow the public values to flourish (see Chapter 6). These civic virtues include tolerant and respectful attitudes towards those whose beliefs, values and commitments differ from one's own. This is roughly the stance adopted in the Final Report of the Advisory Group on Citizenship (AGC, 1998), on which the National Curriculum for Citizenship is based. A substantial list of values and dispositions is included as an essential element in the active citizenship which is being promoted. These include concern for the common good, belief in human dignity and equality, a proclivity to act responsibly, the practice of tolerance, courage, openness, civility, respect for the rule of law, commitment to equal opportunities, concern for human rights, and so on (AGC, 1998, pp. 44–5).

The methods and strategies most likely to be successful in achieving this aim are those which include experience of practical activities. Such activities may be either inside or outside the school. Inside the school, students may be encouraged to work co-operatively towards developing a democratic ethos in the school; school councils may be set up, students may be involved in making rules at class or school level or in other forms of democratic decision-making, including, more ambitiously, the formation of Just Communities (Halstead and Taylor, 2000b, pp. 175–89). These possibilities will be discussed more fully in Chapter 9. Outside the school, students may be involved in various forms of community service and community activities, charitable work, environmental action and other kinds of voluntary activities. These experiences give students opportunities to put into practice their commitment to values such as social justice, the peaceful resolution of conflict, equal opportunities and antiracism. Such activities are most likely to be an effective introduction to active, committed citizenship when they are combined with opportunities to reflect on their social and moral implications, as we shall see in the next section.

This aim overlaps significantly with Moral Education (cf. Beck, 1998, ch. 4). Indeed, Crick argues that 'any teaching of Citizenship not based on moral values and reasoning would either be mechanical and boring, or even dangerous' (1998a, p. 19). The precise relationship between Citizenship Education and Moral Education may be unclear. Torney-Purta claims that 'both moral education and civic education are sub-categories within the larger category of values education' (1996), whereas Crick describes 'PSE, moral education or whatever we call education specifically for values' as 'necessary but not sufficient conditions for good citizenship' (1998a, p. 19). But the fact that there is a relationship is not seriously open to question. In a survey of teachers' attitudes to Citizenship Education a few years ago, teachers regularly maintained that the moral dimensions of citizenship mattered far more than the legal or political dimensions. They referred to the importance of being conscious of the interests of others and the wider society and acting accordingly, and used the language of caring, unselfishness, cooperation, meeting community obligations and demonstrating respect to give substance to their view of citizenship (Davies *et al.*, 1999, p. 50).

To produce autonomous, critically reflective citizens

In the previous section it was suggested that Citizenship Education requires commitment to the public values of society and practical activities based on these values (cf. McLaughlin, 1995, pp. 27–30). However, there is a danger that this could produce passive citizens, citizens who obey the law of the land, who recognize the need for a well-ordered society, who accept assigned duties and responsibilities, who are patriotic and accept the importance of authority in human affairs, but who never think of questioning or challenging laws that they consider unjust or engaging in any form of political campaigning. What is missing here is a critical component in Citizenship Education. As the Council of Europe project on *Education for Democratic Citizenship* reminds us, '*Education for Democratic Citizenship* is not mainly and essentially the inculcation of democratic norms, but more essentially the development of reflective and creative actors, the strengthening of the ability to participate actively and to question' (quoted in Bottery, 2003, p. 116). It is when commitment to the public values of society is combined with critical reflection and a willingness to challenge authority that it is most effective both for individual citizens and for society. Let us look more closely now at what such critical reflection might involve.

If students are to be encouraged to explore, discuss and critically reflect on the public values of society, and on the nature of active citizenship, there are at least three areas where reflection is vital. First, there must be reflection on the nature and obligations of citizenship and on its implications for personal development. This includes reflection on:

- the self, including one's personal sense of identity and worth, and one's links with the broader community;
- the practice of citizenship, the skills, dispositions and understanding needed for this, and the lessons that can be learned from active citizenship;
- civic values including justice, fairness, personal autonomy, responsibility, respect, tolerance and openness, and why these are important in the lives of citizens.

Secondly, there must be reflection on the needs of society, particularly, for example, those needs that arise from the increasing diversity in society (e.g. challenging racism and religious prejudice), from the abuse of power (e.g. human rights abuses and unjust laws), or from a growing awareness of the significance of fundamental principles like equal rights (e.g. challenging sexism and homophobia). Thirdly there must be reflection on dilemmas and controversies relating to citizenship: for example, is there a right under any circumstances to opt out of the rights and responsibilities of citizenship? How should the responsibilities of citizenship be balanced against one's responsibilities to other groups or institutions, including family, religion, employer, even football team? Do economic values ever conflict with the values of citizenship? How is one to reconcile one's own interests with the duty to respect and care for the interest of others?

Just as commitment to the values of society is best seen in practical, community activities involving participation and co-operative action, so critical reflection may be associated with various forms of campaigning and what Print and Coleman call 'enlightened political engagement' (2003, p. 130). Parker seeks to establish the connection between critical understanding and reflection (which he calls 'democratic enlightenment') and political engagement:

> Political engagement refers to the action or participatory domain of citizenship, from voting and contacting government officials to deliberating public problems, campaigning, and engaging in civil disobedience, boycotts, strikes, rebellions, and other forms of direct action. Democratic enlightenment refers to the moral-cognitive knowledge, norms and commitments that shape engagement: knowledge of the ideals of democratic living, the commitment to freedom and justice, and so forth.
>
> (2001, p. 99)

In the survey of teachers' attitudes to Citizenship Education mentioned earlier, a number of teachers concurred with the view that while social harmony is important, citizens should not seek social harmony at any price. For example, one teacher said, 'I think sometimes it's [being] a good citizen to cause ripples . . . and I think sometimes a good citizen is one who rebels against authority' (Davies *et al.*, 1999, pp. 53–4).

How far can students engage in this kind of active citizenship? It seems that there is often a gap between the rhetoric of schools' provision (which emphasizes the need for critical reflection and an understanding of political engagement, lobbying and protest) and the reality (which is more to do with learning conformity and the acceptance of authority). In their study of civic education across 24 countries, Torney-Purta *et al.* report that the 'vision of Civic Education often emphasises the development of critical thinking or education about values, but the reality is often about knowledge transmission' (1999, p. 34). Our own view is that a fundamental aim of Citizenship Education is to produce critically reflective citizens who participate in political debate and discussion and who campaign actively for change where appropriate, and in Part Two of this volume we place a strong emphasis on the role of the Arts and the Humanities in developing the skills of critical awareness and critical reflection.

Aims of Moral Education

Whereas the values with which Citizenship Education is concerned are the public values of society, Moral Education is just as concerned with private virtues or qualities of character as with public values. The aims of Moral Education are often defined in simple terms – to help children to know right from wrong, to teach children to be good, to get children to behave morally (cf. Houghton, 1998). But even a moment's reflection makes one realize that these simple aims mask a great deal of complexity. Are 'right' and 'wrong' relative or absolute terms? What does it mean to 'be good' (cf. Straughan, 1988)? Is the requirement 'to behave morally' satisfied if children have been trained to follow moral rules, even if they do not understand the reasons why – or must they do the right thing for the right reasons? Is morality a matter of conforming to certain externally imposed rules, or is it a matter of autonomous decision-making, learning how to apply moral principles to particular situations, or is it a matter of being a certain kind of person?

In view of these complexities, a number of writers on moral education have argued that we can only gain a proper understanding of what is involved in moral education by clarifying the end product, the 'morally educated person' (Wilson, 1973, pp. 21–5; Elias, 1989, ch. 2). In other words, what sort of qualities, attributes, skills, abilities, knowledge and understanding does a person need in order to be considered morally educated? In what follows, we define the aims of moral education in terms of three characteristics of the 'morally educated person': such a person is informed, actively committed, and critically reflective. This education of course starts in families, it may be reinforced in faith and other communities, and it continues through life; schools at best are only one among several influences on moral development.

To produce informed moral agents

This aim may be achieved at three different levels. The first is initiating students into a specific moral tradition. This may be a formal, often religious, tradition, or an informal, family-based tradition (cf. Harris, 1989, ch. 2; Thompson 2004a, 2004b). There is research evidence to suggest that this happens anyway, whether or not it is conscious and planned by adults; children probably develop a moral sense within the first two years of life (Kagan and Lamb, 1987), and relationships and interactions within the family (such as incidents of play, conflict and family rituals) familiarize them with a generally informal moral tradition from an early age (Dunn, 1987). From an educational point of view this is necessary so that they can learn what it is to behave morally. A religious upbringing may be an effective way of introducing children to a clear framework of moral beliefs and practices, so long as their future autonomy is respected and they are free as they grow up to accept or reject the tradition. Internalizing the tradition is important, because moral learning cannot develop in a vacuum.

However, Wilson and others have argued that the second level is neither the progressive refinement of family-based or faith-based morality to ensure that it conforms with the expectations of the broader society, nor habituation of this virtuous behaviour through repeated opportunities to practise it until it becomes second nature (cf. Aristotle, 1953, p. 56; Lickona, 1991, p. 62; Straughan, 1982, pp. 221–2). Indeed, Wilson argues that moral education does not involve passing on specific content to students in the form of 'right answers' to moral questions at all (1996, p. 90). What is ultimately important in moral education is understanding principles and procedures, and if this is done properly 'the content will look after itself' (Hare, 1979, p. 104). The second stage according to Wilson's view thus consists of developing students' understanding of moral principles and procedures; he calls these the 'equipment' they need to make good (i.e. rational) moral decisions (1990, p. 128). This 'equipment' consists roughly of the following:

- understanding of relevant concepts such as the nature of virtues or the concept of a moral issue;
- identification of the rules or principles which individuals believe they ought to follow in their behaviour;
- awareness of other people's (and one's own) feelings and the ability to identify with others and show concern for them;
- knowledge of surrounding circumstances and factual knowledge relevant to any given moral situation;
- practical wisdom in dealing with people and in moral decision-making.

(Wilson, 1996, pp. 85–92)

These components of the morally educated person are derived from a consideration of what it means to think and act morally and what is necessarily implied by this. Lickona (1991, pp. 56–61) puts a strong emphasis on the links between understanding and moral feelings (including conscience, self-esteem, empathy, loving the good, self-control and humility).

The third level is the more academic study of morality, including ethical theories such as utilitarianism and Kantian ethics, and the skill of applying these to practical moral issues and dilemmas. Other areas of academic study include psychological theories of moral development, the relation of morality to religion and to the law, and links with spirituality and the emotions.

To produce committed, active moral agents

Most people would agree that the aim of developing moral understanding is insufficient in itself: unless it leads to moral action, it has not achieved its purpose. Wilson, for example, argues that the various elements of moral understanding should be brought to bear on practical situations in such a way that people actually act in accordance with the decisions made (1990, pp. 128–9). In fact, moral action is both a means of moral education and an outcome of it. Family, school and local community provide important contexts where the normal interaction with others carries many opportunities for moral learning. In fact, any co-operative social activity, including interactive sports, organizing a charity event, sailing a ship or running a business can be morally educative, especially if specific moral issues that arise are the focus of discussion and reflection.

However, the link between moral understanding and moral action is not always a straightforward one. Commitment to a set of rules or moral principles (by accepting the universalizing nature of concepts like 'good' or 'right') does not guarantee that a person will always live up to these principles in practice – though many people do continue to behave morally when it is easier not to do so. To live up to the principles involves both motivation and strength of will. In his book *I Ought To But*, Straughan (1982) examines the complex relationship between moral understanding and moral action, focusing particularly on the problem of weakness of will in education. Wilson's view is that moral motivation is a matter of encouraging students to take seriously the entire form of life or thought that we call morality, to appreciate it for its own sake and to want to become a part of it (Wilson and Cowell, 1987, p. 35). It has nothing to do with getting pupils to act on 'right answers' because a certain kind of moral behaviour 'pays off' (ibid., p. 34). One of the goals of moral education therefore is to ensure that students understand the importance of morality in their own lives, so that they have the moral courage to do what they know and feel is right.

To produce autonomous, critically reflective moral agents

It would clearly be a mistake simply to present students with a range of alternative moral views and leave them free to select whichever took their fancy. Teachers have to steer a path between on the one hand implying that there are no right answers in matters of morality and that it is all a matter of taste, and on the other trying to impose right answers on students. To deny the possibility of 'right answers' would overlook the considerable difficulties with moral relativism (cf. Wilson, 1990, ch. 3), but to serve up the right answers to students on a plate would be unacceptable, as already stated, because they need to reach these answers by the autonomous exercise of their own reason via the appropriate procedures. The ultimate aim of Moral Education is to create independent, critically reflective, moral reasoners. This involves (*inter alia*) learning the proper use of language, so that students can think and discuss moral issues clearly and rationally and be enabled to approach any moral issue without prejudice, fantasy or other irrational feelings.

The skill of critical reflection may be developed initially through reflection on practice and moral action; it was suggested earlier that any co-operative social activity can be morally educative so long as the specific moral issues that arise are the focus of discussion and reflection. Reflection involves asking, for example, whether I should have done this, what else I could have done, why that would have been better, and what others thought of my action. The same kind of reflection lies at the heart of Kohlberg's approach to moral education, with its emphasis on the development of moral reasoning through the discussion of moral dilemmas (Kohlberg, 1969; Colby and Kohlberg, 1987). Moral imagination is an important part of reflection, helping both to enter into the worldviews of others and see how actions and decisions will affect them, and to envisage possibilities that are outside the scope of one's present experience (Harris, 1989, pp. 72–4; Kekes, 1999). This discussion of critical reflection has re-emphasised the link between Citizenship and Moral Education, for it is the key skill needed in dealing with moral issues in citizenship (such as whether there is a moral duty to vote, and whether one should obey an unjust law) or indeed any social controversies.

Achieving the aims of Citizenship and Moral Education

Need for an open approach

It will be clear from what has been said so far that we reject any crudely inculcatory approach to Citizenship and Moral Education. Just as Religious Education in England has been transformed in the last thirty years from a subject that by and large took for granted the truths of Christianity to one that seeks to encourage interfaith understanding and respect for people from all faiths and none, so we would reject any form of Citizenship Education which sought to reinforce a narrow patriotism either through nationalistic rituals or through any kind of teaching that discouraged critical reflection and would argue strongly for a more open approach that recognised diversity and included global and cross-cultural issues. Bottery paints some bleak scenarios of possible future developments in Citizenship Education, where the curriculum is used either to produce a pliable, compliant, contented workforce or to 'quietly, insistently and subconsciously point the individual to unthinking identification' with crude nationalist values (2003, pp. 118–19). There can be a similar danger in the approach to Moral Education known in the US as Character Education that students may be taught and made to practise certain character traits such as honesty or courage until they become second nature, without ever understanding the reasons for such behaviour, without engaging in any form of moral reasoning and without any reference to underlying democratic values (cf. McLaughlin and Halstead, 1999). The problem is that instilling the values (whether these gain their authority from scripture, from consensus or whatever) seems to take priority over respecting the students and helping them to become autonomous moral agents. Indeed, any content, even controversial values, may be internalized by students using this method. This does not apply to all programmes of Character Education; Lickona, for example, has shown himself willing to draw eclectically from a range of different approaches to Moral Education, even values clarification (Lickona, 1991). However, in many cases Character Education seems to reject the critical independence of students and to be constructed on the basis of prescription and prohibition. Kristjansson has worryingly suggested that Citizenship Education in England has much in common with Character Education (2004, p. 210). What is wrong with all such approaches in our view is that they lack respect for the individual by failing to encourage understanding and critical reflection, and the exercise of free will.

A more open approach to Citizenship and Moral Education involves recognition that one cannot transmit moral 'knowledge' in the way one can transmit mathematical or historical facts. Moral 'knowledge' is always a matter of judgement, and there are no easy routes to developing students' capacity to make moral judgements. It is not a matter of agreeing a list of desirable behavioural outcomes and then training teachers in the best way of achieving these. As we have seen earlier in this chapter, the capacity to make moral judgements involves a complex range of skills, including an understanding of and commitment to moral rules or principles, an awareness of other people's emotions, knowledge of the context and of specific factors having a bearing on the decision, and the motivation to take morality seriously. These skills will be developed over a period of time through guided participation and reflection, so that students come to understand why some behaviours are preferable to others and how judgements about preferred behaviours may vary depending on specific circumstances, the people involved and the likely outcomes.

Implications of an open approach for types of schooling

One question that arises is whether faith schools are permissible on this account. At first glance, it might be thought that faith schools are likely to trap their students in a closed worldview, forcing on them a predetermined package of beliefs and values which militate against their development as autonomous, critically reflective citizens (cf. Halstead and McLaughlin, 2005). According to this view, it is preferable to have a form of common schooling for all children, and if common schooling is to respect all children equally, it cannot promote any essentially controversial religious or other worldview as true or expect children to become committed to it. The only values the common school can promote are the public values of the society such as justice, truth, tolerance and respect for others. However, we argue (i) that the public values provide only a part of moral education, and that familiarizing children with a more substantial religious/moral tradition from an early age can help them to learn what it is to behave morally; (ii) that numerous groups continue to base their moral understanding on religious teaching, and it would seem oppressive to deny them the right to pass on such beliefs and worldviews to their children, forcing them instead into schools where their moral beliefs may be undermined; (iii) that a strong sense of self, identity and community attachment are important prerequisites to full citizenship, and these can be effectively developed in faith schools; and (iv) that there are important parallels between being a member of a faith group and being a citizen. We argue therefore that subject to two conditions there should be no problems with faith schools: they must not undermine the core values of citizenship, and they must teach cross-cultural understanding and respect (Halstead, 2003; Pike 2005a). The existence of faith schools protects children's freedom to maintain their primary identity in a way that does not presuppose that it is based on their nationality (Halstead, 2005b).

Implications of an open approach for teachers

Although knowledge and understanding are an important part of both Citizenship and Moral Education, teachers can never simply be the transmitters of information. If they are to support the open development of students as active, committed and reflective citizens and moral agents, they must recognize that students will learn not only from formal teaching but also from informal situations, including the example teachers set and the way teachers capitalize on unplanned events that inevitably occur in the classroom. Jackson *et al.* claim that informal learning is the most significant: 'We believe that the unintentional outcomes of schooling, the ones teachers and administrators seldom plan in advance, are of greater moral significance – that is, more likely to have enduring effects – than those that are intended and consciously sought' (1993, p. 44). This makes a great diversity of demands on teachers, and also has significant implications for teacher training (cf. Davies *et al.*, 1999, ch. 7). Teachers must be helped to reflect critically on their own views on citizenship, and be willing to bring to consciousness their own values and assumptions. They also need to understand the implications of their role as moral exemplars; this includes not only the professional care and responsibility that they bring to their role, but also the moral persona they present to their students and the respect they show them. Part of respecting students is a willingness to listen to student voices, to know where their students stand and what they believe and value about citizenship and ethics. All this will be discussed more fully in subsequent chapters, especially Chapter 9.

Implications of an open approach for the curriculum

Every subject has a potential contribution to make to the teaching of Citizenship and Moral Education. To take just one example, science has an increasingly significant impact on the economic, political, military, medical and cultural life of nations, and so it is inevitable that there are links between Science education and Citizenship. Indeed, there is a growing literature about the relationship between the two subjects (an excellent critical overview is provided by Davies, 2004). Science education equips young people with much of the knowledge and understanding they need if they are to have an influence in public life, and also helps to train their critical capacities such as weighing evidence before drawing conclusions. Science can make people more aware of the global dimension of citizenship, aware that our responsibilities as citizens include loyalty to the whole of humanity (Bourn, 2004). Rotblat (2002) draws attention both to some of the recent scientific advances that have had a positive impact on world citizenship (such as developments in transportation, communication and information technologies) and to some of the negative dimensions of scientific progress, which again have global consequences (such as weapons of mass destruction). Many of the most challenging ethical issues of contemporary life with which young citizens should engage are rooted in science: energy and resource usage, the use of fossil fuels, stem cell research, gene therapy, nuclear fuel and nuclear power stations, cloning, CFCs, GM foods, pollution, environmental issues, sustainability, the screening of unborn babies, genetic engineering, immunization, and the siting of electric pylons, power stations and mobile phone masts. Science, far from being 'value-free' as it has sometimes been presented in the past, thus provides much of the raw material for ethical debate and Moral Education (Jones, 1998). But the very nature of science and the way that scientific enquiry is conducted also encourages critical, rational thinking. Rational and open-minded thinking, basing judgements on the best available evidence, asking questions, seeking information, drawing balanced conclusions, understanding consequences, considering other people's views as well as one's own – all these are skills which are central to young people's development as citizens, and skills that Science education can help to develop.

In fact, however, the relationship between Science and Citizenship is two-way, because Citizenship can encourage public engagement with Science, so that 'citizens had a positive (rather than negative) attitude to science and technology, and understood the basic *process* and value of the scientific method – with its ultimate appeal to experimental methods and predictive power' (Edmonds, 2005). If citizens are to develop cultural literacy, this must extend to a general understanding of key scientific ideas, and the training they receive in critical reflection and debate through Citizenship will help them to engage in informed discussion and democratic debate about scientific issues.

But Citizenship and Moral Education can also influence and enrich the way that other subjects are taught. In Part Two we explore the links between Citizenship and Moral Education and (in turn) Language and Literacy, the Arts, the Humanities, and Religious Education and PSHE. These subject clusters have been chosen because of the rich insights they can bring to Citizenship in particular, but also because of the opportunities they allow for the development of the many dimensions of citizenship and moral understanding that have been explored in this chapter, including key concepts and principles, rational understanding, critical openness and key values such as active commitment, personal autonomy and critical reflection.

Part 2

Citizenship and Moral Education in the Curriculum

Chapter 4

Language and Literacy in Citizenship and Moral Education

Why should an entire chapter in this book be devoted to the relation between language, literacy and Citizenship? It will be helpful at the outset to consider recent statements made by leading scholars and researchers of literacy in order to begin to appreciate the increasing importance that is being attached to language and literacy within Citizenship and Moral Education:

> Literacy has transformative potential in a democratic society.
> (Hall, 2003, p. 178)

> A democratic agenda requires a critical literacy – one that acknowledges the differentials of power in society and seeks to realize a more equitable, just, and compassionate community . . . critical literacy assumes that literacy instruction can empower and lead to transformative action.
> (Powell *et al.*, 2005, p. 13)

> We have a moral duty to read . . . if learning to read opens significant additional possibilities in terms of understanding how we might live, then we can argue that we have a moral duty to read, and, therefore as teachers, a moral duty to teach reading.
> (Harrison, 2004, p. 6)

Why is language an issue when discussing moral education? Why is the relation between democracy and literacy receiving fresh scrutiny now? How does the language used by teachers or textbooks promote specific values? These are some of the questions to which answers are sought in the following pages. In the present chapter a number of key areas will be considered. Firstly, in the section 'Critical literacy for democratic action and social justice', the potential synergy between critical literacy and Citizenship Education in the classroom will be explored. A case study is reported which illustrates the ways in which literacy can facilitate children's political engagement and involvement as environmentally aware citizens. Secondly, in 'Language learning and values', the relationship between language and beliefs is examined and attention is devoted to how children who have English as an Additional Language (EAL) should be taught so that their voice is heard and their rights are respected. Thirdly, in 'Language and the identities of citizens', the emphasis upon values is developed by looking at the disparity between communication in the home and school and the ways in which language can be used to promote mainstream values which may not be supported by the homes or communities of some children.

Critical literacy for democratic action and social justice

Critical literacy seeks to foster critically literate citizens. It is now accepted that one does not learn to be literate and then, afterwards, somehow learn to be critical. From an early age becoming critical, being able to read and interpret the world, goes hand in hand with becoming literate. As the title of Friere and Macedo's seminal text *Literacy: Reading the Word and World* (1987) suggests, understanding words and world go together. If one is to be an active citizen, not only does one need to be empowered to communicate, but one needs to be sufficiently discerning about the world one inhabits in order to communicate effectively within it.

The term 'reading' thus ceases to denote only phonological decoding or the ability to sound out words and comes to signify the decoding of bias and hidden agendas in society and the understanding of beliefs and attitudes within the broad range of 'texts' produced by a number of cultures. It has been noted that 'critical literacy challenges inequalities in society and it promotes social justice and a strong participatory democracy, the kind of democracy where power is with, not just some people (like special interest groups or the wealthy) but all people,' (Hall, 2003, p. 175). Children who become discriminating readers and are able to identify injustice and exclusion are in a position to strive for justice and inclusion. Critical readers are not passive recipients but come to texts and interrogate them. When reading, they are likely to ask the following sorts of questions: Who is powerful? Who has resources? Who has the ability to bring about change? Who is weak? Who is dependent? Who is powerless to effect an alteration in circumstances? Who is the leader? Who is the follower? What or who is omitted from the text? What or who has been chosen to be included? Who or what is portrayed as natural and who or what is depicted as unnatural? Who espouses which values? Where do they get these values from? Wray and Lewis (1997) provide another simple list including questions such as 'Who produced this text?' and 'What are his/her qualifications for doing so?'. Critical reading seeks to identify the values which inform the position advocated by the text, where they come from and how they are legitimated. Indeed, reading is inescapably a socio-political activity (Harrison, 2004).

Non-neutrality is a characteristic of literacy education but it should be pointed out that those who adopt a socio-political perspective on literacy may not necessarily strive for democratic ends. Goebbels understood the power of propaganda only too well as do regimes today which oppress their peoples. Understanding that literacy has socio-political significance will not automatically produce a more equitable and just distribution of power in society. Highly literate people can use their knowledge for good or ill, to manipulate society in one direction or another. The discipline of critical literacy has, however, become associated with democratic transformation.

As 'critical literacy assumes that the teaching of literacy is never neutral but always embraces a particular ideology or perspective' (Powell *et al.*, 2005, p. 13) it provides the Citizenship educator with the opportunity to explore the perspective being embraced. The 'critical view of literacy takes holistic teaching into the political domain' (ibid., p. 14) and addresses issues of religion, ethnicity, disability, gender, socio-economic status and democracy.

Critical literacy, including critical media literacy and the ability to 'read' the 'texts' and artefacts of popular culture, should be promoted within Citizenship Education where there is the opportunity to foreground its political dimension. 'Contrary to skills-based models that assume literacy instruction can be neutral, critical literacy is 'consciously political' in that it intentionally promotes the basic tenets of democracy: freedom, justice, equality' (Powell *et al.*, 2005, p. 14). The aims of critical literacy are certainly congruent with those of current Citizenship teaching as both seek to promote certain forms of behaviour and foster 'active readers and writers who can be expected to exercise some degree of agency in deciding what textual positions they will assume or resist as they interact in complex social and cultural contexts' (Hall, 2003, p. 187).

The National Literacy Strategy and Citizenship in the UK

Both literacy and citizenship initiatives were introduced by New Labour at roughly the same time and it is likely that at some point in the future scholars will look back and reflect upon this irony. While the socio-political stance on literacy promotes the view that 'literacy has transformative potential in a democratic society' (Hall, 2003, p. 178), an aim subscribed to by Citizenship educators, the National Literacy Strategy seems more preoccupied with linguistic skills. As 'literacy policy in England is hugely influenced by the cognitive-psychological perspective' (ibid., p. 109), rather than the socio-political perspective outlined above, this militates against the potential for literacy and citizenship to work comprehensively together. In its most undiluted form 'the cognitive-psychological take on reading considers it to be value-free and more about skills than cultural knowledge' (ibid., p. 189) and it is this that appears to be the lot of most state-educated school children in England and Wales (Pike, 2003b, 2003f, 2004a). The emphasis is upon phonological awareness and word recognition with younger children and the comprehension of information texts with older students.

The dearth of critical literacy is illustrated by one of the most recent documents issued by the Key Stage 3 National Strategy entitled *Literacy in Citizenship* (DfES, 2004c) which accompanies training provided by Local Education Authority literacy consultants. The introductory session of this document appears promising and claims that the 'training is intended to build on, and disseminate, current good practice in supporting pupils' literacy skills as part of citizenship teaching'; one of the aims is supposed to demonstrate 'how focused literacy teaching can enhance understanding in citizenship' (ibid., p. 1). Citizenship educators who have their hopes raised are in for a disappointment.

To give a flavour of *Literacy in Citizenship* it is sufficient to note some of the objectives from *Key Stage 3 national strategy – framework for teaching English: year 7, 8 and 9* (DfEE/QCA, 2001) that are singled out for attention. The focus is on 'distinguishing between everyday uses of words and their subject-specific context e.g. bill, lobby, convention and race' (Year 7, W21) and on the ability to 'define and deploy words with precision, including their exact implication in context' (Year 7, W14). While understanding such homographs as 'lobby' and 'bill' may be supportive of citizenship it hardly qualifies as 'critical literacy'. Attention is directed to the objective for Year 8 (SL10) from En1 (Speaking and listening) where talk is used to 'question, hypothesise, speculate', and to the Year 9 objective, from En3 Writing, to 'integrate diverse information into a coherent and comprehensive account'. Knowing how to spell key words such as 'government', 'committee', 'democracy', 'parliament' and 'sustainable' is helpful but will not in itself foster readers of the *world* with such an emphasis merely on *words*. In fact, the emphasis on words can lead to a trite and misleading oversimplification. A game of word bingo is used to teach definitions of words but whether such a game is the best place to learn that 'holocaust' is 'a huge slaughter or destruction of life' or that 'justice' is the 'administration of law' is questionable.

A few of the suggested activities provided by *Literacy in Citizenship* clearly support Citizenship Education. The work on questions to ask prospective parliamentary candidates and on charities such as Shelter and Oxfam is valuable. So too is the approach to rules in society and how they are enforced. Leadership qualities are explored with reference to Jack and Ralph's respective leadership styles in William Golding's *Lord of the Flies* as the novel provides a 'stimulus on what constitutes the basics of organising a society' (DfES, 2004c, p. 27). Encouraging children to reflect on the implications for democracy of voting patterns for 11–14-year-olds (statistics for which are given on the BBC website) is relevant and the focus in Section 5 on writing for enquiry and issues such as motor vehicle congestion, considered at different levels (school, town, national, global) is appropriate. While learners who complete the work suggested by *Literacy in Citizenship* may be able to spell correctly words that will be useful in their citizenship lessons and will have the ability to extract information from websites describing issues of political importance such as voting patterns, there is little to suggest they will become more critical readers as a result of it.

The promise of critical literacy in a multicultural democracy

Having reviewed the cognitive-psychological approach to literacy in the UK a case study usefully illustrates how literacy and citizenship can work together where 'literacy is more a matter of making meaning out of words than developing a set of skills' (Powell *et al.*, 2005, p. v). These authors acknowledge that literacy instruction is commonly associated with the achievement of economic aims and enhancing GDP through having a more skilled workforce but believe that critical literacy is 'important in realising a strong democracy' (ibid., p. 12) for 'in a multi-cultural society, realizing the goal of equity would mean that everyone had a voice' (ibid., p. 13).

The case study is of children in the poor southern Appalachian region of the US, where economic and cultural exploitation has been rife and mountain land is sought by large corporations for its rich coal and timber reserves. One of the most recent examples of this pattern of exploitation was the plan to cause environmental havoc by strip mining Black Mountain, the highest peak in Kentucky. Once children at Rosenwald-Dunbar Elementary in Jessamine County found out in a social studies lesson that the mountain was designated to be strip mined they became involved in a project to halt the environmental destruction after engaging in responsible democratic enquiry. The children 'took a critical stance, talking with those in the region who benefited from strip mining as well as those who opposed it' (Powell *et al.*, 2005, p. 16). They interviewed miners and families who depended on the mining for their livelihoods and who wanted the strip mining to continue. One child remarked 'we did go against strip mining, but we knew what the other people's perspective was' (ibid., p. 16).

These children from the fourth grade became involved in a public hearing. They met with representatives of the mining company, studied the company website, and found out how the mining application process worked and how companies present information on the environmental impact of their operations. These children engaged in a range of purposeful literacy activities which facilitated their development as citizens who recognized the way in which different sections of society have different priorities which need to be evaluated and balanced. Children who read critically and can detect bias within commercial texts (such as company websites that are designed to persuade) and differentiate between fact and opinion in media texts are an asset to democracy. Clearly such 'critical literacy involves confronting the non-neutrality of knowledge and texts (both spoken and written) and is consistent with a strong democratic system' and it has been argued that the Black Mountain project 'exemplifies critical literacy in that the children learned about the transformative potential of literacy in a democratic society' (Powell *et al.*, 2005, p. 18). The children attracted media attention and eventually a compromise deal was reached and 1,850 acres of the mountain were saved from logging and strip mining.

Given the emphasis upon skills within UK literacy policy and the ways in which critical literacy is often marginalized (in documents such as *Literacy in Citizenship* and in many classrooms) we should attend to the conclusions drawn by the teachers involved in the project in Appalachia and the implications for democracy in the UK:

> As teachers of literacy in a multicultural society, we have a choice. We can either teach literacy as a series of skills, or we can teach as if words matter. Through the Saving Black Mountain project, the students who were involved discovered that words – their words – could have the power to effect change.
> (Powell *et al.*, 2005, p. 19)

That children from southern Appalachia (an area considered by the rest of the country to be backwards and far removed from the centre of political power) contributed to transformation and were active citizens should provide inspiration for educators in the UK working in challenging contexts.

Language learning and values

Language cannot be acquired in a moral vacuum for it is by far the most sophisticated symbol system humanity possesses. While language influences the meanings we create, our beliefs and values can be detected in the language we use. Indeed, this symbolic knowledge is always based upon beliefs and values about the world and therefore 'language and culture courses may effectively support or challenge political agendas which serve to exclude' (Osler and Starkey, 2000, p. 220). Language is not a neutral medium and one example from Osler and Starkey's *Citizenship and Language Learning* (2005) illustrates how one's view of the world can be betrayed by the language one uses even if it appears neutral to start with. A French course provided the following sentence which was to be the subject of tense modification: 'On the whole, if immigrant families speak French they will adapt more easily to their new life' (ibid., p. 34). We could just as easily substitute the word 'English' for 'French' and expect to find the sentence in a Citizenship textbook. The statement might be assumed to be neutral by many readers. Upon further examination certain assumptions are exposed: the emphasis here is upon what the immigrants rather than what the host population should do and implicit within the statement is a deficit model of immigrants. The emphasis is upon the adaptations to be made by immigrants rather than by the indigenous population. Many immigrants to France have French as a mother tongue and enhance the place to which they go but this is not emphasized. A very different starting point could be 'If French people are welcoming, immigrant families adapt more easily to their new life' (ibid.).

Stereotyping often occurs in language education texts and the need for cultural understanding and language learning to be acquired together is highlighted by a recent project on intercultural learning. American students learning German worked collaboratively over a semester with German students studying English via email so that each student was able to have direct contact with a native speaker in the country whose language was being studied. Yet some of the US students 'ended up hating their partners, withdrawing from participation and developing fresh prejudices against Germans' (Smith and Shortt, 2005, p. 4). The reasons for such reactions have to do with simple but profound cultural differences in patterns of social interaction:

> In German conversation, it is normal to express criticism more directly and earlier in a conversation than is the case with typical American communication patterns. In average American conversations, criticism tends to be expressed more indirectly and to be preceded by positive comments. As a result of unawareness of this basic difference in communication styles, some American students concluded that their German counterparts were rude and unsympathetic. It seems likely that some German students likewise had their stereotypes of American students as shallow and insincere reinforced.
>
> (Smith & Shortt, 2005, p. 4)

Credence is lent to the case for Citizenship to be integrated across the curriculum, made throughout this book, when it is understood that language is the medium through which all instruction takes place; the non-neutrality of the medium renders it essential to consider culture and language together rather than separately.

For Citizenship to seek to promote an understanding of other cultures at a time when study of modern foreign languages is decreasing dramatically is, to put it mildly, incongruous. The recent political decision that modern foreign languages need not be studied after the age of 14 is

> rather at odds with the Citizenship programme of study recommended at Key Stage 3 (11–14 year olds) which includes references to 'local to global', 'human rights' and 'debating global issues' (Qualifications and Curriculum Authority, 2001b, p. 6). Citizenship is implicitly international but, presumably, all other nations will speak/act/think in English.
>
> (Leighton, 2004, p. 168)

Evidently, the teaching of both literacy and languages in the UK could be far more supportive of the aims of Citizenship Education. Starkey points out that the Council of Europe advocates multidisciplinary approaches with 'all disciplines having a bearing on ethical, political, social, cultural or philosophical aspects' of learning. The UK's current promotion of segregated rather than integrated citizenship (see Chapter 8 below) is perhaps another instance of how un-European citizenship in the UK can be.

How we teach sends important messages to learners and the 'participative learning styles which characterise good practice in language teaching and learning are also those which support education for democratic citizenship' (Osler and Starkey, 2005, p. 21). It would be entirely inconsistent to teach children in their Citizenship lessons about the diverse religious and ethnic identities in the UK and the need for mutual respect and understanding (QCA/DfEE, 1999a, KS4 1b, p. 15) if teachers do not model an understanding of the linguistic needs of all pupils including those from minority ethnic groups in their classrooms. Skills of enquiry and communication are to be taught in Citizenship lessons and pupils are required to 'express, justify and defend orally and in writing a personal opinion' (ibid., KS4 2b, p. 15) about 'a political, spiritual, moral, social or cultural issue, problem or event' (ibid., KS4 2a, p. 15). There is little point in waxing lyrical about the benefits of an inclusive society where the needs of minorities are respected if teachers do not show children in their teaching what such an inclusive approach looks like.

It is especially important that the work of teachers of Citizenship is informed by guidance such as that contained in *Aiming High: Understanding the Educational Needs of Minority Ethnic Pupils in Mainly White Schools* (DfES, 2004a) so that the needs of children with EAL are met. Valuable work in this area has been carried out by Professor Lynn Cameron at the University of Leeds for Ofsted (Cameron, 2003) and guidelines for working with pupils learning English as an Additional Language are also published by the National Primary and Key Stage 3 Strategies. The material in *Access and Engagement in English: Teaching pupils for whom English is an additional language* (DfES, 2002a) is especially useful as is *Unlocking potential: raising ethnic minority attainment at Key Stage 3* (DfES, 2002b). There is not the space in this chapter to summarize in detail the excellent work that has been done in this area. Chapter 8 describes some key strategies and approaches which are indicative of inclusive classrooms which seek to model what is taught in Citizenship.

The need to adopt strategies which support the learning of ethnic minority pupils may be especially necessary in the two-thirds of UK schools where the 'proportion of minority ethnic pupils is less than five percent' (DfES, 2004a, p. 2) which are often referred to as 'mainly white' schools. The need for a democracy to respect those who are in the minority is a key theme of this book and 'mainly white' schools generally need to address specific issues in order to show respect for the different ethnic minority groups represented in the school. Being aware of and respecting this diversity within the minority ethnic population, rather than treating all ethnic minority pupils as a homogenous group, is central to any genuinely successful inclusion.

Language and the identities of citizens

It is taken for granted by sociolinguists that language is intimately related to identity but it is virtually unheard of for teachers of Citizenship to teach children about language, accent or dialect. Students of Citizenship who must become informed about 'the origins and implications of the diverse national, regional, religious and ethnic identities in the United Kingdom and the need for mutual respect and under-standing' (QCA/DfEE, 1999a, p. 15, Strand 1b) cannot do so if the significance of language for different groups is not appreciated. If the importance of certain ways of speaking and communicating in different communities is not understood then the identities of these groups cannot be properly understood either. Language is not an optional extra for Citizenship educators.

That cultural identity is defined by language can be illustrated by a few lines from the poem 'Search for My Tongue' by Sujata Bhatt which is studied by many pupils as part of GCSE English each year. The potential of literary texts such as this one in Citizenship lessons should be drawn upon far more as they can help students to explore the importance of language to the identities of various minority ethnic groups in the UK. In this short poem Sujata Bhatt writes:

> I felt as if I had spat out my tongue and whole language
> Because, at night in the dream, my language returns
>
> Like a flower – my language, my tongue, blossoms in the mouth.
> Like a flower – my language, my tongue, ripens in the mouth.

These lines appear in the poem in the modified Devanagari script used to write Gujurati and other Asian languages and the inclusion of lines in the poem in both Roman script and Gujurati reflect the tensions between Bhatt's two languages and two cultural backgrounds. Bhatt articulates the fear that she had lost touch with her own mother tongue, Gujurati, and feels that it has died in her mouth; she has rejected it and spat it out, only to find it growing again like a flower inside her.

The fear of losing touch with one's culture by losing fluency in the family language is addressed by the poet and can provide an introduction to the notion that a plural Britain is linguistically diverse. Although some children will be aware of other children in their school for whom English is not a first language and teachers may even be planning lessons with EAL in mind the religious and cultural significance of language is often missed. The central importance of the Arabic language for Muslims, for instance, can be appreciated by pupils when they understand that for Muslims the Qur'an cannot be read in any other language.

If 'we find it easy to make harshly critical judgements about ways of speaking which we perceive as alien' (Crystal, 1995, p. 305) it is clear that the study of linguistic variation deserves a place on the Citizenship curriculum in schools. The more we know about regional variation

> the more we will come to appreciate the striking individuality of each of the varieties we call dialects, and the less we are likely to adopt demeaning stereotypes about people from other parts of the country, or of the world.
>
> (ibid., p. 305)

Any citizenship course seeking to foster an understanding, appreciation and tolerance of different groups within UK society, which ignores linguistic background, bilingualism, community languages, accent and dialect, is incomplete.

In Citizenship lessons children can evaluate whether it is necessary for all UK citizens to speak and understand English. Indeed, whether children from groups where English is not the first language should speak English at school is a highly relevant topic. The arguments put forward are generally the same whether the language of Asians in Bradford or Hispanics in Florida is discussed. Whether a diversity of languages should be accepted or conformity to the language of the majority should be promoted is the key issue. Whether any UK Citizenship test should include a test of competence in the English language is an especially relevant and provocative but necessary topic. We should remember that 'schools historically have reinforced the standards of those who have the power to define appropriate language use' (Powell *et al.*, 2005, p. 13). There are parallels between the practices of speaking and believing and some of these will now be discussed.

Language and values

The ways in which the language of the dominant or most powerful group in society can marginalize other groups and their ways of speaking if they differ from the 'standard' parallels the ways in which schools can transmit and reinforce the 'standard' beliefs and values held by the majority of people. Mainstream values which are not those of the homes or communities of some children can easily be reinforced in schools. As we have seen, texts are often considered to endorse, privilege and foreground certain beliefs, values and attitudes and can influence us to see the world in certain ways rather than others. Many texts that reflect mainstream culture in a democracy can marginalize and exclude those who do not subscribe to the values of that culture. Although a 'continuing focal point of public and scholarly debate is the matter of overt moral and cultural content of early childhood reading materials' (Luke *et al.*, 2003, p. 251) and 'our choice of texts is a political decision' (Powell *et al.*, 2005, p. 13) those making the decisions regarding text-choice may have little awareness of the values implicit in the text and may be quite ignorant of the impact they might have on children.

Writing over half a century ago in *The Abolition of Man*, alternatively entitled *Reflections on education with special reference to the teaching of English in the upper forms of schools*, C. S. Lewis suggests 'we are insufficiently attentive to the importance of elementary text books' (1943/1978, p. 7). One textbook written by two English teachers is taken as an example. C. S. Lewis argues that the pupil is impressionable and the values implicit in the text are especially potent because they are hidden so that a child 'has no notion that ethics, theology, and politics are all at stake' (ibid., p. 9) when a simple homework task is being completed. Lewis discerns clear 'Disapprovals' and 'Approvals' (ibid., p. 61) in the 'real (perhaps unconscious) philosophy' of the authors who reflect 'the whole system of values which happened to be in vogue' in their circles at the time of writing. C. S. Lewis' assessment seems to be proleptic of the 'socio-political view of literacy' which 'takes it that no knowledge is neutral but rather is always based on some group's perception of reality and on some group's perspective of what is important to know' (Hall, 2003, p. 176).

It has been cogently argued that school texts offer a 'portrayal of the world from a mainstream perspective' (Hall, 2003, p. 179) and Lewis suggests that such a portrayal is immensely subtle. Although the child is not overtly being taught a theory about life certain worldview assumptions implicit in the text or teaching will be profoundly influential:

> It is not a theory they put into his mind, but an assumption, which ten years hence, its origin forgotten and its presence unconscious, will condition him to take one side in a controversy which he has never recognized as a controversy at all. The authors themselves, I suspect, hardly know what they are doing to the boy, and he cannot know what is being done to him.
>
> (Lewis, 1943/1978, p. 9)

The point I should like to take up is the way teachers and textbook writers can be oblivious to the values and specific vision they are promoting and may even assume they are adopting a neutral stance. That writers sought to communicate specific values (through textbooks and reading materials) in previous ages is well-known but it is more widely assumed than we might expect that this does not happen today. In former times, early literacy textbooks in the West were 'strongly tied to religious and moral training' (Luke *et al.*, 2003, p. 250). Comenius' *Latin Primer* or Webster's *Spelling Book* promoted Christian values and an awareness of eternity while teaching reading. Indeed, 'before the advent of mass commercial print culture, the influence of the textbook on moral and ideological formation was profound' (ibid., p. 251). It is assumed that textbooks today do not have such a strong ideological bias for 'the very premise of the modern textbook' is that it should be 'designed on the basis of psychological theories of instruction' rather than on 'religious values per se' (ibid., p. 251). Indeed: 'In contrast with the Protestant and colonialist traditions, the designers of modern textbooks consistently have focussed on literacy instruction qua scientific method rather than ideological and moral training,' (ibid., p. 251). Of course the point is that what appears to be a neutral focus on skills is in fact a highly ideological intervention in children's lives. Earlier in this chapter the focus on technical skills rather than critical literacy in the UK's approach was seen to marginalize more critical forms of engagement in a democracy.

The 'mainstream perspective' does not only, of course, come from the books children read in school. The texts of popular culture to which children respond today may well perform a very similar function to Comenius' *Primer*. It should be recognized that 'where earlier generations of children were socialized primarily within the boundaries of family, school, religious organization and community, consumer and popular culture is now the principal mode of early childhood socialization' (Luke *et al.*, 2003, p. 254). To think that Barbie and Ceebeebees may rival Comenius or Webster for ideological impact is not an exaggeration for 'a deluge of texts now claim the authority to instruct children in how to participate in childhood and consumer culture' (ibid.). If the Bible is revered in the homes of devout Christians and the Qur'an has an exalted position in the homes of observant Muslims and both influence the behaviour of believers, the texts of popular culture may well have an ideological influence upon secular materialists in late capitalist post-modern societies. The impact of such texts as 'Big Brother' upon society cannot be ignored. As the majority in the UK is neither Muslim nor Christian, it is secular, liberal values that are 'mainstream' and Wolterstorff (2002) has observed that societies get the schools they deserve in the sense that schools are not simply *for* society but also *by* society.

In the light of this, Citizenship educators need to be especially careful with regard to their 'assumptions' as these can, unwittingly, betray a monopoly of mainstream beliefs. A recent Citizenship lesson taught within History provides a good example of this. The aim of the lesson was to compare the beliefs and values of those living in medieval times with those of people today. An extract from Boccaccio's *Decameron* was used as the Citizenship lesson was situated within a sequence of lessons on the topic of medieval religion. The class was learning that in the Middle Ages people had a profound belief in the reality of Heaven and Hell. When the teacher asked how people's beliefs were different now, in the twenty-first century, the class and teacher appeared to work from the 'assumption' that no one could possibly entertain such beliefs now. The secularism of the majority of the population in the UK had found its way into the Citizenship lesson. The lesson worked on the assumption of shared secular atheism with the danger that a child from a devout Christian or Muslim family might be made to feel distinctly out of date, medieval even.

When teachers or texts address topics such as contraception, abortion, sex or drugs they can operate on assumptions that serve to perpetuate and extend the view of the majority. On the wall of one Citizenship and PSHE classroom the following pupils' views were displayed in large letters: 'I won't be forced into it before I'm ready' and 'I want to have a baby with someone I can trust'. The statements reflected the view that trust in relationships was important and that adolescents should not be forced by peer pressure into having sexual intercourse before they wanted to. The word 'marriage' did not appear on the wall nor did the statement 'I want to be a virgin when I get married'. The words making up the display on the wall enshrined commonly-held twenty-first century attitudes to sexuality and denied a voice to others. We should be aware that literacy and communication in general are the means by which a child is enculturated into a specific group with particular values. In a democracy with a system of state-controlled education it is essential that we do not crush religious minorities under the weight of secular culture.

Learning has been compared to an apprenticeship and this would suggest that children are especially good at tuning into the patterns, habits, procedures, attitudes, values and beliefs of those they see around them; Mary Hilton notes that long 'before you are locked into what you might call a generalised intellectual culture of the West, all you know, all you bring to school as a 5-year-old, is your family culture' (Hilton, 2003, p. 131). Given that this is the case we need to consider what happens when there is a mismatch between the values of home and school. The current emphasis upon continuity between 'in-school' and 'out-of-school' literacy activities is valuable but the same degree of attention has not been given to the continuity of values between home and school. Pedagogy is never neutral and if the messages a child receives from the home and those which come from school differ the result can be damaging. As schooling is an ideological intervention in children's lives there are often good reasons for the school to come into line with the home and not vice versa although professionals in education, such as teachers, often expect the opposite to be the norm. Citizenship in a plural society must ensure that its teachers and textbooks respect the families and communities of all children.

Chapter 5

Citizenship and Moral Education through the Arts

In this chapter the potential of Arts subjects to inform Citizenship and Moral Education is evaluated with reference to both aesthetic theory and classroom practice. Innovative perspectives on cultural literacy and approaches to contemporary and canonical works of art that may prompt moral engagement are explored. Particular relevance to the Citizenship curriculum is found in the study of satirical works which expose society's vice and folly and in the topic of public art for contested public spaces. How the Arts can help young citizens to become informed and active is described with reference to the moral significance of responses evoked by a range of works.

Art for active Citizenship

To date 'very little has been written about the link between art and citizenship' (Hills-Potter, 2004, p. 39) within schools in the UK which might be surprising given the capacity of art to foster reflection upon action and bring about change in behaviour as a result of changed ways of seeing. The potential of art to alter one's behaviour and augment experience was recognized by Vygotsky in *The Psychology of Art* (1971), where the close relation between action and art is made plain: 'From the most ancient times art has always been regarded as a long range programme for changing our behaviour and organism' (ibid., p. 253). Arguably, most current approaches to Citizenship fail to draw significantly upon the arts within the school and community. Vygotsky, however, draws our attention to art in ancient times and the significance of the rich cultural and aesthetic context in which the democracy of ancient Greece thrived. In the fifth century BC issues of importance to the citizens of Athens were explored in public through the arts. Just as the plays of Sophocles, Euripides and Aeschylus addressed issues of political importance and enabled Athenian citizens to reflect upon their actions and their society, so too can works of art today which engage with the concerns of our society. The capacity of art to bring about a change in the way citizens perceive themselves and their society (which is a prerequisite for changed action) is the focus of attention in this chapter.

Art and the reflective citizen

Art is 'a central and essential human and social activity' (Stibbs, 1998, p. 202) and it is 'art's ability to shock and inspire, to change vision, ideas and feelings' (ibid., p. 210) that can be morally educative. Robert Browning notes in his poem 'Fra Lippo Lippi' that 'things we have passed/ Perhaps a hundred times' can be 'better, painted – better to us' because in the painting we can experience what we have overlooked (or never cared to notice) in life; according to the poet, 'Art was given for that'. Aesthetic activity and response can enable children to re-evaluate their attitudes, values, expectations and also enable them to confront their prejudices (Pike, 2002) and yet the potential of the Arts to aid reflection appears to be largely untapped in the current methodologies of Citizenship teaching in schools. When children reproduce their perceptions through art, regardless of the medium, the act of representation tells us about far more than what was seen; it reveals the lens through which it was seen, a theme taken up later in this chapter. Encouraging children to reflect upon their own particular perspective as an element of aesthetic response can have dramatic effects (Pike, 2000a, 2000b) for 'knowing how we see or read things helps us to see and read things differently' (Stibbs, 2000, p. 43). When children see differently they can make choices about action in the public domain on the basis of their fresh vision.

Educating for life

Not all of our pupils will become playwrights, poets, painters or film directors. Nor will all our pupils directly use what they learn through arts subjects when they gain employment. Why then should they gain experience of the Arts while at school? One answer is that the adults our pupils become will not spend all of their waking hours at work. Outside the workplace they will enjoy leisure time and participate in family and community activities and should be prepared for these pursuits. To emphasize this is especially important at a time when the quest for economic efficiency, material profit and technological advancement privilege more determinist areas of the curriculum. The forces of utilitarianism are militant and the justification for studying a particular subject is often reduced, by hard-pressed teachers, to its potential for helping the child gain employment. Andrew Motion has recently called for 'creativity time' in the curriculum and it is essential to recognize a central feature of arts education in schools: it provides schooling for *life* and not simply *work*. Children have aesthetic needs:

> Were they not able to be moved by feelings of awe and wonder at the beauty of the world we live in, or the power of artists, musicians, and writers to manipulate space, sound and language, they would live in an inner spiritual and cultural desert.
>
> (SCAA, 1995, p. 4)

Those living in such a spiritual and cultural desert are unlikely to become responsible, informed and engaged citizens who participate in a range of cultural activities which benefit their communities. If one accepts the link between personal and public life, whether it is possible to become a discerning citizen without a proper sense of aesthetic appreciation is doubtful. Nurturing aesthetic experience should be the task of every school and yet the close relation between such experience and the education of citizens appears to be only rarely appreciated.

Aesthetic experience and social engagement

The Arts are integral to the community culture of which future citizens are the custodians as well as the beneficiaries. Galleries, museums, theatres, libraries, workshops, as well as many public spaces, house or provide a context for the appreciation of art and citizens are responsible for such facilities. Whether a citizen believes public money should fund institutions such as the Royal Opera House or British Museum is related to the value he or she attaches to the arts. Many community art projects as well as specially commissioned works are also publicly funded and if citizens see no need of them they will be at risk. Artists also depict public events and are often commissioned to do so. Responding to works of art depicting contemporary events entails a response to current issues of public interest. Recently reported research on the use of works of art as an initial stimulus for teaching Citizenship has concluded that lessons about artworks 'might prompt greater social engagement and nurture attitudes helpful in promoting active citizenship' (Hills-Potter 2004, p. 39) but those which engage with and critique moral matters of wide public concern would appear to have special merit within the Citizenship lesson. One of 'the main benefits of teaching about artworks' can be 'increased levels of social engagement' with the concomitant that 'alienation from society decreases' (ibid., p. 39). Indeed, using art has been found to 'sharpen sensitivity to emotions' and has even fostered 'enhanced feelings of empathy, an important quality in the development of active citizenship' (ibid., p. 41). That the Arts can promote engagement with society is not seriously in doubt; whether the Arts can help children to become *good* citizens is another matter.

The art of good Citizenship

Bold claims have been made over the years for the civilizing influence of the Arts. If we take great literature as an example, the civilizing and humanizing power of the classics, the canon of literary art studied on most English Literature degree courses, has often been advocated. The confidence in the moral efficacy of great literature was promoted by the Romantics and reached its apotheosis in Victorian England. For Matthew Arnold the 'poetic' element in poetry could not be abstracted from the poem without destroying the 'moral' significance of the poem (Arnold, 1879/1988, p. 499). Similarly, T. S. Eliot considered that a literary work of art 'affects us as entire human beings, it affects our moral and religious existence' (1935, p. 396). Indeed,

If we, as readers, keep our religious and moral convictions in one compart-
ment, and take our reading merely for entertainment, or on a higher plain, for
aesthetic pleasure, I would point out that the author, whatever his conscious
intentions in writing, in practice recognizes no such distinctions.

(ibid., p. 394)

Subsequently the beliefs of F. R. Leavis (1948, 1975) were influential in education.
For Leavis, great authors bring an unusual and rare degree of profound honesty to
their depiction of humanity. This is relevant to Citizenship and Moral Education
because great writers, so the argument goes, can help us become discerning *people*
not just discerning *readers* as they enable us to discriminate between the true and
the false in the *world* as well as in the *text*. While aesthetic experience can foster
engagement and empathy we should be cautious not to claim too much for the
power of art to humanize and civilize. The Nazi commandant at Auschwitz relaxed
after a day supervising the gas chambers by reading Goethe. He was not alone;
many of those responsible for the most barbaric acts have been highly educated
people with a sophisticated understanding of the high art, music and literature
of the West. That those responsible for genocide appreciated Goethe, Schiller
and Beethoven would appear to disprove the hypothesis that one develops greater
sensitivity to moral issues as a result of aesthetic engagement. Evidently we must
be careful not to claim redemptive power for great works of art (or education and
democracy for that matter) or imply that our society will become a better place by
simply exposing children to works of art. How children are taught in the arts and
how their responses are channelled can make a significant difference to the moral
education occurring in the lesson. Much art does not seek to resolve questions of
good or evil or claim to present truth. Artworks often present life's paradoxes and
ambiguities and leave the observer to act in the light of reflection. Exposure to art
is insufficient in itself to make us good citizens, and teachers need to consider how
responses to works of art can be guided in order to fulfil the requirements of
the Citizenship curriculum to promote empathy, respect and tolerance (Pike, 2003a,
2004b).

The decisions taken by artists and those with responsibility for artworks are
never neutral. The artist's choice of subject matter and viewpoint represent value
judgements, and reflection upon such judgements or aesthetic statements can reveal
to students what their own values are, whether they are congruent with those
of the artist or opposed to them. Calvin Seerveld goes so far as to argue that art
is 'worship' or an 'attempt to bring honour and glory and power to something' for
it expresses 'with what vision the artist views the world' and 'telltales in whose
service the artist stands' (1995, p. 21). Clearly, if the appreciation of the artwork
entails a value judgement this represents something akin to 'worship' too; it can
help young citizens understand what their own values are and what they believe
is important, valuable, worthwhile and ultimately, perhaps, worthy of worship. Art
is in no sense neutral if it is the 'intuitively perceptive metaphoric grasp of something's final meaning' (ibid., p. 32) and we need to recognize that the views of the

artist and the person apprehending the art may differ markedly; it is this contrast or 'aesthetic distance' (Jauss, 1982) that can be so valuable in Citizenship and Moral Education.

If a student believes the artist has fallen into temptation and is siding 'with those sinning' (Seerveld, 1995, p. 52) this reveals certain of that student's values. If a violent scene from a war or human conflict is depicted and responded to, this can be of tremendous value in the Citizenship lesson where the morality of war is the subject and the responsibilities of the UK government are considered. If students are discussing whether war is justified, and in which circumstances, or who bears the responsibility for the deaths and suffering of people in Iraq, art can provide a valuable stimulus. When young citizens are rightly disturbed by human suffering in war and are seeking to understand who is responsible for causing such pain it might be appropriate to study works such as Picasso's *Guernica*:

> a screaming woman burning to death in a closet, an aghast, fleeing shocked-awake head viewing a dismembered, exploded warrior, a mother in naked anguish with the dead body of her child in her arms crying out bootlessly under the impassive nose of a double eyed bull.
>
> (Seerveld, 1995, p. 47)

This work conveys a value judgement about where the ultimate blame for such suffering lies; for Seerveld it is sinful or immoral not because it is ugly but 'sinful is its ruthless God-damning spirit' as the message conveyed is that 'the helpless people do not deserve this misery so who does whoever is in charge think he is, a sacred bull? Who but a beast could let such inhumanity go on?' (1995, p. 47). While we would endorse Picasso's view of the horror of war there may be considerable variation in our interpretations of the causes of and responsibility for such suffering. Students can be led through their response to this work of art to consider the economic, political or territorial motivation for war and human conflict. Seerveld's theology is in direct conflict with Picasso's but the 'aesthetic distance' (Jauss, 1982) provided by the work provokes an exploration of the views held by each. We bring with us a set of beliefs when we view a work and with appropriate teaching and guided reflection in response to art, students can become aware of their own beliefs as citizens and those of others as well as evaluating the actions of their government.

Citizenship, the Arts and cultural literacy

The notion of cultural literacy, of being able to 'read' one's culture and communicate effectively within it has long been associated with Citizenship education. E. D. Hirsch's theory is that being culturally literate enables a citizen to read and interpret the texts that are produced by society. In the famous work *Cultural Literacy* he claims that 'literate culture has become the common currency for social and economic exchange in our democracy, and the only available ticket to full citizenship' (1987, p. 22). Being concerned about school-age children's lack of 'cultural literacy' (which he defines as the background knowledge required to interpret the texts vital to effective communication and interaction in society) Hirsch has called for the teaching of a national cultural canon in US schools. In the appendix to *Cultural Literacy* a list running to sixty-three pages is given and from this it is clear what culturally literate people should know about classical and Christian culture: Scylla and Charybdis, the Ten Commandments, Samson and Delilah and so on. The emphasis in Hirsch's list is associated with the resurgence of traditional values and is bound up with beliefs concerning the Christian faith, the family, patriotism and freedom.

The search for a unified cultural identity in the wake of the events of 11 September 2001 in the US may well increase the desire to ensure citizens possess such knowledge. It is interesting to note that, just after the First World War, when values and ways of living were being evaluated, the Newbolt Committee in Great Britain produced an influential report which stated that 'a liberal education should be not only a gift within the reach of every child, but the very gift purposed by the State in the elementary training of its citizens' (1921, p. 342). Whether or not one agrees with Hirsch's particular brand of 'cultural literacy' it is important for Citizenship educators to consider what cultural knowledge it is important for its citizens to acquire. Once this is decided the Arts have a key place in facilitating the acquisition of such knowledge. When pupils design their own 'National Curriculum for Citizenship', which sets out the knowledge they think citizens should acquire, this can reveal the curriculum designers' priorities and facilitate reflection. In much the same way students can be asked to design their own Citizenship test and reflect upon its value, although a reasonable degree of cultural literacy is required to make informed choices about the content of Citizenship.

The promotion of 'cultural literacy' is often associated with what writers such as Beck (1998) describe as neo-conservative politics seeking to promote classical and Christian 'texts' as a unifying basis for our society. On this view 'the teaching of the majority culture, with the emphasis on the English language, English history and literary heritage, and the study of Christianity and the classical world' should be part of the education of every pupil because it enables them 'to develop a sense of where they are as people living in Britain' (Tate, 1995). Questions certainly have to be asked about which texts it is necessary for citizens in the twenty-first century to be familiar with and the notion that citizens should be culturally literate or possess the ability to engage with a specified range of cultural texts requires careful analysis. There are strong religious reasons, for instance, why some Muslims may not want to become 'culturally literate' in Western music, dance and, perhaps, drama, preferring Islamic poetry, calligraphy and recitation. The place of the Arts in a multicultural society requires careful evaluation (Burtonwood, 1995). The extent to which good Citizenship is based upon a common culture is certainly worth discussing in the Citizenship lesson. Children in a multicultural society should learn about more than the majority culture for this can only give a partial sense of where they are as people living in Britain; they should also learn to appreciate the views of citizens whose cultural literacy is quite different to their own.

The motives for promoting the canonical works of art that explore classical and Christian themes have to be carefully evaluated. Paradoxically, one of the most compelling justifications for children from diverse backgrounds studying works of art from the classical and Christian past is to help them understand themselves in the present (Pike, 2003c). The cultural difference between pupils and the works of art they respond to can provide them with 'aesthetic distance' (Jauss, 1982; Pike, 2002) that many contemporary works may offer to a lesser degree. The chrono-logical, social, religious and cultural *difference* between a classical or Christian work of the past and the child itself can help that child to reflect upon their particu-lar way of living and values in the present if appropriate pedagogy is adopted. Pupils may be more likely to have their horizons changed in diachronic transactions than in synchronic ones (Pike, 2003c) and appreciating the work of artists who inhabited a very different time and culture to their own can be enriching, given appropriate pedagogy, for children from very different backgrounds.

While some critics seek to authorize the study of traditional, canonical works of art in the search for a unified cultural identity (Bloom, 1987; Hirsch, 1987) there are cogent and morally defensible reasons for advocating the study of such texts alongside those from a range of cultures and traditions. Those who suggest that canonical works promote anachronistic attitudes tend to miss the point some-what. Such views are often based on the assumption that works of art are morally authoritative but it is important to recognize that 'works of art are artificial (and, therefore, not necessarily authoritative and truthful)' (Stibbs, 2001, p. 42). Consequently, it can be the *difference* between the world of the work of art and the world in which children find themselves today that is a resource for both Citizenship and Moral Education. A work of art, whether literary or visual, 'neither describes nor constitutes real objects' for by definition it 'diverges from the real experiences of the reader in that it offers up views and opens up perspectives in which the empirically known world of one's own personal experience appears changed' (Iser, 1971, p. 8). In this way it can provide a morally educative experience.

Citizenship and Moral Education through Art and Design

The opportunities for Art and Design education to inform the teaching of Citizenship are extensive. The art classroom is a unique environment and it is here that a sense of achievement in both individual and group work can be fostered. The art room can provide a context that helps children value the contributions of others. They can learn about different ways of representing the natural and built environment and develop an understanding of how works of art, craft and design reflect cultural and ideological beliefs and values. Creating works of art for the local community can help children to appreciate the social and political dimension of aesthetic activity. When children see how artists, designers and craftspeople have reacted to and been stimulated by important issues in society and the way they have expressed their beliefs in creative work attention is being given to their citizenship. The process of decision-making and engaging in collaborative projects which help children reflect on the significance of art and design in their society is also especially important for future citizens. In the following sections examples will be given of how both classical and contemporary works of art can contribute to the Citizenship curriculum. Firstly, the work of graffiti artists will be considered as their work appears in public spaces and can be related to issues of rights and responsibilities. Secondly, the social satire of Hogarth from the eighteenth century and the value of *The Harlot's Progress* in particular will be discussed.

Graffiti: art or vandalism?

Whether or not graffiti is capable of being art and where it should be allowed is a fascinating subject for the Citizenship lesson considering freedom of expression, public and private ownership of space as well as competing rights and responsibilities. Some adolescents might ask why it is against the law to create murals in public spaces which they consider show an appreciation of space, line, symmetry and colour. They may ask why work which celebrates the beauty of life on a dull, monotonous and unimaginative stone building (the surface of which is considered to be public property) is disapproved of. Indeed, discussing the whole notion of 'public' property can be fruitful. Some interesting points are often made by the most perceptive, and sometimes most challenging, students who have been known to point out that a commercial billboard 'invading' public space (and advertising cigarettes or clothing made by exploited children in southeast Asia) is considered to be private property as it belongs to the commercial enterprise that owns the hoarding when their protests and demands for social justice, expressed through graffiti in other public spaces, are illegal.

Artists such as Jean-Michel Basquiat (1960–1988) achieved fame and success with his Graffiti Art in 1980s New York and can be studied to illustrate some of the issues concerning art and the use of public space. Basquiat challenged the art world establishment through his use of African American iconography and was simply dismissed by some critics who rejected the whole movement. A discussion of graffiti art can be especially valuable within the Citizenship curriculum if the democratization of art is explored. Some artists have suggested that walls, where graffiti is encouraged, should be set up throughout urban centres so that this can become an egalitarian form of expression and a democratic cultural activity. The 'Keep Britain Tidy' campaign, on the other hand, argues that graffiti makes people feel unsafe and causes towns to appear squalid. Debate about what is acceptable to different people in public spaces and how agreement can be reached about the visual culture of such areas is a suitably provocative stimulus for Citizenship lessons. The uses of taxpayers' money (it cost £27 million to clean up graffiti in the UK in 2004) can also be debated and ways of tackling offenders should be considered.

Whether graffiti should be celebrated as a democratic art form which brings people together or whether it should be seen as vandalism to be restricted or even banned are views that students can consider. When the themes of graffiti are recognized, the ways in which graffiti reflects personal, social, political and cultural values and beliefs can be analysed. Respect for property, and for that matter anything belonging to other people, should be taught by teachers and it should be made clear that deliberate marking, however artistic, is illegal vandalism if it is done without the owner's consent. The experience of having one's property damaged is common in most classrooms where bags or equipment have been taken without permission and if students are aware of how this feels they are in a position to evaluate the impact of graffiti in communities which have not requested the services of a resident graffiti artist. How we seek the common good in public space has numerous parallels relating to human rights and the need for people who have different values to live together without causing offence. Visual culture in general and the visual culture of the school is currently receiving increased attention (Prosser, 1998). The ways in which the school's visual culture communicates its ethos and values, the extent to which there is a democratization of public space and how different sites (toilets, workshops, common rooms, staffrooms, entrance foyers) are differentially controlled can provide fascinating and controversial subject matter for Citizenship lessons. Issues of control, power, values and rights which feature in discussions of graffiti and visual culture can also be foregrounded, as we shall see, in the study of more conventional if not less controversial art. The relevance of art to the moral education of citizens is not by any means restricted to contemporary works.

The Harlot's Progress

Hogarth's series of painting *The Harlot's Progress* tells the sordid tale of what happens to a young girl who arrives in London from the countryside with nowhere to go – a situation not dissimilar to that faced by countless teenagers even today. Homelessness and the plight of those in such a predicament are often dealt with in Citizenship lessons where the responsibilities of local councils to provide shelter and the work of charities, who seek to help those who are destitute, are studied. Moll is friendless and vulnerable, falls in with the wrong company and ends up working as a prostitute. When students perceive that society seems to have changed very little in important respects since 1732 and that poor and vulnerable teenagers arriving in cities are still exploited, valuable lessons can be learned.

Such a situation is paralleled today when young girls, transported from rural areas in eastern Europe, are promised a better life in the UK by criminals who then exploit them and force them to work as prostitutes. When such illegal sex-traffic has been discovered in some of the UK's cities, it has become clear that many of the prostitutes, from poor villages in formerly communist countries, have been duped and then blackmailed. Threats of violence to be carried out on family members back in Romania or Bulgaria ensure compliance by the victims and protect those organizing the activity from prosecution. As many of the prostitutes are illegal immigrants and often speak little English they find it extremely difficult to exercise the most basic of human rights. This raises a number of important questions about the law, immigration and customs within the EU. It also raises issues concerning economics and the way wealth and poverty can operate to oppress the most vulnerable. The proposed solutions to such illegal activities, the rights of women and the progress made in other countries to tackle prostitution are all legitimate and important areas of study within Citizenship.

Looking at works such as *The Harlot's Progress* prompts students to consider the sort of society we live in that permits such exploitation and has singularly failed to improve the lot of such vulnerable teenagers since the time of Hogarth. The experience of Moll, depicted in these paintings, is both realistic and harrowing. The story can be summarized as follows: Moll is a simple country girl who is met by a well-known procuress when she arrives in London. Moll first becomes a fashionable courtesan and then a street prostitute who is imprisoned. Some years go by and then Moll is depicted in a terrible state as venereal diseases, contracted by plying her trade, ravage her body. By this time, however, Moll is the mother of a little boy. Later we see Moll crouching in agony, diseased and dying while her few remaining possessions are stolen from her. Finally, Hogarth depicts the funeral of Moll, aged twenty-three, where her small son is the chief mourner.

Such a work of art is morally educative as it shows the consequences of actions, but this work and others can be used in Citizenship lessons to raise many questions in teenagers' minds: What will happen to Moll's son, the little boy, who we see as her chief mourner? What kind of life can he expect to lead? Will he receive an education? If not, will he be exploited like his mother? What are his prospects as an illegitimate orphan? Would Moll have fallen into prostitution if she had had another means of support? Should prostitution be legalized and regulated today? How should society deal with it? What role does the government have at European, national and local levels in the prevention of such activity? What are the economic implications of prostitution? How can inequalities in wealth lead to exploitation of the poor? If Moll lived today would she be on drugs? How would her drug habit keep her working as a prostitute? In such a situation should a local council provide free needle exchange? What are the moral implications of such governmental action? What laws would the class make to attempt to ensure that suffering like Moll's is not repeated? What exactly does the law say at the moment regarding prostitution? Using art as a stimulus and fostering empathy for Moll and those like her through such a work would appear to be a better approach to take to this topic than beginning with a barren, factual study of the law concerning drugs, prostitution or homelessness.

Hogarth explores a moral situation that is re-enacted today and can lead children to a consideration of sexual ethics, the law, the duty a local authority has to look after and house those who are destitute and so on. Social satire should be an essential element of any Citizenship course. The satire exposes human vice and folly but does more than this; it exposes the faults in society and prompts us to consider what our responsibilities as citizens are and how our society should protect the most vulnerable. The value of studying a work of art such as *The Harlot's Progress* is that it foregrounds important social issues such as destitution, prostitution and sexually transmitted disease. These are important issues and exploring their public dimension can be illuminating within the Citizenship lesson. Social satire is especially relevant to work in Citizenship and there are many contemporary examples that can be drawn upon. What is brought home very forcibly in *The Harlot's Progress* is that 'it is the utter waste of a young life and the despoiling of innocence by the corruptions of a sick society that have provoked Hogarth's indignation' (Benton, 1995, p. 36). It is the sickness of society and the social issues that Hogarth depicts which are so relevant to the Citizenship curriculum and also to moral education. Studying such a work can arouse children's curiosity and enable them to express important moral questions. Hogarth explores the values of a desperately corrupt society in his work and this can enable children to reflect on the values and actions of their own society and their responsibilities as members of that society.

Censorship of art displayed in public places is another valuable topic to be addressed in Citizenship and Moral Education. Totalitarian regimes generally impose censorship and the 1937 'Degenerate Art' exhibition in Munich is a good example of a government exercising censorship in order to promote a worldview and attitudes that that would support the Nazi regime. On the other hand, democracies recognize that some members of the community are deeply offended by works of art that are praised by others. Feminists may deem certain works to be pornographic or degrading to women and religious groups may find certain works blasphemous and yet such works are displayed in galleries supported by the taxes of these groups. While recognizing that freedom is a central value in a democracy and that we must often tolerate the views of those we do not share, the issue here is the extent to which the offence caused to some people should limit the freedom of expression of others. In Citizenship lessons especially we should be aware of the need to protect children and the most vulnerable members of society and this will necessitate some restrictions on the freedom of others, especially within public places.

Citizenship and Moral Education through English

Although both English and English Literature in schools are closely related to the Citizenship curriculum the focus here will, in the main, be upon the potential of literature (rather than literacy or language which are explored in Chapter 4) to provide young readers with morally educative experiences. It is not possible, however, to ignore the contribution English (sometimes referred to as 'English language') can make to Citizenship education. Consider for a moment the second half of the AQA GCSE Foundation tier English paper sat by candidates on Friday 10 June 2005:

The Minister for Schools is making a list of skills which young people should have in order to make them good citizens.

Write a letter to the Minister for Schools in which you review some of the skills you have learned and comment on how useful you think they will be for you, as a citizen, in the future.

Transactional writing where arguments are presented to a public representative are common in English lessons. Although the GCSE examination in 2005 was explicitly relevant to the Citizenship curriculum it is not unusual for contemporary issues concerning Citizenship to be the subject of discussion in English both inside and outside the examination. Recently students have been required to express their views about the arming of the British Police and to comment on truancy and car crime. Moral issues such as genetic engineering, abortion, advertising, gender stereotyping, vivisection, euthanasia and fox hunting are all regularly debated in English lessons. Furthermore, the skills of communication, and especially small group discussion (assessed for GCSE English) contribute to the development of students' moral understanding and are relevant to the Citizenship programme of study.

Despite the relevance of such topics within English language it will be suggested here that it is literature which offers the greatest potential for fostering morally aware and responsible citizens. In view of this it is especially regrettable that the subject of English in the UK appears to be moving away from the literary arts (or language arts as they are called in the US) and experiencing a shift towards nonfiction such as transactional writing as a result of the advent of the National Literacy Strategy. The result of the Strategy is that the focus in English is increasingly upon utilitarian forms of reading and writing that give value for money in the market place (Pike, 2004c). The significance for children's moral education, and their citizenship, of any diminution in their experience of literature (or the language arts) will be appreciated when some of the claims made on behalf of literature are considered. It has been suggested that 'Literature, more than any other subject in the curriculum, offers the fullest possible picture both of the complexities of the moral situation and the consequences of action' (McCulloch and Mathieson, 1995, p. 30). It is particularly important, at a time when Citizenship is assuming such importance in schools, that the value and potential of literature is understood by policy makers. Literature opens the way to a different way of being, a 'secondary world' where new possibilities exist. W. H. Auden put it like this:

> Present in every human being are two desires, a desire to know the truth about the primary world, the given world outside ourselves in which we are born, live, love, hate and die, and the desire to make new secondary worlds of our own or, if we cannot make them ourselves, to share in the secondary worlds of those who can.
>
> (1968, p. 49)

Arguably, making new secondary worlds is the key to renewing our primary world. Such a task is an essentially ethical activity and is central to moral education as it involves envisioning new ways of being. For A. S. Byatt (1998), reading literature is so potent because it augments a child's experience in quite specific ways: it enables them to explore the moral and spiritual consequences of human action and to appreciate its complexity and interrelatedness. Recently a number of scholars (Trousdale, 2004; Kirk, 2004; Halstead and Outram Halstead, 2004; Witte-Townsend and DiGiulio, 2004; Smith, 2004; Pike, 2004c) have demonstrated in a special issue of the *International Journal of Children's Spirituality* how reading literature is related to children's spiritual and moral development.

The promotion of the sort of reflection that is vital to moral development can be fostered through aesthetic reading where readers are actively encouraged to see the connection between their experiences and those depicted in the work of literary art. When 'the reader's attention is focused on what he is living through during the reading event' (Rosenblatt, 1985, p. 38), moral education is possible. This can be illustrated by some readers' responses to the poem 'Vultures' by Chinua Achebe. The poem explores the nature of evil and was first published in 1971 in *Beware Soul Brother* (published in the US as *Christmas in Biafra*). Achebe wrote 'Vultures' while working for the Biafran government at a time when this region declared itself an independent state and was then starved into capitulation by Nigerian armed forces. In the second stanza of the poem our attention is directed to the horrors of the Nazi era and the Kommandant of Belsen Camp is portrayed as being capable of both love and brutality. He is simultaneously a mass murderer and a caring father; the man who stops at the sweet shop on the way home from work to buy his children chocolate has 'the smell of human roast clinging rebelliously to his nostrils'. The teenagers who read the poem found such profoundly contradictory behaviour extremely disturbing and Achebe deliberately presents the reader with a moral choice regarding such paradoxical behaviour at the end of the poem. The reader is left to decide whether humans are essentially evil but capable of good behaviour or essentially good with the capacity to do evil. Readers are forced to complete the poem for themselves by providing the moral interpretation (Pike, 2000b).

Although it has been argued that 'the reader is the final arbiter of a text's morality' (Gallagher and Lundin, 1989, p. 140) some works may have a specific moral agenda and be especially helpful in helping readers to assess their own world. When a group of fifteen- and sixteen-year-olds recently read 'The Latest Decalogue' by Arthur Hugh Clough for GCSE they compared Victorian society and its values with their own. After some reflection one reader wrote:

> This interpretation of Victorian spiritual malaise causes the reader to look at themselves and the way they live. Clough is intending to correct human vice by showing up the immoral newest Decalogue everyone seems to be following. I feel that in today's society we live in a more multicultural, pluralistic world, there is less hypocrisy as people are very frank and open about themselves.
>
> (Pike, 2000c, p. 24)

Texts often explore topical social and moral issues and do so by portraying relationships between the individual and society. Film versions of literary works (such as *The Lord of the Flies* by William Golding or *Holes* by Louis Sacher) can also be put to good effect as a stimulus for the discussion of a wide range of citizenship issues. English literature contributes to children's personal growth, the development of identity and to their spiritual and moral development by provoking and challenging them in the way that only literature can.

Citizenship and Moral Education through Drama

Drama is an important area of the curriculum in which Citizenship and Moral Education can take place as this discipline 'commonly explores moral dilemmas, injustices of various kinds and will consider the implications of specific human actions within a range of ordinary and extraordinary situations' (Winston, 1999, p. 460).

The drama studio provides a space in which to explore the complex nature of moral situations where children can come to understand the consequences of decisions for individuals and whole communities. Diversity can be explored through performance and productions in the community where personal issues engage with broader social concerns so that the feelings of others, and the issues important to them within society, are appreciated.

Encouraging empathy through Forum Theatre

The use of Forum Theatre to explore refugee and homeless issues has recently been reported by Laura Day (2002) who focused on the issue of the refugee child at school and the impact of a performance staged by a theatre company whose actors had experienced being homeless and/or refugees in their own lives. Findings from the research indicate that the workshop was highly relevant to students and provided them with the opportunity to rehearse moral responses and behaviour which could be enacted in their daily lives. Such work enabled students to empathize with both fictional characters and peers at school. The actors' life histories of homelessness and their experiences of being refugees brought the workshop experience to life. The tremendous potential of such dramatic activity to contribute to children's moral education and their understanding of a range of issues relevant to their citizenship was, however, militated against by the lack of an integrated cross-curricular approach and exemplifies why throughout this book an integrated approach to Citizenship and Moral Education especially through the Arts and Humanities has been advocated:

> The Forum Theatre workshop aimed to encourage the students to become moral agents in their own lives. However, its ability to do this was limited by the lack of both moral reflection upon the issues raised, and guidance in appropriate moral action following the workshop. This absence of follow-up

relates to the fact that the workshop was perceived by teachers as a drama activity, and no attempts were made to address its moral content which, teachers felt, belonged to the domain of Personal, Social and Health Education (PSHE).

(Day, 2002, p. 21)

Drama is concerned with meaning and values and can be used to explore rights and responsibilities but cross-curricular links are essential if there is to be continuity in children's moral education and understanding of their responsibilities as citizens.

Meaning-making and active citizenship through Drama

The range of experiences that the Drama curriculum provides is extensive: students can 'improvise or work from script; they might invent their own work or study play texts; they might create drama, perform it, read it or watch and respond to it; they might work physically, through representation, or through talk' (Winston, 1999, p. 460). A central feature of all of these activities is that they deal with meaning-making. How meanings are ascribed rather than passively received and how beliefs, values and attitudes are enacted is directly relevant to notions of 'active citizenship'. The relevance of Drama to wider social and political concerns is apparent when one considers its different aspects. Anton Franks considers Drama to have three dimensions and all three are pertinent to Moral and Citizenship Education. According to Franks, 'drama as art, text and performance selects, shapes and actively materialises aspects of personal, social and cultural life'; secondly, 'involvement in drama is to engage the personal with wider social concerns and interests'; thirdly, 'modes, structures and forms of drama, as text and performance' have 'particular values' attached to them (1999, p. 44). Drama is concerned with meanings and values which are exchanged and reviewed and as such is both creative and critical.

Story drama and moral dilemmas

Drama is valued for 'its techniques and conventions which facilitate children's engagement in, and response to, texts' (Grainger, 1998, p. 29) and one common approach, relevant to Moral Education, is to involve children in the prediction of action; when children engage in such thought or when they adopt roles their appreciation of complex issues and moral dilemmas can be enhanced. When they are engaged in story drama children can respond aesthetically and fill 'gaps in the tale' (ibid., p. 30). Grainger has provided examples of this approach at work which is about a 'search for meaning' where 'options can be left open and multiple meanings accepted' (ibid., p. 33).

Social interaction for citizens

It is easy to miss the significance of social interaction, which is uniquely fostered in Drama, for Citizenship and Moral Education. It is not just that Drama departments regularly organize school plays which are whole-school events of some scale and are often attended by those in the community. Children do learn to participate as a team when they are involved in putting on a 'show' whether they are engaged as lighting engineers, front-of-house ticket sellers, publicity distributors or catering assistants in a way that is rarely experienced within the formal curriculum. Yet social interaction is also routinely a distinctive feature of lessons where self-control is to be exercised in a space devoid of desks and chairs. Working together in close physical proximity where there is the potential for disruptive behaviour is a challenge most pupils rise to in Drama. Group work also involves children in an evaluation of their own performance as well as that of others and the way they work as a group. Relating this to the way society works ensures that drama addresses key concerns of the Citizenship curriculum. By focusing on speaking and listening skills and personal expression drama also contributes to the ability of future citizens to have a public voice.

Aesthetic distance and the moral journey of citizens

Having considered some of the ways in which issues of concern for Citizenship and Moral Education can be approached through Arts subjects it is important, in concluding, to look briefly at ways of knowing in the arts. It has been suggested that aesthetic encounters have the power to transform as they can help us see in new ways but just how this happens is worth considering. A key concept, already alluded to in this chapter, is that of 'aesthetic distance' for it is this which can provide children with a fresh perspective upon their world, puncture their complacency and galvanize them into action. Hans Robert Jauss defined 'aesthetic distance' as the difference between the 'given horizon of expectations' and what happens at 'the appearance of a new work of art' (1982, p. 25). According to Jauss, one judges a new work of art against the backdrop of one's own past experience. If a work fails to force 'horizonal' change and only serves to fulfil or reinforce expectations then 'no turn to the horizon of yet unknown experience' is required (ibid., p. 25). Such a work is merely of entertainment value and will be of little use in fostering active citizens committed to seeing their community improved.

Response to a new work of art can reconfigure as well as augment the learner's experience and can result in a 'change of horizons' (Jauss, 1982, p. 25). Aesthetic response can move the learner away from the personal to consider the public dimension with which Citizenship is concerned. Arguably, 'aesthetic distance' maps out the territory within which active citizenship can take place in the arts. Works which provide 'aesthetic distance' enable important, even ultimate, questions to be asked by learners which 'do not need to be couched within the ground rules of a competitive game' (Palmer, 1983, p. 76). Works of art that depict 'challenging experiences, such as death, suffering, beauty, and encounters with good and evil' have the capacity to cause profound horizonal change as they often lead the learner to 'search for meaning and purpose and for values by which to live' (SCAA, 1995, p. 3). Arguably, 'the significance of the Arts lies in their fundamentally ontological character, in other words, their ability to raise issues of existence and being to the level of consciousness' (Pike, 2004b).

Moral Education through the Arts which informs learning about one's citizenship is likely to have several distinct features. It may be characterized by communal understanding rather than competition as aesthetic appreciation rarely takes place in isolation and is generally enhanced and augmented by social interaction (Pike, 2003a). Further, in an aesthetic environment the learner cannot be construed as object and the teacher cannot be seen as the 'deliverer' of knowledge for 'aesthetic teaching' is founded upon a special sort of relational consciousness (Pike, 2004b). The study of the Arts can also teach children that there are aspects of human culture which cannot be explained and neatly defined as the sum of their parts. Although 'the picture is made by deploying pigments on a piece of canvas' it is indisputably the case that the art is more than the materials from which it is created and 'the picture is not a pigment and canvas structure' (Langer, 1957, p. 29). In other words, art is an activity that transcends the sum of its parts. Learning the value of aesthetic activity in our culture should be an integral part of the Citizenship curriculum because it helps young learners understand that as citizens they will not always be able to exercise their citizenship in exclusively rational ways. Aims and objectives in such lessons may prove especially problematic for in the Arts one is 'moving towards meaning and not starting from it' (Gardner, 1949, p. 57). McLaughlin reminds us of 'the significance of implicit and intuitive elements in human action', the limitations of 'technical rationality' as a form of reflection and 'the inappropriateness of conceiving of teaching as a *techne*' for the aims of education are 'neither clear, fixed, unitary nor evaluatively straightforward' (1999, p. 13). As well as logical and rational analysis it is sense, feeling, intuition, creativity and expression that are important to children's Citizenship and Moral Education.

The Arts, according to Martin Heidegger, one of the twentieth century's greatest philosophers, often express truths that cannot be apprehended in other ways (Pike, 2003f). Heidegger's notion of existence as *In-der-Welt-sein* (Being-in-the-world) is helpful to Citizenship and Moral Education (where one's place 'in' society is considered) because 'in', for Heidegger, is taken to mean involvement and engagement (such as being 'in' love) rather than physical placing or presence. This distinction is important. If students feel connected to their world this will necessarily have an impact on the way they exercise their citizenship. A profound appreciation of their duties as global citizens and a lasting desire and commitment to play their part in eradicating third world debt or child abuse may often be brought about through the aesthetic encounter more readily than through a factual explanation of the needs of other people. The aesthetic encounter can enable children to appreciate their common humanity with those they have never seen and help them care about places they have never been to. Children may learn more through the Arts that will prompt them to become active citizens, who strive to bring about change and social justice in their world, than in more conventional ways.

Chapter 6

The Humanities and the
Moral Education of Citizens

The place of the Humanities in the moral
education of citizens

The term 'the Humanities' refers broadly to 'the analytical engagement with human cultural settings and relationships, in individualized and collective contexts, and to the educational activities founded on this engagement' (Donnelly, 2004, p. 765). These subjects are, therefore, especially close relations of Citizenship but this chapter specifically examines the potential of the Humanities to foster children's awareness of themselves as citizens who have obligations as moral agents; it shows how they may better discharge these obligations if they have engaged in appropriately guided reflection upon human behaviour in different times and places to their own. Here the focus of our attention is on History and Geography, the two Humanities subjects generally given greatest curriculum time in schools, as the important contribution of Religious Studies is dealt with separately in the next chapter and literature has been considered in the previous chapter on the Arts.

According to Woff (1991) the Humanities are closely linked to moral education and their overall aim is to achieve 'some understanding and appreciation of the wealth of different ways in which humans have lived and expressed themselves' (Woff, 1991, p. 23). History and Geography share a common concern to address questions about the nature of humanity itself and, at their most vital, they explore *why* people live as they do. This may encompass the reasons for people living as they did in the past or it may involve the study of the behaviour and beliefs of people in different places but the humanities address our shared humanity. Evaluating the morality of the actions of citizens and governments is vital for a democracy. Governments need to understand humanity in order to govern justly with the consent of the governed; as a government in a democracy responds to the vision and values of citizens, the teachers of citizens have a sobering moral responsibility.

A survival simulation for citizens

Citizenship addresses the public dimension of life but concerns individual as well as corporate moral responsibility. How the behaviour of groups relates to individual values can be illustrated by reference to a simulation often undertaken in Humanities or Citizenship lessons. Students are divided into two groups and must imagine that they have been on an adventure holiday in a remote part of Africa. A garbled BBC news broadcast has been received by satellite; it reports a catastrophic environmental disaster which has made extensive areas of the world uninhabitable. When the students return to base they find it deserted; as far as they know they are the only people left alive.

The two groups find themselves in very different situations and this simulation provides insight into the morality of how rich and poor nations make decisions and into the values and priorities underpinning those decisions. Important lessons regarding global citizenship can be learned from this simulation which also prompts many children to reflect upon the morality of their own behaviour within the group. How resources should be used and whether they should be shared are decisions each group needs to make. One group is the 'haves' and the other is the 'have-nots', although at the start neither group realizes this.

Group A are in a better position than Group B. They find themselves in a quiet valley with mountains on all sides. A fresh-water river flows down from the mountains and uncontaminated farm crops (oats, wheat, potatoes and other vege-tables) are ready to be harvested. The abundant vegetation includes fruit trees. There are most common farm animals such as cows, pigs and hens and there are also rabbits and foxes in the wood. The climate is mild throughout the year and Group A have a small farmhouse. Farm tools and machinery as well as ordinary DIY tools are found in outbuildings for the animals. The group has a supply of chopped wood and 250 gallons of diesel oil. They have enough food to last them until the end of the summer and a supply of clothes suitable for doing farm work in.

Group B are rather less fortunate than Group A and find themselves on a wide flat plain with little grass. In the east there is a fast-flowing river with steep banks. It is clearly polluted and has dead fish floating on the surface. There are some wild blackberries and blackcurrants in the woods and on the plain they can see a pack of wild dogs which seem to eat most of the remaining rabbits. In the woods are a few squirrels. The summers are very hot and winters especially inhospitable. There are no buildings and the only tools they have are what they have in their pockets and rucksacks. The only fuel is wood which they will have to collect from the woods. They have enough food for four days at the most and the only clothing they have is what they are wearing.

After the initial twenty minutes where procedures for making decisions and group leadership are established the groups are given some new information. They are told that after several weeks of travelling, a scout from each group has returned, having discovered the existence of the other group, and a meeting is arranged. The inequitable distribution of resources between Group A and Group B parallels global inequalities between G8 nations and those in Africa, and the inter-actions between rich and poor as well as within the groups can be reflected upon by stu-dents after the simulation. Surprisingly few survivors seem to want to make decisions within the group by majority voting. A consensus after lengthy discussion is normally the preferred option as everyone then feels as though they have had their say. Systems of government and voting can also be discussed by considering the way each group made decisions and how leaders emerged and such scenarios are especially helpful because they enable learners to see the relevance of such issues to their own lives and help them to discover the values that motivate them.

Further, the mistrust with which each group views the other is often palpable; everyone seems to want to survive above all else. If the two groups do not know each other and are from different classes or even schools the lack of compassion for those in the other group is likely to increase. On one occasion the 'haves' made the 'have-nots' their slaves. Those who had least had no option but to agree to a humiliating pact whereby they would serve their masters who had greater resources. Afterwards the 'haves' attempted to defend their behaviour and just a little probing at this point revealed the values underpinning their actions. The attitude witnessed among Group A was one of 'Why should we give away what we have?'

The attitudes and decisions advocated by members of the group are often the subject of sustained and sober reflection after the workshop and students can be prompted to consider global citizenship and the obligations that rich countries have towards poorer countries as well as the responsibilities of those who are affluent, in our own country, to those who are in need. Of course, the simulation is a simplification of a complex situation and children should not believe that natural resources are all that determines prosperity or poverty. Attitudes towards labour, law and order, debt, leisure, investment, education, family life and government among others all contribute to inequalities of wealth across our world. Studying countries that were formerly within the USSR and seeking to understand why some are prospering and others are struggling is a valuable topic for both Citizenship and Geography. We would suggest that the worldviews of citizens are related to the realities of their daily lives and that fostering an understanding of beliefs and values should be an important focus of attention within Citizenship Education.

The Humanities are relevant to Citizenship because they pose questions about what it is to be human; these subjects can help children consider how humans *should* behave as compared to how they *do* behave. These questions are of seminal importance for the fostering of active citizens as 'what one thinks about human beings is of determinative significance for his or her programme of action' (Hoekema, 1986, p. 2). Immanuel Kant famously observed, 'Out of the crooked timber of humanity no straight thing can ever be made' (1784).

Whether or not we agree with Kant's assessment of the 'crookedness' of humanity we should never forget that the character of the timber determines what we can build both in the world and in our lessons. Learning about the timber and the structures built with it is the task of the Humanities. If we are, as Kant believed, handling 'crooked timber' it is all the more important that we should strive to build, in our curriculum and teaching, something which is as straight and true as we are humanly capable of.

If striving to act ethically and build what is true, teachers of Geography and History will need to make learners aware of the moral implications of the issues they study. Seemingly mundane matters such as where to locate a supermarket or a new road need to be seen by children to involve ethical choices, just as the election of local and national governments and the making of laws are moral activities. One's values and vision of the good life have a direct bearing upon such decisions. When children learn about how data is represented, how processes are described, how reliable evidence is considered to be and so on they must pay heed to the daily lives behind the data, the people behind the processes and the ethics of those who analyse the evidence.

When a child is led to reflect upon his or her own moral choices and how these relate to public concerns, it is their citizenship which is necessarily being reflected upon but it is also more than this: it is the nature of being human. There are numerous opportunities in Geography and History to consider the social and political context of human decision-making. In helping children to think about the ways in which groups of people live today, or have lived in the past, questions of values and morality can be addressed which are relevant to the Citizenship curriculum. It has been argued, for instance, that 'Geography is par excellence the discipline through which global notions of citizenship can be studied' (Walkington, 2000, p. 55). The focus in Geography upon places and environments, whether on a local, national or a global scale, can help children to see themselves as citizens who live and make decisions within different contexts. Some of these decisions and contexts will now be explored.

Citizenship and Moral Education through Geography

The potential for synergy between Geography and Citizenship is immediately apparent from a comparison of the National Curriculum requirements and programmes of study for each subject. According to the leaflet 'Citizenship through Geography at Key Stage 3' (QCA, 2001d), which maps where the two programmes of study are compatible, Geography can contribute to Citizenship by helping pupils to 'understand how decisions are made about places and environments' and 'the consequences of their own actions in situations concerning places and environments'. It also enables children to 'understand the diversity of cultures and identities in the UK and the wider world' and to understand the 'issues and challenges of global interdependence'. Broadly, Geography also helps children to 'reflect on and discuss topical social, environmental, economic and political issues' and to understand 'their rights and responsibilities to other people and the environment'.

Children can learn about aspects of the 'legal and human rights and responsibilities underpinning society' (Citizenship Programme of Study 1a, QCA/DfEE, 1999a) when they investigate environmental issues such as water pollution, acid rain, tourism and trade (Geography Programme of Study 3e, QCA/DfEE, 1999b).

They can find out about 'basic aspects of the criminal justice system' (Citizenship Programme of Study 1a, QCA/DfEE, 1999a) when learning about the degree and prevalence of crime in their community. Within Citizenship children need to learn about the 'diversity of national, regional, religious and ethnic identities in the UK' (Citizenship Programme of Study 1b, ibid.) and this can be addressed in Geography when they 'describe the national, international and global contexts of places studied' (Geography Programme of Study 3b, QCA/DfEE, 1999b) and learn about the 'human features that give rise to the distinctive character of places' (Geography Programme of Study 3c, ibid.).

Opportunities exist for each subject to inform the other when children explore the ethnic and religious dimension of housing and employment patterns when studying settlement and economic activity. In Citizenship children learn about central and local government and how public services are financed and this can be supported by work in Geography on why services in settlements vary (Geography Programme of Study 6g ii, QCA/DfEE, 1999b), why attempts are made 'to plan and manage environments' (Geography Programme of Study 6j ii, ibid.) such as new housing in South-East England, the location of wind farms or the route of a new bypass. Learning about the 'key characteristics of parliamentary government' (Citizenship Programme of Study 1d, QCA/DfEE, 1999a) can include the study of parliamentary debates on such environmental and economic issues as the countryside, flooding, fuel taxes and so on. Evidently there are far more opportunities to find connections between Geography and Citizenship than is indicated by the Crick Report which recommended that between the ages of 7 and 11 children should understand 'the meaning of terms such as poverty, famine, disease, charity, aid and human rights' and 'know about the world as a global community' (AGC, 1998, p. 48).

As Geography 'synthesizes many disciplines' it has the capacity, especially in the primary school, to give children a 'foundation for cross-curricular learning where much values and citizenship education takes place' (Walkington, 2000, p. 65). At Key Stage 3 as children become progressively better 'informed citizens' they will learn in their Citizenship lessons about 'the world as a global community, and the political, economic, environmental and social implications' (QCA/DfEE, 1999a, p. 14, strand 1i) of this interdependence. They should also learn about 'the role of the European Union, the Commonwealth and the United Nations' (ibid.) and a degree of congruence is apparent between such study and what is prescribed by the National Curriculum for Geography lessons (to be precise strands 3b, 3e, 5a, 5b, 6f, 6h, 6i, 6j and 6k). At Key Stage 4 students learn about 'the wider issues and challenges of global interdependence and responsibility' (ibid., p. 14, strand 1j) which is an important aspect of the Citizenship curriculum. Especially at 'secondary level, Geography exposes pupils to global issues and to processes that contribute to a politically, economically and ecologically interdependent world' (Walkington, 2000, p. 65). Yet, paying insufficient heed to the contribution that learning in Geography makes to the Citizenship curriculum is regrettably common.

The value of establishing close ties in school between the Humanities and Citizenship is that teachers can develop an 'issue-centred approach, where understanding geographical processes forms the basis for learners to explore their own feelings and attitudes' (Walkington, 2000, p. 56). The potential for the sort of values education that helps learners to reflect upon how their behaviour affects others can be fostered by Geography lessons which enable them to identify the influence of their beliefs and actions. Indeed, 'the role of the Geography teacher is of fundamental importance in describing and explaining patterns and processes and helping each individual learner to understand his or her role within this complex and dynamic system'(ibid., p. 65).

Although the public dimension is central in Citizenship Education and is therefore necessarily concerned with issues on a large scale it is important that pupils think about the implications of actions 'for their own lives' as well as for other 'people, places and environments' (Geography Programme of Study 5b, QCA/DfEE, 1999b). An essential feature of geographical enquiry is to 'appreciate how people's values and attitudes, including their own, affect contemporary social, environmental, economic and political issues' (Geography Programme of Study 1e, ibid.). Further, as children in Geography should be taught to 'clarify and develop their own values and attitudes about such issues' (ibid.) this aim can be fulfilled within Citizenship. Such values-clarification necessarily needs to take into account the results of one's actions on a global, national and local scale. In the following sections we will move from an exploration of global to local citizenship.

Geography for global citizens

It is essential that 'pupils make connections between their own actions, the actions of their local community and what happens globally' and that they 'identify ways in which they can contribute to sustainable development' (QCA, 2001b, p. 1). Investigating the Amazon rainforest in Brazil is a popular topic and illustrates the ways in which learning about an international issue in Geography can contribute to the development of global citizens. One approach to this theme has been suggested by the Qualifications and Curriculum Authority and is described below.

Faith and the forest

Pupils should come to 'appreciate how the values and attitudes of the different groups affect their stance on the deforestation of the rainforest' and should 'explore the idea of sustainable development and recognise its implications for different people, places and environments' (QCA, 2001b, p. 1). In order to do this students often work as a group and make a presentation to the rest of the class which is divided up so that members of different groups take on roles as members of the Brazilian government, poor migrant farmers, tribal people, environmentalists and so on. Each group researches 'their' viewpoint using the internet. As they prepare their presentations children can produce leaflets, displays or even videos promoting the viewpoint they are representing. Children can then be asked if they believe the Amazon rainforest is being developed or destroyed. In answering this question their reasons can incorporate reference to the beliefs and values of different groups who have a vested interest in this region. This is a reasonably common approach and in itself can provide valuable moral education but it can also be developed significantly.

The reason the Amazon rainforest is studied is because it is important to the whole world. People in different parts of the world, whether in Pakistan, India, Britain, China or the US have views about its deforestation and the global environmental consequences this may have. This sequence of lessons can be developed further to show a range of ideological and religious perspectives on the deforestation. Classes can be encouraged to consider what a Jewish, Christian, Muslim, Hindu, Secularist, Marxist or New Age view of the destruction of the environment might be. Whether the devastation is considered to be destiny, the result of economic forces alone or caused by human sinfulness and greed should be considered. For instance, if one believes that 'The earth is the Lord's and the fullness thereof, the world and they that dwell therein' (Psalm 24:1) this may have an impact upon how the environment is treated. Such a belief could be a powerful motivation to care for the Earth one believes God has created rather than polluting it.

Geographical skills for citizens

In Citizenship children can learn about how to resolve conflict fairly (Citizenship Programme of Study 1g, QCA/DfEE, 1999a) and about 'the world as a global community' as well as considering the 'political, economic, environmental and social implications' and becoming more informed on this issue (Citizenship Programme of Study 1i, ibid.). Helping learners to see that international social justice issues are personally relevant through discussion ensures that what has come to be known as the 'local-through-global dimension' of Citizenship is fostered. As a result of such thinking and response pupils can take action in their school or local community. They can help to develop a school policy on environmentally sustainable practices, write letters to DEFRA (the Department for Environment, Food and Rural Affairs) or write for their school newspaper or environmental magazine and learn how they can manage their own environments sustainably.

Learners engaged in such tasks also develop skills of enquiry and communication. They 'justify orally and in writing a personal opinion about such issues, problems or events' (Citizenship Programme of Study 2b, QCA/DfEE, 1999a) and 'contribute to group and exploratory class discussions' (Citizenship Programme of Study 2c, ibid.). Further, they develop 'skills of participation and responsible action' by using 'their imagination to consider other people's experiences' and explaining 'views that are not their own' (Citizenship Programme of Study 3a, ibid.). Although these skills are fostered it is especially important that children understand, 'develop and clarify their own values and attitudes' (Geography

Programme of Study 1e, QCA/DfEE, 1999b) and appreciate how these affect their views on an issue. Learners can reflect upon why they hold the views they do and how they justify and legitimate these.

The language of global citizens

It is easy to overlook an indispensable skill at the disposal of global citizens which facilitates research and communication and gives us a powerful voice: the English language. We should not forget that the ability to communicate in English was a key to the establishment of democracy in many parts of the world (Pike, 2003c). Although the teaching of English and English literature on a global scale can be seen as a legacy of colonialism 'the English literary icons used in oppression and domination have also provided a language for resistance and opposition' and many 'African, Indian and Malaysian intellectuals who received an English literary education were at the forefront of the struggle for independence' (Maybin, 1996, p. 252). In places such as Africa and Asia the English language provided a common language and enabled disparate peoples who were linguistically divided to work together. The power of a common language to unite people from different backgrounds in resisting oppression is just as significant today where English is the language of the Internet, which often provides unmonitored access to uncensored news from international media organizations in countries where there are tight controls on national media and routine censorship.

In our dealings with the rest of the world we should not forget the value citizens of other nations attach to English which is the language of international politics as well as of travel, science, commerce and technology. To be literate in the world's most powerful language is to be empowered indeed. The ability to communicate in the global language enables the individual to function politically in the global village (Pike, 2004a, ch. 5). The importance of literacy to democracy has already been explored in some detail in Chapter 4 of this book but a word of caution is advisable here; just as children should not assume that most of the world's population is 'white' they should avoid making the assumption that everyone speaks English. The growing importance of other people's languages and the cultures they represent should be appreciated in an interdependent global community. Learning Mandarin could prove to be invaluable in the twenty-first century.

Global status, personal responsibilities

Children studying Citizenship should learn to identify the links their country has within the wider world. They should understand that the country of which they are citizens is a member of the Commonwealth and has links with countries such as Canada and Australia as well as African nations such as Kenya and Nigeria. They should also appreciate that Britain is a leading participant within the community of nations known as the United Nations. Understanding the responsibilities their country has as one of the few countries with the status of permanent Security

Council member at the UN should similarly be understood by citizens. They should learn that the country they reside in is a member of the G8 and has certain responsibilities as one of the richest nations in the world, although the efforts of Sir Bob Geldof and Live8 may have already helped them to appreciate this. Learning about the relationships their country has with other parts of the world is necessary but the challenge for Citizenship educators is how to make such relationships on a global scale applicable to the lives of learners who may never have been to most of the countries their own nation is so intimately involved with.

Oxfam's definition of a global citizen is of one who along with other attributes 'has a sense of their own role as a world citizen' and 'is willing to act to make the world a more equitable and sustainable place' (Oxfam, 1997, p. 2). The reality is, of course, that we are all already acting for good or ill. Bringing to learners' attention what might be termed 'sins of omission' and enabling them to see the results of their existing actions is very important indeed. Walkington reminds us of the phrase 'think globally, act locally' and that 'Geography is a subject of huge potential in alerting learners to the interdependent nature of our planet' (2000, p. 65). Its value also lies in its capacity to help learners reflect on the morality of their own actions as global citizens.

Geography for national citizens

In Citizenship children should learn to respect the 'diversity of national, regional, religious and ethnic identities in the United Kingdom' (Citizenship Programme of Study 1b, QCA/DfEE, 1999a, p. 14). Teaching children how they can respect opinions, beliefs and practices that they may not share and do not necessarily agree with should be a key element of Citizenship Education. Indeed, how children should be taught to respect the views of others when these views may actually be in opposition to their own has been the subject of some controversy (Halstead, 1998). It has been demonstrated that tolerance need not be based upon acceptance of views one does not share. This area will be considered in greater depth when the teaching of controversial issues is considered in Chapter 8 below. What is important to emphasize here is that respect for others whose views one does not share is at the very heart of a plural society where the rights of minorities are respected and majority culture is not imposed on minorities in neo-imperialist fashion. Given the importance of this element of the Citizenship curriculum, research is urgently required to consider appropriate pedagogy through which respect and tolerance for a plural society and the views of others can be fostered.

Learning about the diversity of the UK population and the identities of different groups contributes to the fulfilment of the learning objective in Geography to 'appreciate how people's values and attitudes . . . affect contemporary social, environmental, economic and political issues' (Geography Programme of Study 1e, QCA/DfEE, 1999b). A range of resources, from the Channel 4 Black and Asian History Map to the cleverly named 'Show Racism the Red Card' and 'Kick Racism out of Football' campaigns, are available. An issue raised in the campaigning before the UK General Election in May 2005 was whether a quota system should operate to limit immigration into the UK. What a good Citizenship lesson can bring to such a topic is the moral dimension and a focus on how competing claims and rights can be reconciled in society.

If some people want new homes to be built in the southeast of England and others wish to preserve the countryside from such development, geographical knowledge and research skills can provide the backdrop for a stimulating discussion of values and rights in Citizenship. Similar topics include where to build a reservoir, how to manage coastal erosion (Geography Programme of Study 6jiii, QCA/DfEE, 1999b) and whether alternative energy sources should be developed in the UK. Comparing the decisions made here with those of the Netherlands, for instance, can tell children a lot about national values and priorities. Investigating the work of environmental groups such as Friends of the Earth and Greenpeace on a national level can similarly highlight the differences in values between governments and such organizations. National policy towards such alternative sources of energy can only be studied effectively if Geography and Citizenship teachers join forces. Coastal environments and tourism are regularly the subject of study in Geography lessons and the conflicting views about the management of physical and human resources provide good raw materials for lessons where the children are required to 'use their imagination to consider other people's experiences' (Geography Programme of Study 3a, QCA/DfEE, 1999b). The detailed background knowledge needed to make informed judgements can be acquired in Geography and the Citizenship teacher can then augment and enhance children's understanding of the topic by emphasizing the ethics of public policy.

The role of the UK government and the extent to which it should protect and look after its citizens is a profitable area for discussion when topics such as flood disasters are investigated. Children can carry out a case study and discuss the extent to which government should be held responsible for managing the environment. The role of insurance companies and individuals' own rights to choose where they live can be debated. As understanding how an ecosystem works is unlikely to be achieved in the time allotted to Citizenship in schools, this topic could be investigated in Geography. Students can use desktop publishing to produce leaflets to persuade others of the validity of their views, can exchange fieldwork data using email and use the internet for research purposes. The moral implications of the uses of ICT have been examined recently (Pike, 2004a; Smith and Shortt, 2005) and further attention is devoted to this area in Chapter 8. Students can study oblique and aerial photographs of areas, analyse statistical data, evaluate publicity leaflets and acquire new geographical vocabulary such as 'urban regeneration' or 'drainage basin', but in the midst of all this activity the expert teacher of Citizenship can direct attention to the interpretation of this data and to the value positions underpinning and influencing such interpretations. Understanding how data is manipulated and for which purposes tells us about more than the nation we live in: it tells us about the values of those who are its citizens.

Geography for local citizens

The local scale is perhaps the most appropriate setting for the exercise of school-based active citizenship as it is here that community can be experienced on a daily basis. Children can reflect on their participation in school or community-based activity relating to sustainable development. They can become involved in environmental projects within their school grounds after they have justified their opinions, drawn up plans and decided upon an appropriate course of action which gains widespread support in their community. Pupils can 'negotiate, decide and take part responsibly in both school and community-based activities' (Citizenship Programme of Study 3b, QCA/DfEE, 1999a) and reflect upon it. Geographical research and mapping skills can be drawn upon in both the planning and evaluation stages of such activities.

The beliefs, values and priorities underpinning local actions and decision-making can be explored at a local level by looking at school issues such as litter or the use of shared space or community issues such as the location of a new housing development or skateboard park. Children can learn how decisions are made on this scale and become actively involved in making their views known. Children's involvement in their local area with reference to the 'Saving Black Mountain' project is described in Chapter 4. The work of the local community, voluntary organizations and their own school can be examined when investigating conservation, sustainability and Local Agenda 21. The ways in which such activity relates to national and EU aims can help children to see that such issues are part of a national dimension; they can then learn about the global community and the ethical and economic implications of local and national actions when studying the environment.

All of the issues dealt with on a national scale such as the building of new houses, roads or supermarkets and out of town retail parks can be studied 'close-up' in the local area. This provides a superb opportunity to gauge community response and engagement in the processes of planning, consultation and governmental decision-making surrounding such initiatives. When competing needs are identified in a local area, conflict resolution is essential and learning about this is an integral part of the citizenship curriculum (Citizenship Programme of Study 1g, QCA/DfEE, 1999a). When studying developments in a local area well-known to the children it is possible to become involved for real in issues such as the 'changes in urban land use' (Geography Programme of Study, 6g iv, QCA/DfEE, 1999b). Children can also visit and observe for themselves 'how and why changes in the functions of settlements occur and how these changes affect groups of people in different ways' (Geography Programme of Study 6g iii, ibid.). Studying how public services are financed and the choices made about their deployment is very much related to Geography, where economic activity is studied and understanding 'how and why the distribution has changed' together with the 'effects of such changes' (Geography Programme of Study 6h iii, ibid.) is important. The advantage of work undertaken on the local scale is that the beliefs and values of a child's own community can be understood when these may have been hidden previously.

Problematizing scale

At the end of this brief exploration of Citizenship and moral responsibility exercised on a global, national and local scale, this ready-made division according to scale might appear to be rather too neat and straightforward. The process of foregrounding scale can be problematic for many citizens. Carrington refers to second-generation Bangladeshis living in the East End of London to exemplify the changing nature of community and belonging and refers to 'the multiple identities of this group' (Carrington, 2002, p. 118). The notion of 'multiple identity' may be used to problematize notions of citizenship based too exclusively upon physical location and context. Geography educators are concerned to represent all manner of relationships and patterns, and the potential exists for identities forged within 'socio-space' (Carrington, 2002) or derived from religious faith (Pike, 2005a) (which transcends geographical boundaries) to be explored in Geography and to inform a person's citizenship.

Spiritual rather than physical geographies are of prime importance to many people of faith (Kirk, 2004) and a 'worldly' or material approach which privileges scale may pay insufficient heed to the spiritual and moral aspects of Citizenship Education through Geography. Where we begin sends important messages to children and a 'worldly' approach is likely to promote secular rather than faith-based interpretations of the world we live in. The fundamental principle of Augustine's *City of God*, for instance, is that the primary allegiance of Christians is to the City of God and that such believers owe subordinate and more limited allegiance to human rulers and governments. Many Muslims living in the UK have an allegiance to the *umma* (worldwide community of Islam) as well as to the government of the UK. If the state education system of a liberal democracy should not privilege either secular or religious perspectives in order to maintain neutrality, teachers cannot proceed on the assumption that the most obvious way to explore a child's citizenship is according to geographical scale. Although the primary allegiance or sense of belonging of some children will be defined in relation to a 'spiritual' faith rather than a 'worldly' area, how children with disparate world-views believe they should behave on a global, national and local level should be very much the concern of all educators.

Citizenship and Moral Education through History

The congruence between Citizenship and History is evident from the Programme of Study for Citizenship at Key Stage 4. This states that children are required to learn about 'legal and human rights and responsibilities' and 'the role and operation of the criminal and civil justice systems' (QCA/DfEE, 1999c, p. 15: 1a). They also need to study the 'work of parliament, the government and the courts in making and shaping the law' (ibid.,1c) as well as the importance of playing 'an active part in democratic and electoral processes' (1d). In addition, children need to know 'how the economy functions' (1e) and 'the importance of a free press' as well as its 'role in society' (1g). In addition to acquiring knowledge children should develop skills of enquiry and communication by researching a topical political, social or cultural issue, problem or event by 'analysing information from different sources' which is, in general, the starting point of any enquiry in the History classroom. Other skills honed in History are the ability to persuade, to develop and express opinions and to engage in discussion and debate (ibid., 2b and 2c). There are many opportunities for young people to become informed and active citizens through such study.

History has been defined as the 'study of human society and citizenry in the past' (Stow, 2000, p. 67) but it is also more than this, and as the curriculum is an ideological intervention in children's lives it is only fair that children should be given the opportunity to engage in sustained reflection upon the aims of a discipline they follow and the values it may engender. According to Heater (1990) there are three ways in which schools transmit values to children: in the choosing and selecting of resources and materials to be studied, in the identification of objectives to be achieved (as these provide a specific moral outcome) and through the hidden curriculum. Value judgements are implicit when decisions are made about what is to be studied and the reasons for doing so.

The twin issues of choice of subject and allocation of time send important messages to children. If the period 1750–1900 is to be studied, does the teacher emphasize the achievement of the British Navy at Trafalgar or an inhumane maritime endeavour so many British ships were involved in – the slave trade? Indeed, Slater observes that: 'Selection involves a value-judgement which gives public importance and status to those who are selected and implicitly, sometimes deliberately, denies it to those who are not. History is not a value-free enterprise' (1993, p. 45). What messages do we transmit if we spend one lesson on the Battle of Trafalgar and six lessons on the Battle of the Somme? If the British Empire is studied, is the focus upon India, Africa or the Americas? Further, which perspective is privileged if one studies the British Empire? Is the overall perspective celebratory or condemnatory? Do children come away with a sense of achievement or of shame? And are they encouraged to apply assessments of trade or power to their country's responsibilities today? Is a link made, for instance, between the plight and potential of Africa today and Britain's role in that continent in the past?

It is not only in the topics studied that one finds the common ground between Citizenship and History. Enquiry and communication are skills which are common to each subject. Becoming critical and being able to sift evidence in order to express their own views as well as to understand the points of view of others are skills which children develop in History. Enabling children to develop these skills is at the heart of History teaching. They are also integral to citizenship in a democracy. Understanding and critically analysing different interpretations of the same event or policy are skills which are developed when historical sources are studied. Such skills are essential for citizens. Perceiving and evaluating bias in the media and in the presentation of issues generally is of great importance if the citizenry of a nation today is to assess policies and the actions of politicians.

By enabling children to gain a better understanding of current affairs, political systems, and the legal and criminal justice systems, History has a powerful contribution to make to Citizenship Education. To pay insufficient attention to the cross-curricular links between History and Citizenship is to deny pupils the opportunities that exist for this alliance of subjects to contribute together to a rich and sufficiently discriminating appreciation of the complexities of their nation and their place within that nation. Arguably 'the heart of the school history curriculum, encompassing for example: war, genocide, exploitation, revolution, suffering, persecution, martyrdom, sacrifice, triumph and celebration leads students beyond a simple study of facts' (Cottingham, 2005, p. 46) towards a deeper exploration of the fundamental issues which can be the basis of much moral reasoning and reflection within Citizenship.

History teachers, as a matter of routine, present pupils with historical (and moral) dilemmas in order to elicit pupils' opinions and to encourage them to justify their opinions. These dilemmas often concern the morality and ethics of decisions that have been taken by governments. When a question such as 'Was the USA justified in dropping the atomic bomb on Nagasaki and Hiroshima?' is asked one requires more than historical knowledge to come up with an answer. On the other hand, one needs historical knowledge to be sufficiently well-informed to exercise a judgement. When children wrestle with the question 'Should Dresden have been bombed?' in History, it makes no sense at all to have this discussion without reference to their activities in Citizenship. These questions give pupils opportunities to reflect, discuss, debate and act in response to current events that are directly related to political and moral decisions being made as they sit in their classrooms. The study of History is not simply concerned with understanding the public and political past in order to understand the present, it is about gaining an understanding of decisions made today in the light of those made in the past. The difference is subtle but important.

One of the most important keys to unlocking children's understanding in this area is how the learning experience is framed. If children are to appreciate the relevance of History to Citizenship and Moral Education the nature of enquiry questions employed by teachers require careful evaluation. The way in which an enquiry question is worded can make an enormous difference. For instance, a study of Oliver Cromwell could be entitled 'How did Cromwell rule England?' or students could spend their time attempting to answer the question 'Was Cromwell a dictator?' The former is a perfectly valid assignment for the History classroom but the latter has the greater power to inform Citizenship. We shall now turn our attention to a brief exploration of seven areas of importance to the relation between History and Citizenship.

Reading texts from other times

We should, perhaps, ask what the particular moral benefits of reading texts from other times might be (Pike, 2003c). After all, 'we do not live by the ethics of the

Iliad, or by the politics of Plato' (Bloom, 1994, p. 40). In answering this question it should be remembered that understanding the difference between one's own views and those common in another time (be they political, social, cultural, ethnic, religious or moral) can provide a standpoint from which to appreciate that certain of our beliefs and values are temporal and merely products of our time. Gaining an appreciation of other generations and cultures has been observed to contribute to the moral development of adolescent readers in the present (Pike, 2000c). The relation between the political past and the public present is especially close because the past can only be 'grasped through the limited perspective of the present' and 'we cannot make our journey into the past without taking the present with us' (Selden and Widdowsen, 1993, p. 54). Reading texts from other times can 'address the needs and realities of the world our young people actually inhabit' (Davies, 1996, p. 9) if an appropriate pedagogy is employed (Pike, 2000c, 2004a) across a wide range of topics, some of which will now be briefly described.

Democracy and human rights

When studying Citizenship within History pupils can learn about different forms of government such as democracies and dictatorships and the differences between Sparta and Athens in the fifth century BC. They could also learn about the transition from Tudor Government (monarch and parliament) to Victorian Parliament (partial democracy) to the more comprehensive democracy of Britain in the twenty-first century. A possible route might be as follows. In Year 7 children might study King John and the origins of parliament and democracy in England. In Year 8, a more detailed understanding of the characteristics of parliamentary and other forms of government could be gained when studying the English civil war and the rule of Cromwell. In Year 9 children might learn about the electoral system and the importance of voting when they research why people were prepared to die to gain the right to vote. This could be a good point at which to hold a mock election. From about the age of fourteen when the children have gained greater maturity they could encounter a unit on human rights and the Holocaust. Before leaving Year 11 they might learn about the global community, conflict resolution since 1945 and the role of the UN.

Immigration and diversity

In the primary school there are numerous opportunities to combine Citizenship teaching with a range of topics in History. At Key Stage 2 children learn, in History, about the different groups of people who have lived in the British Isles, from the Celts and Anglo-Saxons to the Vikings, Romans and Normans. Gaining such an awareness of the mixed ethnic background of the UK population is a good way of combating racism and introducing children to the diverse makeup of UK society as part of their Citizenship education. Immigration during the twentieth century from India, Pakistan and the Caribbean as well as more recently from eastern

Europe is helpfully put into historical context and can be combined with work in literacy on the vocabulary English has acquired from other places. Learning how words have been imported can provide the introduction to learning about other cultural imports. The personal relevance of such work can be understood by children when they consider the cultural influences at work in their own identities. Understanding one's cultural roots and inheritance as well as allegiances and loyalties that one has chosen can be explored in this way.

Law and order

In History at Key Stage 2 children learn about how laws are made and how changes in the law have been brought about. There is the opportunity here to relate such work to the non-statutory guidelines for Citizenship at Key Stage 2 (QCA, 2000a) which suggests, for instance, that in preparing to play a role as active citizens children should be taught how and why rules and laws are made and enforced, why various rules are needed in different situations and how to take part in making and changing rules. Policing and the enforcement of the law is another common topic in the primary school. Children can be taught how societies have been policed in the past, from self-policing Athens to the feudal duties of the Anglo-Saxons and the military policing of Roman Britain. They can then learn about the private watchmen of the Tudors and the introduction of the modern police force in England in Victorian times. The development of policing today, from the use of ASBOs to the use of firearms by specialist officers, can be discussed.

The rights of the child

When the child poverty of the Victorian era is encountered at Key Stage 1 this can be compared with child labour and poverty today in other countries. Later on, older children can be faced with serious moral issues surrounding the products that they buy and whether child labourers, much like those of Victorian England, have provided them with the goods they desire. It is inconceivable that the legal rights and responsibilities of children and young people as laid out in the UN Convention on the Rights of the Child would not have emphasis and be given some scrutiny within any World Study or Twentieth Century Study. The social and historical context of the introduction of the UN Convention on the Rights of the Child is important from the perspective of learning about Citizenship.

Cottingham (2005) reports on the use of a passage from *Jude the Obscure* with the nineteenth-century painting *The Haymakers* by George Stubbs with a Key Stage 3 class. The painting portrays a rural idyll and appears to confirm children's preconceptions of rural nineteenth-century life. Conversely the passage from *Jude the Obscure* describes Jude feeding the birds in the field he is employed to protect and receiving a beating from his employer as a result. Pupils in this lesson wanted to know why the farmer was so cruel and this led on to more general questions about whether all employers were cruel at that time. Subsequently 'students moved beyond the abstract or academic question of how children lived and worked in the nineteenth century, to consider questions of morality' (Cottingham, 2005, p. 7). Citizenship educators will immediately identify the potential of such a topic as a way into considering the treatment of children today who have employers who do not respect their rights. The reasons for the legislation restricting the hours children are permitted to work in the UK today and employment rights generally can be examined after the conditions endured by labourers in other times is reflected upon.

Economics

Case studies can be valuable especially if children can visit the places they learn about. The philanthropy of Josiah Salt (Salts Mill in Bradford, which was built by Salt, has recently been designated a world heritage site) provides a case study of an industrialist with a social conscience and can be compared to the actions of Bill Gates, CEO of Microsoft, who recently donated £750,000,000 from his personal wealth to provide vaccines for children in third-world countries. The medical facilities that Josiah Salt provided for his workers in Saltaire, Bradford or those established by the Rowntree family in Birmingham can show how wealth generation can be combined with a social conscience. When economic issues such as wealth generation and taxation are discussed examples can be drawn from the Saxon payment of the Danegeld required by the Vikings to taxation in England in Victorian times and what taxes pay for today, from waste disposal to schools that employ teachers to provide Citizenship lessons.

Reading against racism

One of the best examples of a History lesson that teaches children about citizenship and fosters their moral education is based on materials from the Imperial War Museum's *Teaching the Holocaust* pack (Cottingham, 2005). The dilemma of the Polish sewer worker who discovered twenty Jews hiding in the sewers beneath Lodz while the city was occupied by the Nazis is studied in one lesson. If he gave the Jews up to the SS he could expect a reward but if he was found to have helped them he would be shot. The children in Cottingham's study were asked what he would do and were shown a rather unflattering photograph of the man and given the information that he was an ex-convict. Most pupils, unsurprisingly, predicted that he would surrender the Jews to the SS. In fact, he brought them food and clean clothes every day in exchange for payment. Discussing the morality of earning money in such a way (and other ways of earning money today that depend upon the exploitation of others) made for lively classroom interactions. The children were then told that the Jews' money ran out and were asked what they thought the sewer worker would do next. Most of the pupils predicted that he had handed the Jews in to the SS and were proved wrong again. The man continued to help them until Lodz was liberated in 1945. Getting children to think beyond the stereotypes is an important aspect of the learning in this lesson. This need to get beyond stereotypes and to focus on individuals and the needs of minorities within our society is at the heart of some concerns we have about the power of the history lesson within our schools and democracy, to which we now turn.

Liberal concerns

As one would expect from historians, competing interpretations of their own subject abound but one of the most commonly given reasons for studying History is that it is regarded as promoting a student's well-being as 'an autonomous person within a liberal democratic community' (White, 1993, p. 15). While few may have any reservations about such aims (which are congruent to a remarkable degree with those of Citizenship Education) we should be sufficiently aware of arguments concerning diversity and human rights to recognize that some sections of the population cannot subscribe to such an aim as a primary goal of education (Pike, 2005a). Some parents express concerns about educating their children to be 'autonomous'. Whether the state should contravene the wishes of parents and groups who do not want their children to become critically reflective about their families' beliefs is debatable as 'the civic standpoint does not warrant the conclusion that the state must (or may) structure public education to foster in children sceptical reflection on ways of life inherited from parents or local communities' (Galston, 1989, p. 99). Being a good citizen is 'perfectly compatible with unswerving belief in the correctness of one's own way of life' (ibid.) provided one is prepared to tolerate those who valorize ways of living with which one cannot agree. In the light of the requirement within Citizenship to understand and respect those whose views we do not share it is important that we do not impose a secular, liberal ideological agenda upon those who do not share the worldview of the majority in our democracy. Many would agree with C. S. Lewis that 'an open mind, in questions that are not ultimate, is useful' but that such a mind 'about ultimate foundations' is simply 'idiocy' because such questions are matters of faith (1955, p. 60).

History is also considered to enable 'a more effective participation in a liberal-democratic society' (Slater, 1993, p. 50) which serves the interests of the state because 'the success and stability of liberal politics depends on people's private beliefs and commitments becoming importantly liberalised' (Macedo, 1990, p. 54). Many would not be able to endorse such politics because 'to accept the liberal settlement is to accept institutions, ideas, and practices whose influence over our lives and our children's lives will be broad, deep and relentless: family life, religious life . . . take on the colour of liberal values' (ibid., p. 62). Parents who do not wish to accept such a settlement may be suspicious of the aims of History and Citizenship as they will view the responsibility for moral education as being that of the home. John Beck refers us to the claim from Hardy's *Jude the Obscure* that 'All the little ones of our time are collectively the children of all the adults of our time, and entitled to our general care' and calls this a 'generous and inclusive vision' (1998, p. 92) but there are many parents who regard such 'general care' as interference and an infringement of their parental rights. One of our concerns in this book is the defence of their rights and we see no convincing basis for Beck's dangerous view.

The right of the state to promote the educational aim of rational autonomy has been challenged on a number of counts (Pike, 2005a, 2005b) and while many with a faith-based perspective do believe that thinking for oneself and rational analysis are important capacities for their children to acquire they may also believe that there is more to education than fostering rationality and autonomy. Obedience to God's rule and authority for the Christian, or submission to Allah for the Muslim, can be considered to be more important than the freedom to choose any way of living one likes. Liberals' privileging of personal autonomy often 'assumes the value of autonomous rationality and excludes a theonomous alternative' (Shortt, 1980, p. 76) and while Citizenship educators may consider that few elements of the Citizenship curriculum are at all contentious they should be aware that for a person of faith 'the content of public education invariably is related to religion' in that 'the purpose of education, the notion of what constitutes the good life, morals, ethics, good citizenship, and character development ultimately are all religious questions' (Cox, 1997, p. 113).

In Chapter 2 we alluded to the differences between two sorts of liberalism. Political liberalism is considered to be one of the most important foundations for the political institutions in our society; most would agree that all citizens should have some attachment to it. Comprehensive or cultural liberalism, on the other hand, applies liberal values to all areas of life and believers often find this more or less acceptable depending upon the degree to which they have been secularized. It is our view that both Citizenship and Moral Education should only ever promote political liberalism; if these subjects ever seek to promote cultural liberalism they will be infringing the rights of many believers in our democracy and as such would be an abuse of state power. Liberals who are 'egalitarian' and argue we should treat all alike should be distinguished from more enlightened 'diversity liberals' who acknowledge the importance of communal rights such as those of churches and parents.

On the one hand, Macedo (2000) argues that civic well-being requires a 'tough-minded liberalism' to promote conformity and it has been pointed out that if this is the case, 'Good citizenship on this view is a project properly undertaken by the state and best institutionalized in public schools' (Burtonwood, 2003, p. 324). On the other hand, Callan recognizes that 'the liberal democracy worth having will also respect the right to live in some ways that renounce the stringent ideal of autonomy' (Callan, 1997, p. 11) and that there are ways of life that do not favour individual autonomy that are quite legitimate, morally defensible and worthy of respect. Burtonwood (2000, 2003) terms this 'diversity liberalism' because it accepts that autonomy need not be a right to be valued above all else.

While political liberalism underpins citizenship education for all children in a democratic state it is important that cultural liberalism is seen as merely one of a number of competing ideologies. We would argue that faith-based education that is balanced by attention to cross-cultural understanding may well lead to a more genuinely pluralist and tolerant society than the secular approach of many public schools which pays insufficient heed to the needs of religious individuals. Respecting the faith of children and families rather than expecting them to become secularized would appear to be the way to demonstrate tolerance.

Both History and Citizenship are value-laden and teachers need to be aware of their power to indoctrinate, even unwittingly, in these lessons. For instance, it has been argued that if the history lesson focuses on the relationship between rich and poor and devotes 'a great deal of attention to the disadvantaged and marginalised groups in society' then this 'might be accused of being party political or even socialist in bias' (Stow, 2000, p. 71). Others have good reasons for prioritizing the needs of the least advantaged in society. The promotion of democratic values, pluralism and diversity are necessarily value positions. Teachers of Citizenship need to be explicit about the agenda they are promoting if indoctrination is to be avoided. History teachers may be especially well placed, in this regard, to help children see the historical context of Citizenship in schools.

Conclusion

This chapter has sought to sketch out the close relation between subjects such as History and Geography within the Humanities and Citizenship. Reference to respective programmes of study and numerous topics in lessons have illustrated the potential for an interdisciplinary teaching of Citizenship. Characteristic approaches within the Humanities and Citizenship have also been challenged in order to guard against an insufficiently discriminating 'one-size-fits-all' approach to the moral education of citizens. In the common state school we must guard against inadvertently coercing children to conform to certain ways of seeing their world rather than others. For instance, any overemphasis upon scale (global, national and local) when Citizenship is informed by Geography has been shown to be potentially problematic for those who privilege the spiritual over the physical. Equally, the aim of teaching of History to foster rationally autonomous citizens in a liberal democracy has been problematized and the important distinction between political and cultural liberalism has been made. It has been emphasized that the time has come for cultural liberalism to take its place as one specific vision among many in the marketplace of ideas rather than assuming its right to a monopoly within the Humanities.

It has been argued that in Citizenship through the Humanities children should be encouraged to reflect upon their own values as well as those of others and that this requires the study of worldviews so that the moral and ethical frameworks underpinning actions can be perceived (Naugle, 2002; Pike, 2005a). It has been suggested that the stance adopted by citizens and governments at different times and in various places can be judiciously evaluated by those studying Citizenship through the Humanities. It has also been suggested that the morality of actions taken by governments should be scrutinized by citizens who need to be made aware that legality and morality should not be conflated. Clearly, those who teach citizens have very important moral responsibilities which can be illustrated by reference to a story rich in significance for the teaching of Citizenship through History (where attention is drawn to values in different times) and Geography (where the environment and our responsibility for it is considered).

In *The Magician's Nephew* (1955), the first of the Narnia stories, Digory and Polly are supernaturally transported by Digory's Uncle Andrew, by means of magic rings, to a World beyond their own World. Pedagogy can, of course, be seen as the 'magic rings' by which children are transported in our lessons and enabled to experience environments, times and ways of living beyond their own – but this novel also reminds us that 'what you see and hear depends a good deal on where you are standing: it also depends on what sort of person you are' (Lewis, 1955/1970, p. 125). This chapter has shown that what students see and hear depends on where they are made to stand in lessons, and lessons often carry expectations about the perspectives children should adopt; the stance they take in response necessarily has an influence upon the sort of citizens they become. Certain risks are attendant upon the use of our 'magic rings'; after all, in *The Magician's Nephew* the world to which the children are transported is the dead world of Charn where they arouse a sleeping witch. After landing back in London where chaos ensues they (and other people) are then dragged back through time into a world that is devoid of life and completely barren of vegetation; perhaps this story serves to remind us that in Citizenship teaching informed by the Humanities, 'The task of the modern educator is not to cut down jungles but to irrigate deserts' (Lewis, 1943/1978, p. 13).

Chapter 7

Citizenship and Moral Education through RE and PSHE

Neither Religious Education (RE) nor Personal, Social and Health Education (PSHE) is a National Curriculum subject in England, and this fact may have contributed to their comparatively low status within the curriculum in the decade following the introduction of the National Curriculum. Drawing on fieldwork in ten schools, Whitty *et al.* (1994, pp. 175–7) report that students considered PSE a boring, poorly taught, low status, 'catch-all' subject which they did not take seriously, and similar views were frequently expressed by students about RE (Taylor, 1996, p. 127). Nonetheless, RE is part of the basic curriculum which all schools are obliged to provide, and PSHE's statutory core (health education, careers education and work-related learning) has led the Office for Standards in Education (Ofsted) to the view that schools choosing not to provide PSHE are taking 'an untenable position' (Ofsted, 2005b, pp. 3, 18). In recent years, however, both subjects have been experiencing something of a revival. A national framework for RE has recently been published (QCA, 2004), which sets out non-statutory guidelines for the subject and seeks to support syllabus development in LEAs and religious denominations. RE is also increasingly popular as a GCSE subject, perhaps because its open approach and relevance to life in multicultural Britain appeal to students. PSHE has also received considerable government attention since the establishment of the National Advisory Group on PSHE in 1997, and it is now frequently perceived by students as providing an opportunity to discuss issues currently of importance to them as well as preparing them for adult life.

Both subjects have close links to Citizenship and Moral Education. Both subjects are centrally concerned with attitudes and values, with preparing students for the opportunities and responsibilities of adult life, and with provision for their spiritual, moral, social and cultural development, and both subjects can provide opportunities for students to develop the skills of critical reflection. The links between RE and Citizenship have been explored in a range of recent publications (Baumfield, 2003; Blaycock, 2002; Broadbent, 2004; Draycott, 2002; Jackson, 2002, 2003; Mead, 2000; Pestridge, 2002; Teece, 1998; Watson, 2004). The links between PSHE and Citizenship are even stronger, with the assumption in the Framework for PSHE and Citizenship at Key Stages 1 and 2 (QCA/DfEE, 1999a) and in subsequent guidance for schools (QCA, 2000a) that the two subjects are part of a unified whole that can be planned and implemented as a single provision. More recently, the Qualifications and Curriculum Authority issued further guidance entitled 'Citizenship through PSHE at Key Stage 3' (2001c), arguing that both subjects involve a whole-school approach and the involvement of students in activities outside the school, and this is discussed more fully below. It has also been claimed that there are many pedagogical skills that are common to Religious Education, PSHE and Citizenship (Mead, 2001).

This chapter is divided into four sections. The first provides an overview of current links between Citizenship and RE both in schools and in recent QCA documents and schemes of work, and illustrates some practical approaches where Citizenship can be enriched by a contribution from RE. Secondly, a threefold critique is provided of issues that might arise, particularly relating to pedagogy and underlying approaches to teaching, if close ties are made between the teaching of RE and Citizenship. The third section deals with the relation of PSHE to Citizenship, and the fourth examines the question whether Moral Education can be merged with Citizenship and PSHE.

RE, Moral Education and Citizenship

RE has for many years been regarded as a 'major vehicle for moral education' (Priestley, 1987, p. 107) and for the National Curriculum Council its contribution to the understanding of values was 'too obvious' to merit discussion (1990a, p. 2). However, the relationship between religion and morality is by no means clear. While acknowledging that religions typically have much to say about morality and provide a source of moral vision (cf. Priestley, 1987; Lewis, 1943/1978), many writers argue that religion and morality are logically distinct ways of interpreting experience (cf. Hirst, 1974). If this is so, there is no justification for schools to locate moral education exclusively within RE. The reconceptualization of RE that has occurred in the last thirty years has involved a move away from a 'confessional' approach which sought to encourage the development of faith (and morality through faith) towards a 'phenomenological' approach which seeks to develop a sympathetic understanding of religious beliefs and practices (Lovat, 1995). Students are now encouraged to explore the nature of religious values, beliefs, commitments and personal experiences, and the nature of religion itself, and to see the world through the eyes of believers from different traditions. In line with this change, the contribution that RE makes to the development of students' values now has more to do with providing opportunities to discuss and reflect on the search for meaning and purpose in life and with encouraging the growth of tolerance, understanding and respect in our increasingly multicultural and multi-faith society. A survey of local authority advisers for RE shows that a large majority believe that their subject makes a significant contribution to students' spiritual, moral and cultural development, and among the most frequently mentioned values promoted by RE are tolerance, respect for others and love (Taylor, 1989). RE is also the curriculum area where students are most likely to be introduced to ethical issues like euthanasia, medical ethics, animal rights, sexual ethics, environmental ethics, the treatment of refugees and asylum seekers and world poverty.

The relationship between RE and Citizenship is much more complex. Some teachers, we are told, regard RE 'as a synonym for citizenship' (A. and E. Brown, 1999, p. 17), whereas others 'want to build a fence between RE and Citizenship' (Blaycock, 2002, p. 2). Grimmitt sees Citizenship as a direct threat to RE, potentially undermining 'the educational contribution that RE is making' and suggesting that 'this government, like the previous one, has little belief in RE's personal and community value' (2000, p. 11). There may indeed be some grounds for Grimmitt's concern; the final report of the Advisory Group on Citizenship (1998) makes only passing reference to RE, and Hargreaves (1994) has called for Citizenship Education to replace RE in non-denominational schools. Nevertheless, other RE specialists have chosen to emphasize the 'vital and distinctive contribution' that RE can make to Citizenship Education (Jackson, 2002, p. 162) – a contribution based on the exploration of moral issues, the nature of commitment, the beliefs and values of minority groups, and many other key issues. In any case, RE and Citizenship are often taught by the same teachers in secondary schools. It is entirely appropriate for children to be sitting in class surrounded by wall displays on Wilberforce's Christian commitment to the abolition of slavery (from RE) while learning about human rights (in Citizenship) or to be learning about the multi-cultural issues of identity and diversity in the very room where they have studied world religions. RE Agreed Syllabuses often contain sections on Citizenship (cf. Devon County Council, 2001, pp. 26–8), conferences such as 'Citizens of the Future – their Faiths, Beliefs and Values' held at the University of East Anglia in 2003 are provided, and INSET is available to help tease out the synergy between the two subjects.

The Qualifications and Curriculum Authority document 'Citizenship through religious education at Key Stage 3' (2001c) indicates opportunities for RE to contribute to Citizenship. Pupils can see 'how individual, group and political choices, policies and actions' are influenced by and 'inextricably linked with [. . .] religious and moral beliefs, practices and values'. Local, national, European and global issues cannot be adequately understood without 'understanding of their religious dimensions and contexts'. RE can help children understand 'personal, social and moral responsibility' and to consider how human beings treat each other and their environments. Further, RE can help 'to develop active citizenship by involvement with voluntary religious and charitable activities' (ibid., p. 1). A comparison of RE and Citizenship is complicated by the lack of a national programme of study for RE but reference here is made to the sorts of opportunities provided by RE Agreed Syllabuses as well as the Qualifications and Curriculum Authority non-statutory scheme of work (2000c) and the Qualifications and Curriculum Authority non-statutory national framework for Religious Education (2004).

To give a brief flavour of the possible synergy between RE and Citizenship some examples may be helpful. In Citizenship, 'legal and human rights and respon-sibilities' (1a) can be supported in RE when religious people who have promoted human rights, such as Martin Luther King, are studied. Learning in Citizenship about the diversity of 'religious and ethnic identities' (1b) present in the UK can be related to units of work in RE on beliefs and practices, such as how the beliefs of Sikhs affect their actions. Studying the criminal justice system presents the opportunity for children to learn about the influence of the Judeo-Christian tradition on British society and the importance of the Ten Commandments as a moral framework even today. A fascinating Citizenship lesson recently required Year 10 children to consider whether various actions were right or wrong. The class were unanimous that adultery was morally wrong but something approaching a moment of revelation was witnessed when they realised that the state did not punish everything they considered to be wrong. This then led onto a discussion of whether the state should intervene in what are viewed as private, family matters and the realization that legality and morality are not the same in the twenty-first century. Nevertheless, children should understand that many laws have religious origins and that in the UK the Christian roots of many laws are still apparent today.

When looking at the 'work of community-based, national and international voluntary groups' (1f), children can consider the role of religious aid agencies such as Muslim Aid and Christian Aid and can listen to speakers from such organizations as the Salvation Army which work with alcoholics and homeless people. When considering the significance of the media in society (1h), students can study the portrayal of different religions and religious figures in the media. In Citizenship children are required to use their imagination 'to consider other people's experiences' and to 'explain views that are not their own' (3a) and this fits well with current approaches to RE where children are encouraged to empathize in order to see an issue from the perspective of adherents of different religions. Indeed, it would be difficult to think about 'topical political, spiritual, moral, social and cultural issues' (2a) without understanding and responding to religious teachings and paying heed to the nature of values and beliefs. The 'importance of resolving conflict fairly' (1g) is singled out within the scheme of work (QCA, 2001c) for special attention and Unit 13, entitled 'How do we deal with conflict?' is designed so that most pupils will come to 'know about the major religions' holy sites in Jerusalem'. Many pupils will progress beyond this, however, and will 'critically evaluate the outcomes of continuing conflict or compromise and reconciliation in places like Jerusalem' and will 'understand political situations' and their 'religious dimensions' (Unit 13, p. 1). We would argue that it is impossible to be a well-informed global citizen without an understanding of Islam, Judaism and Christianity, the importance of Jerusalem and its significance in these religions in relation to global conflict and peace.

A critique of the links between teaching RE and Citizenship

It has been asserted that 'world religions must be recognised as the principal foci of disciplined and coherent moral and spiritual life' for they 'remain along with a humanised art, literature and science, the main resources that we have for the *rehabilitation of human life*' (Hull, 2001, p. 8, our italics). The decision to introduce Citizenship is part of the current government's plan to *rehabilitate political life and democracy* in specific ways and directions. Evidently *how* a subject is approached (its characteristic pedagogy and the way it is conceived) can send messages which are just as significant as *what* is studied. Clearly the study of religion has much to offer Citizenship, and the areas that RE and Citizenship have in common (as we have seen) are reasonably easy to identify. What is more complex is discerning the impact upon each subject of the ways in which the other is generally formulated and taught in state schools. This is the task to be attempted now. In this section we shall discuss three issues in particular: the attitudes of the two subjects to cultural and religious diversity; the problematic nature of 'learning from religion' in the light of religious claims to truth; and the danger of superficiality (and even stereotyping) when too many world faiths are studied.

Tolerating or celebrating diversity

The programmes of study for National Curriculum Citizenship include the require-ment for students to be taught about 'the diversity of national, regional, religious and ethnic identities in the United Kingdom and the need for mutual respect and understanding', and to be taught to 'use their imagination to consider other people's experiences and be able to think about, express and explain views that are not their own' (QCA/DfEE, 1999a, pp. 14–15). The contribution that RE can make here is clear and self-evident, and it is all the more surprising that the final report of the Advisory Group on Citizenship (1998) ignores it completely. Watson's view is that the report's authors appear to have a totally different response to diversity from that of religious educationalists (2004, p. 266). The National Framework for Religious Education states that RE 'places specific emphasis on . . . the *celebration* of diversity in society' (QCA, 2004, p. 8, our italics), whereas the AGC Report identifies cultural diversity as a matter of concern and suggests that find-ing 'a sense of common citizenship, including a national identity' is the best way of 'responding to these worries' (AGC, 1998, p. 17). In so far as the Advisory Group for Citizenship represents current thinking on the topic, Watson is surely right to point out that

> the gap between citizenship education and religious education is potentially enormous with each subject taking politically divergent routes to address-ing the challenge of British cultural and worldview pluralism. Citizenship education appears to equate with a conformity to one-nation values, while religious education *celebrates* diversity and encourages dialogue.
>
> (2004, p. 267)

Two points emerge from this. The first is that RE does indeed have an enriching contribution to make to Citizenship by welcoming and facilitating dialogue between different faiths and cultures. The second is that RE should be wary of too close an involvement with Citizenship, because the goals and aspirations of the two subjects are not the same, and RE's primary purposes of developing open-mindedness and respect for all, engaging with the meaning and purpose of life, celebrating diversity and exploring ethics in a global context may provide an important alternative framework of values to those espoused by some of the main proponents of Citizenship Education.

'Learning from religion'

There is currently an emphasis upon 'learning from religion' which is one of the two attainment targets for RE (QCA, 2004, pp. 33–7). The phrase 'learning from religion' indicates a particular approach where religious activity and belief is related to 'common human experience'. It is described in the following terms:

> Pupils should be able to make clear links between *common human experiences* and what religious people believe and do. Rituals, festivals, rites of passage, beliefs about God and the world – all these connect with *common human experiences* of awe, celebration, passage of time, a quest for meaning, purpose and value. *Learning from religion* requires pupils to see how such experiences are understood and interpreted in varying ways by members of different faiths and by those without religious beliefs.
>
> (QCA, 2000d, p. 23, our italics)

While this would seem *prima facie* to be in harmony with the requirement in the National Curriculum Citizenship programmes of study that students should be taught to 'think about topical political, spiritual, moral, social and cultural issues, problems and events' and 'justify orally and in writing a personal opinion about such issues' (QCA/DfEE, 1999a, p. 14), we will suggest that it may present some specific problems at the point where RE and Citizenship meet. One of the points we have emphasized throughout this book is that in a plural and multicultural society an illicitly comprehensive secularism should not be the sole lens through which Citizenship and Moral Education are viewed. Our concern with aspects of teaching legitimated by 'learning from religion' is that the importance of religion to a believer may be insufficiently appreciated. This has clear implications for Citizenship Education. Attempting to make a particular religion relevant to those who are not adherents can be helpful and also deeply problematic; the focus on response and applying religious belief to a child's everyday secular experience can lead to the trivialization of a religion. This is best illustrated by examples from the classroom provided by Thompson (2004) which she terms the 'extraction' and 'distraction' methods. According to Thompson the notion of 'learning from religion' originates in the work of Grimmitt (1987), is founded upon construc-tivism, and may produce 'a thorough-going relativism and hostility to traditional religions' (Thompson, 2004, p. 136).

In the 'extraction' method an idea that is not central is taken out of context. For instance, a lesson on Moses' leadership qualities might be the focus of attention when the burning bush, the Exodus and giving of the Ten Commandments are taught, although the central point of these stories is not Moses' leadership skills but God revealing himself to his people and teaching them how to live. The message and relevance of the stories becomes secularized into a story about leadership. The 'distraction' method (Thompson, 2004) is perhaps more dangerous, however, for in the attempt to make religion relevant, the original meaning may be deeply confused. For example, when teaching the five pillars of Islam non-Muslim children might be encouraged to relate these pillars to their own lives. They complete the sentence 'Five times a day Muslims . . .' but following this the emphasis is on their own 'version' of such behaviour with the task of finishing a sentence beginning 'Every day I intend to . . .'. Subsequently, as the attempt is made to find parallels, they complete a sentence beginning 'Every week Muslims give . . .' and then finish off one which begins 'If I chose to be generous I would . . .'. As they attempt to apply Islam to their own experience the children complete the sentence 'Once a year for self-discipline Muslims . . .' and then add to 'My ambition for the next year is . . .' in the misguided attempt to make Muslim behaviour comprehensible. In this case:

> Attention is immediately taken off Muslims and the possibility of children taking their faith seriously, and put onto matters which have little relation to the Muslim equivalent. What relation has naked ambition to the self-discipline required of a Muslim? And giving to others, a sacred task in Islam, becomes a matter of individual choice for the pupil.
>
> (Thompson, 2004, p. 128)

Not only is secularization promoted here but the self is unduly elevated. Children can easily learn to see themselves as the source of importance and value which only serves to reinforce a humanist agenda. These practices, which in Islam are concerned with self-denial and submission to Allah, are transformed here and seen merely as aspects of human behaviour based on the choices a person makes. We would agree that 'RE should treat religious traditions with great seriousness rather than reducing them to something else, whether that be secularism or essentialism' (Thompson, 2004, p. 149). The problems this approach creates for Citizenship and Moral Education may be especially acute if RE and Citizenship are taught as halves of a whole GCSE. The Qualifications and Curriculum Authority states that 'The GCSE short course has moved awarding bodies towards greater attention to religion as a meaning-making activity, that is *learning from religion*' (2000d, p. 27, our italics). But 'learning from religion' may well have 'become a tool which prevents children from learning the lessons a religion has to teach' (Thompson, 2004, p. 129). It is unlikely that children's understanding of the beliefs and values of religious groups or issues will have been sufficiently enhanced to fulfil the aims of the Citizenship curriculum through the approach described above.

Learning from religion, at least if the 'distraction' or 'extraction' methods are adopted, necessarily shifts attention away from the truth claims of a religion. If a child learns of the various answers to an important issue or question provided by a number of different religions (learning about religion) and then responds freely (learning from religion) this can lead to a situation where there 'are no right or wrong answers; indeed what is praised is the creative use of the data of religions so as to construct something new' (Thompson, 2004, p. 126). This 'pick 'n' mix' approach to religion again prioritizes the self as the determiner of meaning and downplays the notion that a religion may be a revelation by encouraging religious belief to be seen as a human construction. This communicates to children the message that we create our own version of reality, and such a position is antithetical to the teachings of many of the religions being studied. To lend credence to the notion that religions are human constructions and manifestations of political power that should be deconstructed is to adopt a particular value position rather than a neutral stance. We should be wary of any approaches to RE which simply induct pupils 'into the rules of the post-modern game, encouraging them to construct their own realities, on the basis of unrestrained freedom, desire, will and preference' (Wright, 1996, p. 144). Such approaches cannot be justified as the best way to develop tolerance and respect for others. Little is to be gained from obscuring doctrinal differences between Muslims and Christians, for example. Muslims and Christians can disagree on the nature of Jesus and still agree on the importance of the rule of law and the moral duty to live peaceably together. To encourage children to engage with such truth claims is valuable in Citizenship for it promotes a judicious understanding of the beliefs of others while recognizing that tolerance is not based on agreement but can be promoted by an awareness of differences.

Religious literacy and the reflective citizen

One of the dilemmas faced in RE is how many religions children should be expected to study. As we saw in Chapter 2, no single conception of the good life should be promoted in the liberal state school, and official religious neutrality requires that all religious and non-religious worldviews are treated with equal respect. For those who hold this (dominant) view, there are important repercussions for religious education. Given that children will not be fully educated if they know nothing of religion, and given that it is impossible to study all religions, it seems reasonable that children should study a representative sample of religions, and that the sample should be drawn either from major world religions or from the religions with most adherents in the country concerned. For this reason, and to ensure the curriculum is broad and balanced, the Qualifications and Curriculum Authority recommends that the six principal religions represented in Great Britain (Christianity, Buddhism, Hinduism, Islam, Judaism and Sikhism) should be studied in RE across the key stages, and that in addition opportunities are provided for all pupils to study other religious traditions such as the Baha'i faith, Jainism and Zoroastrianism, as well as secular philosophies such as humanism (QCA, 2004,

p. 12). The aim is not only to develop pupils' knowledge and understanding of individual religions and how they relate to each other and to give all pupils a chance to share their beliefs, but also to encourage 'the study of the nature and characteristics of religion' (ibid., p. 11).

On the other hand, this approach can be criticized for providing little continuity and coherence within RE, and a further problem of such a method can be superficiality especially when so little time is devoted to the subject. Attainment Target 1 in RE is concerned with learning about religions and understanding 'issues within and across faiths'. For instance, in the Qualifications and Curriculum Authority schemes of work for RE (2000c), in Year 1 Noah, Jewish and Christian beliefs are taught. In Year 3 Hinduism and Diwali are taught alongside the Bible. In Year 4 Hindu worship is taught next to Easter. In Year 5 Muhammad is explored alongside the Bible. In Year 7 the Buddha, God and the environment are the topics. If many religions are studied from an early age a child may not experience one religion in sufficient depth and subtlety before moving on to others, and may even be in danger of confusing the different religions. The danger of a superficial approach is that it can trivialize each faith's claim to truth and undermine the richness of a faith by oversimplifying it, which can in turn lead to the sort of stereotyping Citizenship seeks to combat. The interests of Religious Education may in fact be better served by studying fewer faiths. One option would be to bring young children up within a particular tradition rather than exposing them to many at an early age:

> If one starts from a position of commitment to one religion, then other religions will be taken seriously, since they challenge that commitment. Not to begin from a position of commitment to one religion, but rather refusing to be committed, may undermine respect for them all.
>
> (Thompson, 2004, p. 158)

Such an approach need not be indoctrinatory for the aim is that children should become critical. Indeed, many brought up within a particular religious tradition are uncommitted to that tradition as adults, although they may have a deeper appreciation of religious believers than those who were brought up with a superficial introduction to an eclectic and contradictory range of beliefs. Andrew Wright has argued children should as far as possible be brought up within their own faith especially when they are in the primary school and Pike (2005c) claims that where there are religious or ideological differences between home and school, it is generally the duty of the school to come into line with the home rather than vice versa. After becoming acquainted with a particular faith tradition children can become critical and make their own decisions. A second option (which may be more appropriate for children who are not themselves from a strong faith background) would be to provide an in-depth study of just two religions, which we would argue should be Christianity and Islam. There are important cultural reasons for children educated in the UK to have a good understanding of the Christian faith, and knowledge of the Bible is an important aspect of cultural literacy in the West (Pike, 2003e). But we would also argue that it is essential that children in the UK are not ignorant about of the teachings of Islam and the Qur'an, both because Islam is the second biggest religion in the UK and in the world and because it is a much misunderstood faith in the West.

At first glance, the multi-faith approach appears to fit in better with Citizenship, since it covers 'the diversity of . . . religious identities in the UK' (QCA/DfEE, 1999a, p. 14), whereas the mono-faith or dual-faith approach may suit the purposes of RE by providing opportunities for the in-depth 'study of the nature and characteristics of religion' (QCA, 2004, p. 11). Yet the situation is certainly more complex than is implied in this straightforward dichotomy. RE is currently committed to the multi-faith approach, whereas the interests of Citizenship may in some ways be better served by a stronger emphasis on Christianity, since this faith occupies a key place in relation to British citizenship and an understanding of Christianity is integral to the study of Citizenship in twenty-first century Britain; as Freathy points out, 'for a considerable proportion of English history and for a considerable proportion of the population, consideration of social and moral responsibilities and community involvement would have been inconceivable without reference to Christian beliefs and ethics' (Freathy, 2004).

PSHE, Citizenship and Moral Education

Personal, Social and Health Education (PSHE) has a much shorter history in the school curriculum in England than Religious Education, and the subject (then called PSE) only began to emerge in its present form in the mid-1980s, largely as a result of initiatives from Her Majesty's Inspectorate (Murray, 1998). In 1999, the National Advisory Group on Personal, Social and Health Education produced its report entitled *Preparing Young People for Adult Life* (DfEE, 1999), and one year later the Calouste Gulbenkian Foundation published *PASSPORT: a Framework for Personal and Social Development* (Lees and Plant, 2000). The terms PSE and PSHE have been used fairly loosely in the past to refer to the contribution which the whole curriculum (and indeed the ethos of the school) makes to children's development (Tattum and Tattum, 1992), though now it commonly refers to a planned range of activities centred on a timetabled course of separate lessons. A Framework for PSHE and Citizenship at Key Stages 1 and 2 is included in the National Curriculum Handbooks (DfEE/QCA, 1999a, 1999b), and initial guidance for schools across all the key stages was produced by the Qualifications and Curriculum Authority in 2000 (2000a, 2000b). HMI have made it clear that they expect PSHE to have a broad curriculum, rigorous planning and assessable outcomes (Ofsted, 2005b). The general aim of PSHE is to support students in issues relating to their personal and social development and to prepare them to lead healthy, independent adult lives and participate confidently in society. It includes such topics as emotional health and well-being, nutrition and physical activity, drugs, alcohol and tobacco education, sex and relationship education, safety, careers education, work-related learning, personal finance, bullying, family life and respecting differences between people. Richard Pring, one of the first educationalists to write in detail about PSE, stresses the need to base the subject on an examination of the concepts of 'person' and 'personal development' (1984, chs 2–3). Like Straughan (1988, p. 24), Pring sees the moral development of students as the heart of PSE (1984, p. 56), whereas White argues that the promotion of students' personal well-being is more central (1989, p. 10). It is White's view that has prevailed in recent official guidance on the subject.

The Final Report of the Advisory Group on Citizenship maintains that of all school subjects contributing to Citizenship, the 'biggest overlap is with PSE or PSHE' (1998, p. 52). A letter from Bernard Crick appended to the main report sets out the common ground between the two subjects, as well as the main areas of divergence. Of the three strands of Citizenship Education which the report identifies, Crick argues that 'social and moral responsibility' is the most obvious area of common ground, though Citizenship will focus more on public values and institutional responsibility; there is some overlap in the area of 'community involvement', though this too may have a different emphasis in Citizenship; but 'political literacy' is 'quite distinct in content from anything reasonably called PSE' (ibid., p. 62). It is for these reasons that the report recommends that PSHE and Citizenship are taught together in primary schools (at Key Stages 1 and 2) and as separate subjects in secondary schools (at Key Stages 3 and 4), and this approach is now current policy in England. As Crick points out, 'Children learn responsibility best and gain a sense of moral values by discussing . . . real and controversial issues' (ibid., p. 64), and such learning is a necessary foundation for both PSHE and Citizenship as they go on increasingly divergent paths at secondary level.

The combined Framework for PSHE and Citizenship at Key Stages 1 and 2 (QCA/DfEE, 1999b, pp. 136–41) includes 'Preparing to play an active role as citizens' as one of the four areas of knowledge, skills and understanding. The focus is particularly on rules, responsibilities, communities, decision-making and resources. However, when the two subjects diverge at Key Stage 3, there are still many links, and the Qualifications and Curriculum Authority has mapped some of these in a recent leaflet (2001c). One obvious area of overlap is knowledge of 'the diversity of national, regional, religious and ethnic identities in the UK and the need for mutual respect and understanding' (Citizenship Programme of Study, 1b) and 'respecting the differences between people' and recognizing 'some of the cultural norms in society, including the range of lifestyles and relationships' (PSHE framework, 3d). There are many ways in which these goals can be achieved together, including inviting guest speakers, engaging in community action, devising anti-racism policies, organizing multicultural events, producing themed drama activities as part of school assemblies, and so on. Another area is learning about the need for rules and laws: the Citizenship programme of study emphasizes 'legal and human rights and responsibilities underpinning society, basic aspects of the criminal justice system, and how both relate to young people' (1a) and the PSHE framework includes 'basic facts and laws, including school rules, about alcohol and tobacco, illegal substances and the risks of misusing prescribed drugs' (2d), 'resisting the pressure to do wrong' (3j), and 'developing and putting into practice school policies about anti-bullying' (4c). Students can cover these issues in a variety of ways, such as participating in the development of school rules or the review of school policies. One activity carried out by Year 7 students was to devise a new board game, which highlighted the need for rules and led on to further activity drawing up ground rules for successful progress and learning (Lees and Plant, 2000, p. 51).

Citizenship and PSHE overlap not only in terms of content but also in the skills (such as decision-making and communication) that are developed and in approaches to teaching and learning. Like Citizenship, the learning associated with PSHE occurs not only in designated lessons, but also occurs across a range of National Curriculum subjects, in tutorial time, in assemblies, in special projects and activities, in whole-school 'focus days', in work experience and mini-enterprise schemes, in extra-curricular activities, sport, residential experiences, community service and other events that enrich students' experience (Ofsted, 2005b, pp. 15–19; QCA, 2000a, pp. 10–14). Both subjects involve learning from the school culture and environment and partnerships outside the school. There is also an emphasis on active learning, enquiry, discussion and debate as suitable ways of developing the knowledge, skills, understanding, attitudes and values of both subjects. As Crick points out, discussion and debate are 'the bases of social responsibility and intercourse and the grounding and practice of active citizenship' (AGC, 1998, p. 64). Both subjects are concerned to develop the ability to act responsibly, and to provide opportunities to analyse and reflect critically on such action.

The Qualifications and Curriculum Authority reports that many secondary as well as primary schools are currently using PSHE as the main vehicle for delivering Citizenship. Twenty-three per cent of primary schools and twenty-nine per cent of secondary schools in the QCA survey report that the two subjects are always taught together, and a further sixty-nine per cent of primary schools and sixty per cent of secondary schools say they are taught together some of the time (2004, p. 5). Many of the advantages of teaching Citizenship and PSHE together have already been touched on. However, both the QCA and Ofsted have also mentioned some disadvantages. Ofsted reports that in too many schools the introduction of Citizenship has adversely affected the curriculum and teaching time of PSHE (2005b, pp. 1, 3, 15). The QCA also mentions that where there are combined programmes of PSHE and Citizenship, 'aspects of statutory requirements may not be met in either subject' (2004, p. 4), and where there is a single co-ordinator for the two subjects (as in sixty per cent of secondary schools) there may be too heavy a workload and 'a failure in many cases to make a distinction between the subjects' (ibid., p. 5; see also Chapter 8 of this book). Researchers have reported that schools often lack a PSHE policy, scheme of work and co-ordinator, and that PSHE is often 'taken off the timetable to make room for other activities' (Mead, 2004, pp. 21–2).

Aside from these practical and organizational issues, Ofsted reports that 'too few schools saw achievement in PSHE as related to their pupils' attitudes, values and personal development', and in fact too little attention is paid to attitudes and values overall (2005b, pp. 1, 3). Other research suggests that this may be related to the deep-rooted fear many teachers have of 'moralizing' (for a recent philosophical discussion of 'moralizing', see Coady, 2005). For example, Passy quotes one teacher who found it very difficult to talk to her pupils about families and family values:

> There's such a diverse range of what is at home really; there are a lot of them [pupils] who have your nuclear family, and then there are those that . . . I don't actually know if there's a dad at home . . . so I find it very difficult . . . because . . . there are some here that have got really difficult situations at home and I don't want to make them feel that they're missing out on something . . . cos I think it's hard to talk about it without making it sound as though this is how it should be . . . So that's the main reason I avoid it. And also it's difficult, there's so much else that we've got to do – I mean it's easier not to do it.
>
> (Passy, 2003)

Teaching about 'the role and importance of marriage in family relationships' and 'the role and feelings of parents and carers and the value of family life' is part of the PSHE framework for Key Stage 3 (3f and 3g), but many teachers especially in secular state schools feel uncomfortable with promoting family values in this way, because they believe that

* such teaching implies the moral superiority of certain kinds of family relationship, and this conflicts with the teachers' view that they should be non-judgemental about things that belong to the pupils' private lives;
* such teaching stigmatizes children from single-parent families, renders them more vulnerable and may damage their self-esteem;
* such teaching is based on an idealized, static, backward-looking notion of family life and pays inadequate attention to contemporary attitudes and lifestyles or to the complexity and instability of some children's family lives;
* families are in any case not always based on love, care, support and commitment, but may equally embody violence, deceit, neglect, abuse, manipulation, rejection, overprotection, dominance and mistrust;
* one of the aims of school-based education, particularly at secondary level, is to encourage children to move towards a greater degree of personal autonomy, and this may include becoming more independent of their families.

The importance of these points cannot be overstressed. However, we believe that it would be a mistake if teachers were to draw the conclusion that it is wiser to avoid the topic of the family altogether in PSHE, for the family (whatever form it takes) plays a hugely important part in the lives of most children. If PSHE is to provide opportunities for children to discuss and reflect on the nature and value of family life, such discussion should obviously reflect the diversity of family structures that exist in contemporary society rather than focusing exclusively on the traditional nuclear family. Clearly, the value of the family as an institution and the values associated with being a member of a family are more to do with the quality of the relationships and the benefits that derive from living on intimate terms with others, and are not tied exclusively to any particular family structure or definition of the family. To acknowledge this will probably defuse many of the anxieties teachers have about teaching family values. But one of the effects of failing to provide any direct teaching about the family is simply to drive the topic into the hidden curriculum, where the influences on children are haphazard and they pick up values and moral messages that may be unintended. For example, mathematics or modern language textbooks may present stereotypical views of family life, whereas literature and drama activities may overemphasize family violence, which makes good drama but is not necessarily a good introduction to family life. Somewhat surprisingly, Ofsted expresses strong approval of one such role-play activity, involving a fourteen-year-old daughter asking her mother if she could go to a club and stay overnight at a friend's house (2005b, p. 9). The pupils and the teacher role-played 'passive, aggressive and assertive responses to the situation', but responses based on a loving, trusting relationship between mother and daughter are excluded, perhaps not even thought of as a possibility.

It is this emphasis on the negative that we find most worrying about current approaches to PSHE. The framework for PSHE at Key Stage 3 includes being taught 'to resist pressure to do wrong' (DfEE/QCA, 1999b, 3j), but moral values like love in family relationships or anywhere else are simply not mentioned. This neglect of love is as apparent in much PSHE practice as it is in the framework and guidelines. For example, it is a practice in some schools to give girls in their early teens a 'flour baby' to take home, or an electronic doll that wakes up crying every two hours in the night (cf. Halstead and Reiss, 2003, pp. 116, 182), with the ostensible intention of putting them off having a baby at too early an age; but the actual effect may be to encourage negative feelings about parenthood generally. At any rate, the practice does nothing to help them understand the joy that many people feel at the birth of a child or the deep bond of love that mothers commonly feel with their newborn child. This is just one of a number of teaching approaches to Sex and Relationship Education in which babies are presented as nuisances or inconveniences, rather than as sources of wonder, love and personal enrichment (ibid., pp. 192–3). The reasons why many teachers feel uncomfortable talking about love to their students are varied and complex (Halstead, 2005c), but since for many people love is a route to personal fulfilment, it seems that PSHE is selling children short by failing to teach them about it.

In this chapter we have been looking at the relationship between four curriculum areas: Citizenship, Moral Education, Religious Education and PSHE. It is in the domain of values that this relationship is most complicated. In his discussion of the relationship between Citizenship and PSHE, Crick concludes that what is needed for good citizenship cannot 'simply be deduced from the principles' that guide PSHE (AGC, 1998, p. 63). In other words, he is drawing a significant distinction between the principles or values underpinning Citizenship and those underpinning PSHE. We disagree. It seems to us that the values of PSHE and Citizenship come from the same stable, both being derived from the framework of liberal values outlined in Chapter 2. It might be tempting at first glance to assume that Citizenship is based on a framework of public values and that PSHE is based on a framework of private values, but of course this is not the case; both are equally based on public values. It is RE which exposes children to a representative range of private values. The question that arises now is where Moral Education fits into this. We argue in the final section of the present chapter that there are dangers in severing the link between Moral Education and RE and tying Moral Education instead more closely to Citizenship and PSHE.

Moral Education: the domain of RE or Citizenship and PSHE?

Everything we have written so far, indeed the very title of our book, implies a close link between Moral Education and Citizenship/PSHE. Crick argues that 'any teaching of Citizenship not based on moral values and reasoning would either be mechanical and boring, or even dangerous' (1998a, p. 19). Of course, he is here referring to public or shared moral values. However, many teachers also link private moral values like caring and unselfishness to Citizenship. Teachers in a survey of attitudes to Citizenship Education a few years ago regularly maintained that the moral dimensions of citizenship mattered far more than the legal or political dimensions; they referred to the importance of being conscious of the interests of others and the wider society and acting accordingly, and used the language of caring, unselfishness, co-operation, meeting community obligations and demonstrating respect to give substance to their view of citizenship (Davies *et al.*, 1999, p. 50). This raises the question of how the curriculum should be organized, which Crick (1998a) discusses in detail. Should Moral Education, Citizenship, PSHE and RE all have a separate slot within the curriculum, or should there be some merging?

In an important pamphlet, *The Mosaic of Learning* (1994), Hargreaves tackles this issue with characteristic forthrightness. His argument is in four steps. First, he claims that 'morality is not as closely linked to religion, especially the Christian religion, as in the past' (p. 34), and that the time has come to acknowledge this and separate religious and moral education. Secondly, he argues that 'non-denominational core RE' is unpopular with children, and trivializes each faith's claims to truth, as well as being unviable as a vehicle of moral education, and should be abandoned in (secular) community schools (p. 34). Thirdly, he supports the establishment of more religious schools (of Christian and other faiths) to meet parental demand, and accepts that such schools could uphold the moral and religious convictions of their communities (p. 35). Fourthly, he argues that all schools should teach 'a common core of civic education' which should include a significant element of non-religious moral education (pp. 35–6).

In response to Hargreaves' first two points, we have already noted that although there are dangers in trying to teach too many religions in the small amount of curriculum time allocated to RE, the subject is becoming more popular with students (in terms, for example of numbers of GCSE entries), perhaps because of its willingness to encourage discussion of contemporary issues in an open way. Students realize that many core liberal values (such as the equal moral worth of all human beings) have their roots in Christianity. On the other hand, they also recognize that scriptural injunctions to look after the poor, the stranger and those who are most vulnerable provide a basis for a critique of governmental policy towards immigrants, the homeless and children in care, and that religions provide strong arguments against the excesses of capitalism and economic liberalism. In any case, people could hardly claim to be educated citizens if they knew nothing of the influence religion has had (and continues to have) on human affairs in every country of the world. The implications of Hargreaves' third point (with which we broadly agree) have been discussed in some detail elsewhere (Halstead, 2003; Halstead and McLaughlin, 2005; Pike, 2005a, 2005b) and need not concern us here. His final point, however, merits detailed discussion, and it is with this that we conclude the present chapter.

A number of writers have supported Hargreaves' final proposal. Crick (1998a), for example, suggests that with young children Citizenship and Moral Education can be taught together (along with RE and PSHE for good measure), through interactive and experiential approaches like Circle Time, and that there is no need for careful conceptual differentiation at this level. However, as children grow older, he claims they will need to distinguish more clearly between issues of personal responsibility (PSHE) and issues of public policy (Citizenship) (Crick, 1998a, pp. 18–19). Haydon (2000a, 2000b) faces up to the challenge of what he sees as a continuing disagreement over what 'morality' is and a declining interest in moral education in both official and professional discourse, and questions whether there is any longer any need to talk about morality and moral education in schools. He suggests that if Citizenship includes education in public values and the agreed norms of a society, and if PSHE includes matters of personal morality, this makes the idea of separate moral education (or moral education through RE) redundant. It would follow from this, Haydon claims, that the concept of moral education could be abandoned in the school context, though the norms and expectations involved in living together in society would continue to be the focus of educational attention.

It is possible to view the matter simply as one of labelling and argue that so long as the issues get covered, it does not really matter under what heading they are taught and learned. This is broadly the line taken by Crick when he says, 'What's in a name?' (1998a, p. 19). However, there are dangers in blurring the distinction between Moral Education and Citizenship/PSHE. Though they overlap, they have different emphases and different cores, they use different concepts and have different goals. Morality is a broad concept, covering much more than matters of Citizenship and the civic virtues. Moral Education would therefore be distorted if it were taught only or mainly through Citizenship/PSHE. We shall argue that a separate form of Moral Education is needed to provide the principles and procedures necessary for developing a critique of some of the values taught implicitly or explicitly through Citizenship.

To start with, in the liberal framework of values which underpins Citizenship/ PSHE, religion is relegated to a matter of individual choice, whereas for many people it is the basis of their moral understanding. Tying Moral Education too closely to Citizenship/PSHE has the effect of secularizing it for these people and thus undermining the basis of their understanding of morality. Citizenship necessarily involves a rejection of the view which some citizens may hold that religious attachments are more important than political ones as a source of identity, or that the Islamic *umma* is more important than the nation state. The aim of education for active citizenship is to help students to take a general perspective as equal citizens, but if this general perspective is expanded to include social, moral and cultural elements, it carries the danger of undermining the social, moral and cultural life of minorities and undervaluing difference (Hall, 2000; Phillips, 1991, 2000; Young, 1989). If Moral Education is to be worthwhile for *all* children, it cannot be based on assumptions which undermine the beliefs, values, commitments and identity of some. The problem is that the more substantial the framework of public values is, the more people there will be who do not share the values and who therefore feel excluded; but the thinner the values framework is, the less adequate it is as a means of moral education.

In any case, the public/private distinction is problematic in a number of ways. McLaughlin discusses the difficulty of distinguishing between public and private values in theoretical terms, and the even greater difficulty of distinguishing them in practice (1995, pp. 28–31). These difficulties arise for many reasons – partly because of the increasing intrusion of the public into the private (Hall, 2000, p. 47), partly because issues which were once considered private (such as homosexuality and disability) are being brought increasingly into the public domain (cf. Young, 1990, pp. 119–21), and partly because more recent approaches to morality and Moral Education, such as the ethics of care, further blur the private/public distinction (Sevenhuijsen, 1998). It is clear anyway that the 'public' values cover only part of the moral life; students will not reach a full understanding of moral issues unless they are addressed from both public and private perspectives. When E. M. Forster famously said that if he had to choose between betraying his friends and betraying his country, he hoped he would have the courage to choose the latter, such a conclusion could not be reached, or even understood, if Moral Education were restricted to public values and subsumed under Citizenship. As Phillips reminds us (1991, pp. 85–6), being a good citizen is not the same as being a good mother, a good feminist or a good neighbour – or indeed a good friend. Feminist research has made further inroads into the public/private divide by drawing attention to the gendered nature of citizenship and to the fact that Citizenship as currently taught in schools contributes to the modern state's valorization of male-oriented public life (focusing on the responsibilities of the citizen) and devaluing of female-oriented private life (focusing on the responsibilities of the carer) (Pateman, 1989; Foster, 1997). This raises moral issues and highlights the need for a moral critique of Citizenship that can only be developed from an external perspective. Once again, it suggests that if Citizenship is intended to prepare children *for* citizenship, then they also need to be able in some way to stand outside what they are taught in order to develop a moral critique of it, and hence there is a continuing need for Moral Education to provide an understanding of moral principles and procedures outside Citizenship.

Finally, it is clear that an understanding of and commitment to the law is central to the notion of Citizenship. But this generates a number of problems if Citizenship then becomes the main vehicle for Moral Education. One problem is that if Moral Education and Citizenship are merged in this way, this might mean that because the law embodies many of society's public values, the law comes to be treated as the authoritative basis by which people decide whether things are right or wrong, rather than, say, religion or a humanist code of ethics (cf. Gilbert, 1997, p. 79). The problem is that the law is inadequate as a sole basis for deciding questions of morality. The fact that something is legal does not necessarily make it moral; apart from anything else, the law is open to frequent change and transformation, whereas ethical values are not. The effect of pinning morality too closely to the law could be to confuse children's moral development just at the age when they need most guidance. Education must make clear the differences between law and morality, and this is not best achieved by teaching morality through Citizenship. A further problem is that though Citizenship will among other things help young people to develop an attitude of respect for the law, to internalize a commitment to the rule of law and come to accept the authority of the law because they understand appropriate reasons for doing so, those virtues in themselves will not provide them with the competence to distinguish a just from an unjust law. If we want individuals to be able to identify an unjust law, this ability will not come from a study of law, but from an understanding and application of principles outside the law, namely, moral principles. It is difficult to encourage commitment to something and an open-minded, critical attitude to it at the same time (McLaughlin and Halstead, 1999, p. 152). Moral Education can provide the critical distance needed to evaluate the commitments required by Citizenship. There is a danger that this will be lost if Moral Education is merged with, or replaced by, Citizenship.

Part 3

Teaching and assessing Citizenship and Moral Education

Chapter 8

Teaching and Learning Citizenship

In this chapter the state of Citizenship teaching in schools will be evaluated and reasons for the current situation will be considered. Recommendations for the development of Citizenship will be made which enable due attention to be given to children's moral education. Different models of Citizenship provision in schools are evaluated and subsequently the effective teaching of relevant texts, with a special focus on ICT and media texts, is described. Following this consideration of texts the teaching of communication in the classroom is analysed. The chapter ends by bringing together the approaches to texts and communication in the classroom by looking at the teaching of controversial issues. To begin, however, an assessment of the current state of Citizenship teaching in the UK will be helpful.

The state of Citizenship teaching

Citizenship teaching has an unenviable reputation in many schools. David Bell, Her Majesty's Chief Inspector of Schools, in his Office for Standards in Education Lecture to the Hansard Society on 17 January 2005 presented sobering findings and unequivocally stated that 'citizenship education is the worst taught subject in secondary schools'. Bell even reiterated his assessment, saying that 'Citizenship is the worst taught subject at Key Stages 3 and 4' and observed that schools 'are seldom judged to deliver very good teaching in this subject' (2005). Clearly, we need to understand the extent of the problem and the reasons for it if solutions are to be found.

The extent of poor Citizenship teaching

The extent of poor Citizenship teaching was officially revealed the month after David Bell's speech in February 2005 with the publication of HMI report 2335 *Citizenship in secondary schools: evidence from Ofsted inspections (2003/2004)*. According to this report 'provision is unsatisfactory' in 'one in four schools' (Ofsted, 2005a, p. 3). Yet not only are a quarter of schools providing unsatisfactory Citizenship Education, even fewer provide inspectors with examples of very good practice. We are told that schools are 'seldom judged to deliver very good teaching'

(Bell, 2005) in Citizenship. Further, it is reported that in Citizenship, 'pupils' achievement and the quality of teaching compare unfavourably with established subjects and there is little that is graded very good' (Ofsted, 2005a, p. 3). Indeed, in just 'one school in seven' was 'provision for Citizenship' actually 'judged to be very good' and only 'in a further one school in four' was the curriculum's newest subject 'judged to be good' (ibid., p. 3). One indication of the lack of satisfactory provision within Citizenship teaching is that 'most schools have not yet established ways of assessing pupils' progress and attainment in citizenship' (Ofsted, 2004a, p. 10) and consequently a chapter of this book is devoted to the complex and challenging practice of assessment in this subject.

Unexpected failure

If the examples found of 'very good' provision appear few and judging a quarter of schools to be 'unsatisfactory' might seem rather harsh (especially when judging such a new subject) we should be aware that inspectors were 'instructed to regard citizenship as an emerging subject' and directed to 'make allowances' (Ofsted, 2005a, p. 4). In other words, even when evaluating Citizenship teaching with a degree of generosity it was weighed in the balances and found wanting. If this was not bad enough even schools judged to have 'satisfactory' provision at this stage 'are based on curriculum models that may not be viable in the longer term' (ibid., p. 4). Some of the models schools have used for implementing Citizenship will be examined shortly. Evidently, though, Citizenship is a subject that is giving senior managers and teachers some concern. Schools will be reviewing their provision in the light of these findings and those responsible for the subject will be reflecting upon current models of implementing Citizenship. This chapter seeks to illuminate (and also problematize) some of Ofsted's findings, suggests reasons for these findings and advocates a direction in which schools may wish to proceed.

Problems of definition

The necessity of a far reaching review of Citizenship Education is apparent when it is evident that such findings were not anticipated by many schools who believed their Citizenship provision to be quite good – until they received their Ofsted inspection. To report that a quarter of all schools were judged to have 'unsatisfactory' Citizenship provision is one thing but what is of particular interest is that many of these schools did not realize that their provision was unsatisfactory. As schools are normally aware of where their strengths and weaknesses lie this might be somewhat surprising in itself. One reason for the unpleasant surprise appears to be that the schools inspected and the Ofsted inspectors had very different views about what Citizenship is. David Bell admits as much when he notes that 'a number of otherwise high performing schools, have found their provision for citizenship to be judged as unsatisfactory by inspectors' and suggests that 'the root of the problem here is often misunderstanding' (2005). This 'misunderstanding' is redolent of some of the competing notions of Citizenship Education discussed in the opening chapters of this book and is of interest because it highlights not only the fact that defining Citizenship is problematic but also indicates the version of Citizenship currently being privileged and valorized by Ofsted. Certain ways of implementing Citizenship are being legitimated and others, it would seem, are disapproved of. Ofsted admits that the 'implementation of citizenship as a National Curriculum subject has been beset by problems of definition' (2005a, p. 6) and these competing definitions are apparent in the different ways schools have chosen to ensure that it is taught.

Models of Citizenship provision in schools

What is clear is that certain models of teaching Citizenship are considered by Ofsted to be more effective than others and Bell notes 'there is good evidence to suggest what is working and what is not' (2005, p. 4). Seven of the most common models or approaches to Citizenship are outlined below. The 'audit-of-what-we-already-do' method is contrasted with the 'integration-in-Arts-and-Humanities-for-moral-education' approach and the 'one-timetabled-lesson-a-week' model. In addition the 'whole-day-event' and 'assessment-driven' methods of implementing Citizenship are considered. Finally the 'married to PSHE' model and 'ethos-citizenship' are evaluated. It should be remembered that, in Ofsted's view, some of these models are 'unlikely to be viable in the longer term' (2005a) and, consequently, models described below which have gained schools a 'satisfactory' report on this aspect of their work look unlikely to achieve similar results in the future. That all but two of the models outlined below are effectively obsolete and appear to be disapproved of by Ofsted provides all the more reason to look into them.

Citizenship by audit

In short, teaching Citizenship through other subjects, the cross-curricular route, is often considered to be unsuccessful in Ofsted's view. David Bell notes that:

> Problems have also arisen where schools have taken a cross-curricular route, seeking to identify or provide citizenship through subjects. Many schools prepared for the introduction of citizenship with an audit of links to citizenship, typically compiling a matrix that showed where citizenship content could be found. But our evidence suggests that, so far, pupils are confused by cross-curricular approaches, and sometimes are not aware that they have had a citizenship programme at all.
>
> (2005)

The approach described and criticized here seems to be one where the school assumes Citizenship must be occurring and simply seeks to audit its curriculum to indicate where the various aspects of Citizenship are occurring. This is rather different to the planned teaching of Citizenship through, for instance, the Arts and Humanities where teachers of these subjects meet together to plan a coherent, integrated and challenging programme of Citizenship and Moral Education.

Citizenship for Moral Education through the Arts and Humanities

Although Bell's statement does not exactly encourage the 'cross-curricular route' where a school seeks to 'provide citizenship through subjects', it should be made quite clear that it is the 'matrix-approach' which is singled out for criticism where schools have attempted to see if 'citizenship content could be found' rather than proactively seeing where aspects of citizenship could be imaginatively taught within, for instance, English, Drama, History and RE. Indeed some comprehensive schools teach Citizenship successfully within one faculty, most commonly the Humanities. It must be stressed that Ofsted is not claiming that the cross-curricular route is unacceptable but rather that the cross-curricular approach is often implemented rather badly. This is one reason for the inclusion of separate chapters in the present volume on teaching Citizenship through the Arts (Chapter 5), the Humanities (Chapter 6) and RE or PSHE (Chapter 7). Ofsted suggests that where this cross-curricular approach is taken schools should 'go with strength, identifying those subjects with the greatest capacity to provide good citizenship units' (2005a, p. 4).

This is considered to be more practical than expecting every subject to contribute to citizenship provision, although there are many reasons why citizenship *should* be taught in disciplines such as Science, PE and Music as well as the areas assumed to have the most obvious links to Citizenship.

Arguably, the integrated cross-curricular route can be the most rewarding for pupils but it is also the most complex and challenging for teachers as it requires extensive liaison between numerous staff especially in large schools. Such a challenge, in terms of planning and assessing, should not prove insurmountable if an effective subject co-ordinator for Citizenship is in place who can work with those responsible for generating schemes of work in the subject areas with which Citizenship is to be integrated. The other barrier to achieving an effective cross-curricular approach is a lack of knowledge of the Citizenship curriculum among 'non-specialist' teachers. It should be stressed that this is normally not a lack of 'subject-knowledge' but of the requirements of the Citizenship curriculum.

English teachers may be far better equipped than a 'specialist' Citizenship teacher to teach about the influence of the media upon public opinion especially if they teach Media Studies to GCSE or A-level students. English departments are also well-placed to teach transactional writing that argues and persuades. RE teachers would appear to be best placed to teach about the beliefs and values of minority ethnic groups in the UK and History teachers are normally better able than others to teach political literacy and the intricacies of the British parliamentary system of government or economics. Drama teachers are most experienced at role-play and are accustomed to helping children develop empathy. If a group of such teachers becomes sufficiently familiar with the requirements of the Citizenship programme of study they could, between them, plan for imaginative coverage of Citizenship. Arguably, all teachers have an obligation to contribute to children's moral education and sharing the teaching of Citizenship could be a valuable way of doing so.

Dedicated Citizenship lessons

It may be due to the challenge that such integrated cross-curricular teaching evidently presents that Ofsted encourages a much simpler and more straight-forward approach. In contrast to the cross-curricular approach, the model that is singled out for praise is the establishment of a core of dedicated Citizenship teachers, often in a new Citizenship department where the subject is explicitly timetabled as 'Citizenship' and taught once a week. While such an approach poses least risk to schools and may be the safest one to adopt it seems unlikely to be the best. The 'one-timetabled-lesson-a-week' model should effectively eliminate the worst excesses of the 'matrix-of-what-we-already-do' approach but will equally effectively deny pupils the best of integrated teaching within subjects which are closely related to Citizenship.

It is clear, however, which model is privileged by Ofsted. Adding Citizenship, as another subject, to the curriculum may be the easiest way to gain a satisfactory Ofsted report. Finding an hour a week on the school timetable and adding 'Citizenship' as a named subject seems to be encouraged. Eltham Girls School in Greenwich has been singled out for praise by the Chief Inspector as an institution 'where citizenship is a strength' because it has an hour a week for Citizenship lessons, a team of specialist teachers and children 'enjoying their lessons spent considering government priorities and writing election manifestos' (Bell, 2005). It is not a coincidence that these are the aspects of Citizenship which are high-lighted because political literacy is increasingly being emphasized within the teaching of Citizenship rather than the broader view of the subject which sees it as an opportunity for Moral Education.

The assessment-driven model: introducing GCSE Citizenship

Where a school has its own Citizenship department it usually enters children as candidates for GCSE Citizenship Studies. The disadvantages of such an approach are explained in Chapter 10 which is dedicated to an examination of assessment in relation to Citizenship teaching. Entering children for GCSE Citizenship is often explicitly commended and we are told that 'Involvement in GCSE citizenship short courses has been generally associated with greater focus, better teaching and higher standards and achievement' (Ofsted, 2005a, p. 3). Specialist teaching in designated timetable periods is advocated and the setting up of Citizenship departments that teach GCSE is praised. Ofsted seems to promote the approach to Citizenship where it is taught as a 'National Curriculum subject', has a 'strong and identifiable core programme' and where 'some or all pupils are following accredited courses including short course GCSE' (2005a, p. 3). Citizenship is praised where 'attitudes to citizenship are good', teachers have 'good subject knowledge and are up to date with subject thinking', 'resources are used critically' and the subject 'involves homework' (ibid., p. 3).

Whole-day-event Citizenship

Many schools put on a Human Rights Day for Year 11 where speakers from outside the school work with children. Representatives from Amnesty International or organizations such as the Red Cross are often helpful in this respect. Alternatively schools may institute a Criminal Justice day where children attend court and participate in a mock trial. In our experience, helpful lawyers, magistrates, probation workers or police officers, who are parents or governors, seem very keen to become involved and readily accommodate schools wanting their pupils to have experience away from the school campus of the way the courts work. Other schools have a Disability Day or an Equal Opportunities Day and teachers devise innovative workshops to broaden pupils' experience and understanding of these issues.

A Media Day is an especially valuable opportunity for children to learn how the media influences public opinion and the local Newspapers in Education (NiE) co-ordinator, normally based at the offices of a local paper, can be a tremendously helpful source of guidance and professional knowledge. On one such day, children from Year 10 worked in teams for the day producing either a newspaper, a radio news programme or a television news broadcast. Groups can be given different perspectives to represent to illustrate the way in which the same event can be reported quite differently depending on the perspective of the team reporting the event. Local businesses and public services became involved at one school in staging events to be reported. One pupil from each team was transported by school minibus around the city to be at the scene of newsworthy events. On this occasion the local community entered into the spirit of the day: an estate agent produced mock particulars of an exclusive residence with a recording studio that was to be purchased by the pupils' favourite band; a supermarket actually closed its doors so that a health and safety hazard could be reported and the Fire Brigade even staged a chemical spill and cut the roof off a wrecked car at the scene of the accident. Learning about bias when reporting and the difference between fact and opinion when writing or speaking about these events on the news gave these children an insight into the workings of the media. They even got to meet real reporters because the local BBC station decided to report the young reporters reporting, who were pleased to end up in the news themselves.

While such days can be the highlight of the school year and provide the opportunity for work on a given Citizenship theme over several hours, rather than just one lesson at a time, there are also disadvantages to such an approach. As teachers know from their experience of INSET days it is all too easy to forget something if it is a 'one-off' and is not followed up throughout the school year. The best approach to the one-day event appears to be to schedule it as the culmination or starting point of sustained concentration upon a Citizenship theme that lasts several weeks or even a whole term. The risk of the one-day event is that it may have little impact on its own upon the lives of young citizens throughout the rest of the year. Integrating Citizenship into the life of school is unlikely to be achieved through one day events alone.

Married to PSHE: a public or private affair?

As noted in Chapter 7, Citizenship is often taught within PSHE or in tutorial time with a form or tutor group. This is often inadequate according to Ofsted, which claims that linking Citizenship too closely with PSHE can cause confusion. This is because the two can be conflated and what we might term 'National Curriculum Citizenship' may not be taught. David Bell observes that 'the perceived close relationship between citizenship and PSHE is proving problematic' and he also offers a helpful definition of the remit of each subject: 'PSHE is about the private, individual dimension of pupils' development, whereas Citizenship concerns the public dimension' (2005). Ofsted's report (2005a) provides useful elaboration on this point as it is explained that 'conflict resolution in citizenship is not about the problems experienced in individual parent-teenager relationships' (p. 6). If one moved from personal conflict resolution to the global conflict resolution role of the UN this would, however, qualify as Citizenship and moving from the personal to the public dimension of a given issue would appear to be one approach to the integration of Citizenship and PSHE. Topics familiar in PSHE such as drug abuse, teenage pregnancy or bullying can only rightly be explored within Citizenship when the public aspects of such issues are considered. In other words they 'take on a citizenship dimension when the questions addressed are to do with topical local and national issues, policy, and what can be done to bring about change' (ibid., p. 6).

Ethos Citizenship

Ofsted appears to have seen most good Citizenship teaching where it was instituted as a distinct subject as this ensures that greater attention is given to the specific knowledge-base or National Curriculum content of Citizenship. Although pupils' participation in charity events, school councils and other community events are praised, the Chief Inspector is at pains to point out that 'National Curriculum citizenship is not about the way a school goes about its business, or its ethos, although these factors are important. Neither is it participation by some pupils in extra curricular or community activities' (Bell, 2005). Citizenship is a defined subject with a specific body of knowledge and set of skills and therefore 'National

Curriculum Citizenship is, and should be, an entitlement for all pupils' (Bell, 2005). What might be termed 'Ethos Citizenship' is not, it would seem, in vogue, although it is extremely important. We consider the importance of ethos in the next chapter for, in our view, it is central to children's acquisition of values. A school with an ethos of tolerance, respect, inclusion and participation which has a culture which promotes moral education is an environment in which all the most important aspects of the Citizenship curriculum can be approached constructively. Further, having some experience of democracy within school is held by some researchers to be central to learning about and participating in democracy outside school.

What's wrong with 'invisible' Citizenship?

Evidently what *is* and is *not* Citizenship is being defined and the models for teaching Citizenship which are being advocated require scrutiny. Three reasons are given as bullet points in Ofsted's 2005 report on inspections to explain what was 'unsatisfactory' about Citizenship provision. It is worth quoting them here. The view of Ofsted is that:

> Where citizenship provision has been judged unsatisfactory, the subject is insubstantial or invisible. Usually this is where:
>
> - citizenship is provided entirely through other subjects, but not distinctively;
> - tutorial periods are used, but without the necessary time or expertise to support effective subject development;
> - the curriculum consists of 'opportunities' for some pupils for enrichment rather than an entitlement for all.
>
> (2005a, p. 4)

The *visibility* of Citizenship to pupils is something that is taken to be an indicator of successful provision. We have seen above that one of the reasons for interdisciplinary Citizenship being criticized is that 'pupils are confused by cross-curricular approaches, and sometimes are not aware that they have had a citizenship programme at all' (Bell, 2005). Ofsted's opinion poll (although the report does not provide details of the sample) indicated that 'more than half of pupils either did not know what Citizenship Education is or could offer no examples of what they had learned' (Bell, 2005) and the unchallenged assumption here is that for Citizenship to be successful children must know they are doing Citizenship. Such an assumption is very much a product of its time and can be challenged on a number of counts. Such a challenge is essential for the assumption within Ofsted that Citizenship should be visible militates against cross-curricular approaches which can be immensely rewarding for pupils.

Visibility should not be taken as an automatic indicator of success as invisibility could be the mark of a highly integrated programme that has been embedded with some sophistication. The influence of 'National-Strategy-Think' has been to place a premium upon explicitness or visibility. At the risk of exaggeration, it is as though every aspect of learning must be exposed for all to see. Children must be told quite explicitly what it is they will learn at the very start of the lesson before learning begins and they are to be reminded of what it is they are learning (the learning objectives) while they are learning. Then at the end of the lesson, in the plenary, they see if they have learned what it was they were supposed to have learned.

This sort of teaching has previously been likened to the 'diagram' as opposed to the 'picture' and we should not forget that pictures, unlike diagrams, leave room for personal response (Pike, 2003b). If our Citizenship lessons become too diagrammatic we may leave insufficient space for genuinely personal moral development. The notion of explicitness is very much in vogue and while not advocating deliberate obfuscation, so that children are constantly kept in the dark and mystified by the ways of their teachers, the dangers associated with the pursuit of explicitness should be made quite clear. Increasingly, explicitness, or 'visibility' as Ofsted prefers (because they are concerned that Citizenship will become obscured from view by other subjects), is perceived as a panacea for all pedagogic ills. As we have seen this is simply not the case.

Teaching cultural interpretation in Citizenship and Moral Education

Having considered different ways in which Citizenship can be implemented, it is important to turn our attention towards teaching in the classroom, a subject taken up again in the following chapter. It was suggested in Chapter 4 that reading was especially important in Citizenship and Moral Education. In this section the use of three types of texts (non-fiction, media and ICT) within Citizenship and Moral Education will be evaluated. It was suggested in Chapter 5 and Chapter 6 that aspects of the Citizenship curriculum could be taught within the Humanities and Arts and one of the reasons for such a view is that these subjects are the specialist areas where students should learn to become discerning readers (see Chapter 4) and interpreters of a very broad range of 'texts' or cultural artefacts.

Non-fiction

When learning to read and interpret such non-fiction texts as newspaper articles, biographical accounts, speeches, advertising, propaganda, editorials, letters or political manifestos, students can become aware of differing beliefs and values to their own. They can also learn to discern the difference between fact and opinion and begin to understand how advertisers and politicians like to blur the distinction and present their own opinions as incontrovertible facts. Children can be encouraged to become discerning readers who seek to discover the motivation and value positions which inform and underpin the texts they read. When they 'read' media texts they must learn to perceive the bias of reporters, news channels and newspapers. Knowing about the ownership of newspapers and the political beliefs of newspaper proprietors as well as the importance of circulation figures is especially necessary if children are to recognize how the media influences public opinion which is a vital aspect of Citizenship.

When children construct their own non-fiction texts and write for a specific audience in order to achieve a specified purpose, they are developing many of the skills the Citizenship curriculum seeks to foster. When the emphasis is on transactional writing and students learn about the importance of tone and register when writing for a specific audience, they are learning how to communicate effectively within their society. Becoming aware of the common conventions of a 'text' that seeks to persuade is a necessary precondition for having a political voice and being heard in a democratic society. Learning how to explain or describe a situation with clarity is also essential if others are to be able to understand one's needs. The current national literacy initiative in the UK (DfEE/QCA, 2001) is highly relevant to Citizenship Education, and if teachers place emphasis upon critical literacy (see Chapter 4) a valuable contribution to children's Moral Education can also be made. Whether schools will perceive the connection between these two recent high-profile national initiatives remains to be seen.

Citizenship Education that privileges critical literacy can be a form of critical education. It has been suggested that this is emancipatory and can empower communities as well as individuals towards 'increasing humanisation, not merely of our minds, but of our social and political structures and systems' (Wright, 2000, p. 133). Those who are marginalized as a result of economic, ideological and political systems need to become aware of the belief systems which contribute to their social and economic plight.

Media texts and visual literacy in Citizenship and Moral Education

Some of the non-fiction texts used most frequently in Citizenship lessons are media texts. Learning how to read media and other visual texts is central to being an informed and critical citizen. For instance, if one watches a television news report of a civil disturbance where police with riot shields are on one side and angry protesters are on the other we might reasonably encourage students to ask where the reporter is standing and where the camera is when we see scenes of violence. When the police hold their shields with their batons ready and the rioters start to throw bricks or petrol bombs it is always important to consider the location of the camera. If it is behind the rioters we gain a rather different impression than if it is placed behind the police line. This is only a simple example but it illustrates one way in which the media can influence public opinion and generate hostility towards the protesters or sympathy for them. The ability to deconstruct images and to analyse how words and images work in conjunction should be fostered if our pupils are to be visually literate citizens. Texts on photojournalism such as *Get the Picture* (Morris, 1998) can usefully inform the teaching of Citizenship as can many of the superb textbooks produced within English or Media Studies which deal with advertising and other texts which seek to persuade.

One of the most important texts on the media for teachers of Citizenship is David Buckingham's excellent *The Making of Citizens – Young People, News and Politics* (2000). The research reported by Buckingham explores the relation between television and the citizenship of young people. The role the media should play in encouraging political participation is considered and, importantly, how young people's views about important political and social issues are represented by the media is also analysed. Buckingham's theory is that we need to redefine what passes as political understanding in our society and he advocates innovative forms of reporting designed to engage with young people's views of themselves as citizens.

The notion of reading the media as meaning-making and an essentially herme-neutical activity has been explored previously (Pike, 2004a), and Andrew Hart's research reminds us that it is all too easy to treat certain media texts, such as advertisements, with 'no reference to social context' (2001, p. 74), which it is especially necessary to interpret within Citizenship. Although the study of the media might appear to be difficult to separate from values and ideology and many teachers 'tended to talk of the media as manipulators whom children needed to be taught to read' what is surprising is that so many seemed uneasy about discussing values explicitly and 'seemed uncomfortable about discussing *who* was manipulating and for what purpose' (ibid., p. 74).

Hart's research is valuable to those concerned with Citizenship and Moral Education because it pays particular attention to values. For instance, it is suggested that it is 'by no means certain that exposing an advertiser's means of exploiting our fantasies in any way reduces our susceptibility' especially when 'teachers no longer feel that they have an alternative set of values to offer in their place' (ibid., p. 74). This research also suggests that when teachers were asked to 'indicate their own ideological position' they were, themselves, manipulated by the media; these teachers 'tended to refer to issues of gender, race and equal opportunities, the agenda set and sanctioned by the media' and made 'no reference to approaches to ideology in terms, for example, of manipulative, hegemonic or pluralist models' (ibid., p. 74). Further research is required into the influence of teachers' beliefs and values upon the children they teach as this is a complex but important area. Whether teachers' values should be communicated to children is discussed shortly with reference to research focusing on children's preferences.

ICT in Citizenship and Moral Education

It has been noted previously that ICT 'should be concerned with the *interpretation and analysis* of information, communication and technology as well as its use' and that we have the opportunity to help children engage in critical and creative rather than merely functional computer literacy and ICT (Pike, 2004a). As David Smith notes, new technology does not simply help us perform the same tasks, instead it 'makes complex alterations to human life' (2004, p. 511) for 'embedded in every tool is an ideological bias, a predisposition to construct the world as one thing rather than another, to value one thing over another, to amplify one sense or skill or attitude more loudly than another' (Postman, 1992, p. 13). New technology does not simply have the power to change *how* we do things but to change our beliefs about *what* we do. Topics such as inclusion and access can be explored in lessons in relation to the Internet and the impact of mobile technology. The uses to which new technology is put and what such use tells students about their own values and those of their society should be the basis of research investigations in Citizenship. New technology is relevant to Citizenship and Moral Education because its use can reveal the values and moral assumptions underpinning behaviour.

Regrettably, official documents such as *ICT across the curriculum – ICT in Citizenship* (DfES, 2004a) do not seem to recognize the potential to foster the sort of understanding suggested above. The focus is upon how ICT can support Citizenship but strategies are suggested which address questions such as 'How can the use of ICT raise standards in citizenship?' (ibid., p. 15). Four ICT key concepts judged to be 'particularly significant for citizenship' are: 'using data and information sources', 'searching and selecting', 'fitness for purpose' and 'communicating' (ibid., p. 15). Promoting a moral evaluation of the uses to which ICT is put or considering how ICT can make our society more equitable is not the focus of attention in this document. The missed opportunity this represents is analogous to the approach to literacy and citizenship discussed in Chapter 4 where the emphasis is upon functional rather than critical literacy and upon skills rather than meanings.

Teaching communication for Citizenship and Moral Education

Having looked at the sorts of texts that children can be encouraged to respond to in Citizenship lessons it is important to consider the nature of the communication that is engaged in. Firstly, the importance of speaking and listening in the cultivation of moral reasoning is considered. Secondly, the ways in which teachers of Citizenship can attempt to ensure that all children have a voice are discussed. Thirdly, the communication of teachers' views is evaluated.

Speaking and listening to cultivate moral reasoning

As Citizenship may be timetabled for only one lesson per week there is often no time for lengthy pieces of writing to be drafted or extensive reading to be engaged in. Consequently, much of a child's learning in Citizenship will take place through speaking and listening, via oral rather than written communication. Paired, small group and whole class discussion are the ways that many moral and political issues are approached. Just how important discourse is to learning in Citizenship Education is apparent when one considers the Vygotskyan perspective that all learning is social and that learners modify their meanings as they collaborate with others. Essentially the development of reasoning is often considered to occur through talk. Children move from 'intermental' to 'intramental' functioning (Vygotsky, 1986). In other words, the reasoning they can engage in with others to begin with eventually becomes the reasoning they can achieve on their own. The importance of discussion and interaction between peers has a special place in Citizenship lessons, for when learners argue, persuade and negotiate, important developmental changes and moral reasoning can occur (Dunn, 1988).

It is important to note that children's abilities to engage in such sophisticated speaking and listening activities will need to be taught. If one is going to spend the majority of a lesson having children discuss sensitive and often emotive issues that are the subject of controversy and disagreement in wider society, it is advisable to give some thought to teaching talk. Certain ground rules need to be established and patterns of interaction need to be modelled and exemplified. A range of strategies have been developed for helping children to discuss challenging issues in groups (Edwards and Mercer, 1987; Pike, 2004a) and Citizenship teachers should be aware of the techniques at their disposal. Citizenship is often taught in mixed ability groups and this is a significant opportunity as well as a challenge for the teacher will need to differentiate and teach inexperienced learners how to interact sensitively and tolerate views they feel antipathy towards. Collaborative problem-solving about a political policy, law or action to be taken is the sort of moral reasoning children should engage in and it can also model the working of society.

Including all: honest voices

It is especially important in Citizenship and Moral Education that teachers do not fall into 'ritual' rather than 'principled' discourse (Edwards and Mercer, 1987). Teachers should ask genuine questions to elicit students' views and this is not always easy because classrooms are places where ritualistic discourse is rife. To illustrate the peculiar nature of discourse in classrooms an example may help. If I dash up to a man waiting on the platform at Leeds railway station and ask what time it is, my fellow commuter will probably assume I have left my watch at home. He will not think I have my watch hidden up my sleeve and that I am merely testing him to check if he knows what I know. If he knew that this was the case he might think I was, at the very least, eccentric. This is the sort of discourse we, as teachers, frequently engage in; we ask questions to which we know the answers. The result is that children often play guessing games. They try to guess what the teacher wants to hear and teachers of Citizenship should be on their guard against such rituals, as they should help students to form their own personal opinions. Only if teachers engage honestly and openly with the child's perspective are they likely to challenge, provoke, guide and augment the child's experience appropriately.

Teaching in Citizenship that seeks to be honest and to engage with the child's experience recognizes that 'children cannot learn things simply by being told; they need to be able to relate such principles to their own actions, experience and conceptions' (Edwards and Mercer, 1987, p. 95). If Citizenship is taught in a way that does not allow children to perceive its relevance to their concerns, an education in Citizenship could turn out to be counterproductive and might even be an inoculation against interest in the public square. While we know that laws influence our lives, children can be quite oblivious to how certain laws impinge on them personally and the challenge for Citizenship teachers is to make public issues and concerns, enacted on a large scale, relevant to individual children's lives. While not suggesting that Citizenship should be reduced to a consideration of the individual's concerns, we are suggesting that the attempt should be made, wherever possible, to set up a 'live-connection' between the world of the child and the topic being studied because this is likely to sustain the child over some difficult conceptual hurdles and boost motivation. Topics like economics can seem rather distant to the concerns of most children until they start to consider who made the branded merchandise they wear and thus consider the ethics of third world production. We have an obligation as teachers of Citizenship to relate complex public issues to pupils' concerns.

Citizenship teaching must ensure that everyone has a voice. Including children with EAL is especially important and the Citizenship classroom should demonstrate inclusion. Documents such as *Aiming High: Understanding the Educational Needs of Minority Ethnic Pupils in Mainly White Schools* (DfES, 2004a) or *Access and Engagement in English: Teaching pupils for whom English is an additional language* (DfES, 2002a) are especially useful and should be familiar to Citizenship teachers who should be aware of linguistic barriers to inclusion. If teachers employ a few basic techniques their classrooms can become more democratic places where no one is denied a voice. Giving children appropriate language to use, such as sentence starters, can help to ensure that more than one-word answers are given. Children can be provided with phrases such as 'I disagree because . . .' or 'Rich countries should help because . . .' or 'We should respect . . .', and if staff and other pupils provide good models of language use, children who are developing fluency have a good example to follow. Group work has to be taught rather than simply assuming everyone knows how to engage in discussion, and the explanation of roles in group talk can prepare the way for successful discussion.

Teaching vocabulary in advance and providing visual material for key words is another way to promote inclusion. Sometimes teachers have a tendency to be too impatient or so concerned with the pace of the lesson that they allow insufficient 'thinking time' to give children with EAL or special needs the opportunity to consider an answer before expressing it. Allied to this is the need to pre-read texts and to allow children to re-read them. Giving copies of texts to pupils in advance and also to the supporting adult (with key aspects of the text highlighted, perhaps) is another strategy for inclusion. How we value someone is related to how we value their language and the Refugee Council has key words available for school life in languages such as Albanian, Kurdish Turkish, Kurdish Sorani, Persian, Somali, Arabic and Bosnian. Valuing a child's mother tongue and awarding it space in a public context is another way of ensuring that his or her voice is heard.

Teachers' views and voices

We should not forget that the teacher's voice is the one that is most often heard in the classroom. When a controversial ethical, social, political or religious issue is being discussed and an animated discussion is in progress within the classroom, pupils often want to know their teacher's opinion. Whether teachers should reveal what they think about contentious issues and tell their pupils what they believe is worth considering. A value-neutral position for teachers is impossible to achieve and the teacher's beliefs will inevitably influence teaching, but whether the teacher should deliberately and consciously articulate his or her views is quite a different matter. Teachers of Citizenship are likely to have strong views about contemporary issues and whether 'air-time' should be devoted to these given the teacher's position of authority is a matter of some debate. A teacher's worldview can be inadvertently revealed for beliefs (about children, the subject, what is important in life) cannot remain hidden for very long when being observed by curious and perceptive children for extended periods of time. The question is, perhaps, how explicitly the teacher's perspective on a given issue should be incorporated into lessons.

Recent research in the Netherlands provides some helpful guidance for teachers. Veugelers suggests that 'teachers will always express values in their teaching' (2000, p. 39) and, with regard to a specific value-loaded topic, that they have the following options:

A   The teacher tries not to express his/her values
B   The teacher makes explicit which values he/she finds important
C   The teacher stresses differences in values without expressing the values he/she finds important
D   The teacher indicates differences in values, but also expresses the values he/she finds important.

(ibid., p. 42)

According to students in this study, approach D is the most common one teachers take and they prefer their teachers to do this (ibid., p. 44). In our view, this is intellectually honest as pupils can filter what teachers say and do if they are aware of the teacher's perspective. In all schools, teachers should be careful to ensure they stay within the law, and due sensitivity is needed if the view expressed by the teacher conflicts with that of the home of a child. A model of teachers as participants rather than impartial and objective umpires may be both realistic and sustainable.

Teaching controversial issues

Andrew Wright has argued that currently there is 'no sustained tradition of using the tensions inherent within any given controversial situation as the starting point for a critical pedagogy' (2000, pp. 131–2). Evidently, critical reflection upon one's own views within the context of a plural society can be brought about by exploring controversial issues and although respect for others and tolerance should be expressed by students, it is important to note that tolerance is not the same as agreement and that a wide range of views are tolerated in plural democracies. If children from various backgrounds are to be educated in common schools it is important that 'mainstream' values or those of the majority are not the only ones that are expressed. It has been argued that it is 'important for schools not to side with one particular world view but rather to adopt a neutral stance towards controversial issues' (Halstead, 1999b, p. 131).

Indeed, 'two of the main tenets of liberal education' are considered to be 'its refusal to side with any contestable conception of the good and its emphasis on equality of respect' (Halstead, 1999b, p. 132). Such a position is congruent with the need in a pluralist society to recognize that there will be issues upon which people will disagree. In our society very different views are heard on such issues as abortion, euthanasia, the death penalty, fox-hunting, drug taking, gay marriage, contraception, corporal punishment, the EU and so on. It has been argued that common schools must take as neutral a stand as possible on controversial issues, but teachers of Citizenship need to recognize that this approach is in itself a particular ideological position and that 'the claim to be culturally neutral or to be a meeting ground for all cultures, is itself a cultural stance' (Halstead, 1995a, p. 268). It is important that children in Citizenship lessons come to understand that where controversial issues are discussed, the needs of all citizens should be attended to. Learning that the beliefs and values of the majority are not to be imposed upon minorities should be a central feature of Citizenship Education in our democracy if the rights of all citizens are to be protected and promoted through the study of Citizenship in schools.

Chapter 9

How children learn values

In the previous chapter we noted Ofsted's apparent preference for dedicated Citizenship lessons and the Chief Inspector's view that Citizenship in the National Curriculum is neither about 'the way a school goes about its business, or its ethos', nor about 'participation by some pupils in extra-curricular or community activities' (Bell, 2005). Of course this makes sense in the context of the first aim of Citizenship Education that we set out in Chapter 3 – 'to produce informed citizens'. Students will learn little in a systematic way about the workings of the criminal justice system or the complexities of local government through school councils, charity events or sporting activities. In so far as Citizenship is defined as a subject with a specific body of knowledge and set of skills to be acquired, and the teacher has expert knowledge of the subject matter, then there is much to be said for an approach which allows for the most effective and efficient transmission of that knowledge and expertise. This does not imply a narrow pedagogical approach where the students remain generally passive. On the contrary, teachers will adopt a diversity of teaching styles, especially active learning and collaborative learning, and a wide range of strategies, which may include the use of guest speakers, computer software, group discussions, guided role-play, simulations, analysis of statistics, lectures, debates, problem-solving, writing reports, brainstorming, teamwork, information searches, reading, critical analysis and research. Citizenship does not presuppose a certain style of teaching, but the teaching must be appropriate to the topic and sufficiently interesting and stimulating to the students. The recent EPPI *Review of the Impact of Citizenship Education on the Provision of Schooling* recommends, for example, that teachers should experiment with teaching approaches, make their intended learning outcomes explicit at the start of each lesson, encourage students to pose questions of their own rather than simply answer those posed for them, and involve learners in structured self-evaluation (Small, 2004, p. 8). None of this is significantly problematic or controversial.

But the second and third aims of Citizenship Education – 'to produce active, committed citizens' and 'to produce autonomous, critically reflective citizens' – present much greater problems. As we have seen in Chapter 2, these aims are grounded in values and attitudes. But comparatively little is known of the processes through which children acquire values. In spite of a number of major research programmes exploring the processes of teaching and learning in recent years, including those sponsored by the Economic and Social Research Council (ESRC), there is little research evidence about how children learn values, whether the public values associated with Citizenship or the private values associated with Moral Education. A small-scale research project into the developing sexual values of children aged nine to ten suggests that 'the main sources of children's sexual learning are the family, the media, the hidden curriculum and peers' (and possibly 'the religious community') (Halstead and Reiss, 2003, pp. 41–8), and that the main role of the school is threefold. The first is to uphold the shared values of the broader society, thus helping to counterbalance any extreme opinions and values children have picked up elsewhere. The second is to fill in gaps in children's knowledge and understanding, including their understanding of core values. The third is to help children to choose a rational pathway as they try to make sense of the variety of influences that impinge on their experience, and gradually, through a process of critical reflection, to begin to shape, construct and develop their own framework of values (ibid., pp. 9–10).

The Moral Life of Schools Project carried out in Chicago from 1988 to 1990 focused on the direct and indirect influence that teachers and schools have on the developing moral values of children and young people (Jackson et al., 1993). This ethnographic research highlights the ways in which moral considerations permeate all aspects of school life and are part of the professional ethos of the school. Every speech, action, response, decision and gesture made by a teacher may convey a moral message, and the research provides detailed yet highly sensitive analyses and interpretations of typical classroom scenarios that highlight the complex processes through which moral learning takes place. Yet this research raises as many questions as it resolves, for if the moral influence of teachers is as wide-ranging and pervasive as it suggests, surely they have a responsibility to raise that moral influence to consciousness (for Jackson et al. imply that it is often buried within the hidden curriculum) and explore in more detail how children learn virtues and values.

The question whether moral and civic values can ever be learned through direct teaching or instruction has vexed philosophers since the days of Plato. The present chapter continues with a brief consideration of this issue, and then examines in turn three other ways in which children may learn values – through observation, through participation and guided action, and through critical reflection.

Learning through direct instruction

'Character Education', which was discussed briefly in Chapter 3, is currently one of the most popular approaches to moral education in the United States (Lickona, 1991; Kilpatrick, 1992; Wynn and Ryan, 1992; Molnar, 1997), and it is slowly gaining ground in the UK (Farrer, 2000; Hawkes, 2001). Its aims are to teach virtue (not just *about* virtue), to shape children's characters, and to produce active, committed citizens and moral agents, and it seeks to do this through direct instruction.

It is based on two core beliefs. The first is that there are 'widely shared, objectively important core ethical values . . . that form the basis of good character' (Lickona, 1996, p. 95; cf. Bennett, 1993); these may include self-discipline, honesty, responsibility, courage, loyalty, tolerance, law-abidingness, patriotism and other qualities. The second is that teachers would be neglecting their duty in the current climate of moral decline and antisocial behaviour if they did not present these core ethical values to children in a direct and unambiguous way. This direct instruction of standards of right and wrong (it is said) enjoys much more widespread support among parents and politicians than other approaches (such as moral reasoning) that fail to 'give unqualified support to the content of any particular set of moral standards' (Pritchard, 1988, p. 470) – though it is open to a number of criticisms including that it emphasizes compliance at the expense of critical reflection (Nash, 1997, p. 31) and that it engages in the illicit and undemocratic shaping of individuals (Gutmann, 1987, p. 36; cf. Purpel, 1997). Direct instruction in civic and moral virtues is most effective when it is systematic and explicit. Such instruction need not involve separate courses, but can be integrated into the existing curriculum. In particular, stories drawn from history and literature are seen to be an effective way of teaching the virtues; Kilpatrick offers a guide to 120 books that may contribute to children's character development (1992, ch. 15). The instructional process may also include 'visual displays with moral content' (Jackson *et al.*, 1993, pp. 8–9) and the study of national heroes and others who have demonstrated a particular virtue, as well as formal teaching, discussion, problem solving, co-operative learning, integrated thematic learning, and so on. Finally, there is what Jackson *et al.* call the 'spontaneous interjection of moral commentary into ongoing activity' (ibid., pp. 9–11), in other words, temporarily suspending a planned lesson in order to talk about a moral issue that has unexpectedly arisen, usually involving praise or blame of a student's behaviour.

But is it really possible to develop commitment to moral or civic values through direct instruction in this way? It is not at all a matter simply of finding an appropriately 'engaging and imaginative manner' of teaching abstract principles like rights, entitlements and obligations, as Arthur and Wright (2001, p. 73) seem to imply. The issues are much more fundamental. Can one instruct children in goodness in the way one can instruct them in physics, or swimming, or driving a car? In an important article entitled 'Can Virtue Be Taught?' (the title, incidentally, is drawn from Plato), Ryle (1972) argues that virtue is neither a matter of knowledge and information nor of skill and proficiency, and that the use of the word 'instruct' is inappropriate. In any case, there are no expert coaches, instructors, demonstrators, lecturers or other professionals in goodness to carry out the instruction. Virtue, if it is to be learned at all, has to be learned a different way. In his book *Can We Teach Children to Be Good?* Straughan distinguishes between 'teaching that', 'teaching how' and 'teaching to' (1988, pp. 105–12). It's 'teaching to' that is central to both Citizenship and Moral Education, because the intention is for children to learn to act as good citizens and moral agents. But, as Straughan points out, no teaching method 'can guarantee to produce the appropriate motivation and subsequent behaviour', for, among other things, children are free agents, 'capable of accepting or rejecting what is taught' (1988, p. 112). Ryle concludes that in asking whether virtue can be taught, we are asking the wrong question. We should be asking 'Can virtue be learned?' for it is less a matter of instruction and more 'about the tasks and puzzlements of growing up' (1972, p. 446). He suggests that in matters of morals we learn 'first by being shown by others, then by being trained by others . . . and lastly by being trained by ourselves' (ibid., p. 437). In more contemporary jargon, we learn through observation, through participation and guided action, and through critical reflection.

Learning through observation

Children observe many things in schools, some of which they are intended to learn from and some not. But all of them may contribute to their developing under-standing of the world, of what it is to be human, and of the nature of good and bad, right and wrong. In this section, we shall look particularly at the ways children can learn values through observing teachers, observing school rituals, observing the school environment, observing the ethos of the school, and observing democracy in action in the school.

Children learn many things by imitating the example of others, and may in this way develop dispositions such as trust (Applebaum, 1995) and respect (Tierno, 1996). Patterns of imitating the behaviour of parents and siblings are established very early (Poulson and Kymissis, 1988), and as they grow older children may also take peers or media personalities as their role models. They also pay close atten-tion to the example set by their teachers. Jackson, after many years of research in classrooms, concludes, 'I can think of no other social arrangement, save parenting of course, in which the modelling component plays as large and pervasive a role as it does in teaching' (1992, p. 404). Certainly, the role of the teacher implies the power to influence students (Hansen, 1993a, p. 668), and since values are inherent in teaching, it seems unlikely that students will be able to avoid the influence of teachers' values completely, even if teachers do not see it as part of their role to set a moral example (Carr, 1993). In fact, research suggests that much of the moral influence teachers have on their students occurs without the students being aware of it, perhaps even without the teachers being aware of the moral consequences of what they are doing (Jackson et al., 1993, p. 2). The indirect moral influence on children is deeply embedded in the daily life of the school, either within normal teaching activities or within the contingent interactions at classroom level (Hansen, 1993b, pp. 397ff). Such moral 'lessons' can be understood only by care-fully observing the day-to-day life of the school and the gradual emergence of shared understandings and values (Hansen, 1992). The process is further complicated by the fact that the same incident may have moral meaning to one observer and not to another (Hansen, 1993a, p. 669). This is particularly the case with what Jackson et al. call 'expressive morality' (1993, pp. 29–42), by which they mean not only teachers' facial expressions and gestures but also the confidence and trust they may inspire, the aura of friendliness and personal integrity which may surround them and the way they convey messages through personal routines and other aspects of teaching style (including prompt arrival, thorough preparation and careful marking of students' work). It is clear that the moral meaning evident in classroom teaching is often 'the expression or enactment of the person the teacher is, which can encompass far more than self-conscious intent' (Hansen, 1993a, p. 671).

Teachers of Citizenship will set an example to their students in a number of different ways. They can reasonably be expected to model enthusiasm and commitment towards their subject. But they should also demonstrate behaviour consistent with the values of the subject, both in and out of school. This may include setting an example of good sense, balanced judgement, wisdom and maturity, as well as exemplifying fairness, justice and impartiality in discipline and the application of school rules, and other civic virtues such as tolerance, respect for the law and acceptance of diversity. Teachers' personal behaviour should reflect the values which underpin school policy statements supporting equal opportunities and inclusion and rejecting racism, sexism and discrimination against minorities, so that students do not perceive an implementation gap between the rhetoric of school policy and the reality of life in the school. In a sense, teachers are passing on an 'inheritance' to their students, an inheritance of 'feelings, emotions, images, visions, thoughts, beliefs, ideas, understandings, intellectual and practical enterprises, languages, relationships, organisations, canons and maxims of conduct, procedures, rituals, skills, works of art, books, musical compositions, tools, artefacts and utensils' (Oakeshott, 1989, p. 45). It is teacher example that helps students to enter this inheritance, and thus become fully and distinctively human.

There is also the expectation that teachers should not just be 'on their good behaviour' in class (Jackson, 1992, pp. 403–4), but should also be a certain sort of person, perhaps better than average, if they are to set a moral example (Carr, 1993, p. 206). This is perhaps an unrealistic expectation, but at least teachers should reflect on the influence they have. This may involve, among other things, reflection on their relationship with their students and reflection on student expectations and the qualities valued by students. There is research evidence to suggest that a secure, supportive relationship with a teacher in early or middle childhood can at least partly compensate for an insecure attachment to a parent (Elicker and Fortner-Wood, 1995; Werner and Smith, 1992). A Mori poll in the UK found that seventy-eight per cent of adult respondents considered that teachers set a good example for young people (SCAA, 1996a). However, a study based on interviews with American teenagers found that only nine per cent of students consider their teachers to have made a difference in their lives (Csikszentmihalyi and McCormack, 1986). Evidence suggests that children are most likely to be influenced by teachers whose qualities they admire. Such qualities include tolerance, firmness but fairness, acting in a reasonable manner and a willingness to explain things (Hayes, 1993) and, for older students, respect and freedom from prejudice (Rhodes, 1990), gentleness and courtesy (Haberman, 1994), and sensitivity and responsiveness to the needs of students (Kutnick and Jules, 1993).

Another area of school life where children learn through observation is school rituals and ceremonies. The most common of these in the UK is the daily assembly (or 'collective worship'), where children may learn about local community activities, moral issues like drug abuse, current events, the lives of famous people, or religious beliefs and practices. Assemblies may be led by staff or students, often celebrate student achievement, and typically seek to strengthen the sense of the school as a community. Other common rituals include special days, prize-givings, sports days, nativity plays, concerts, circle time, outside speakers, school plays and even standing when a teacher enters the room. What makes such activities essentially moral, in the opinion of Jackson *et al.*, are the feelings they seek to engender, including 'pride, loyalty, inspiration, reverence, piety, sorrow, prudence, thankfulness, and dedication', and the fact that they call on students 'to identify with causes, social missions, and social and political entities whose goals and purposes lay (*sic*) outside the framework of the students' individual interests and daily concerns' (1993, pp. 6–8).

The physical environment of the school is something that students observe every day of their school lives, but the moral messages the environment sends may be subtle and covert. Are the classrooms barren, gloomy and off-putting, or are they bright and cheerful, exuding a welcoming warmth? Are they tidy and well cared for, or cluttered and neglected? Do the posters and objects in the classroom celebrate students' achievements, or stimulate their interest, or oppress them with dry information about school rules and regulations? The visual culture (Prosser, 1998) of the classroom and the school in general may present important underlying beliefs and values, and may symbolize the attitude the school has towards its students. Does the layout of desks and tables reinforce hierarchical structures, with the teacher's desk in a position of dominance and control, or are students encouraged to move their chairs into a circle when appropriate, to facilitate democratic participation in discussion (cf. Cunningham, 2000, p. 135)? The broader environment of the school can convey similar messages. One writer describes how children who felt oppressed by the 'pokey playground' of their school succeeded in persuading 'a leading councillor to take up their cause' (Claire, 2001, pp. 109–10).

The physical environment of the school is just one element of its overall ethos. School ethos has been described as 'an imprecise term referring to the pervasive atmosphere, ambience or climate within a school' (Halstead and Taylor, 2000a, p. 17). In its broadest sense, the term also encompasses leadership style, sense of community, the nature of relationships within the school, dominant forms of social interaction, attitudes and expectations of teachers, teacher morale, student morale, ways of conflict resolution, partnership with parents and local communities, patterns of communication, degree of student involvement in the school, discipline policies and procedures, anti-bullying and anti-racist policies, management styles, the extent to which students are listened to and respected, behaviour in the playground and on the way to and from school, power structures, decision-making processes and the school's underlying philosophy and aims. The development of virtues and civic commitments requires a practical human context if it is to flourish, and the school ethos in all its diverse manifestations is rich in its potential to influence this development (John and Osborne, 1992; Mellor and Elliott, 1996). In a sense, the school may be perceived by students as a microcosm of the nation, with the staff representing the government, the students representing citizens and school rules representing the law. When students observe (and participate in) the school's culture, environment and ethos, they are learning more than simply how to live as members of the school community; they are actually learning how to live as citizens.

Closely related to the concept of the ethos of the school is the hidden curriculum. It has long been acknowledged that children learn things at school which are not planned by teachers as part of the overt curriculum, and values and attitudes are perhaps particularly susceptible to being picked up this way ('caught rather than taught'). In the past it has been possible to leave this indirect transmission of values at an implicit level, on the assumption that the values concerned would be broadly shared by parents anyway. However, the growing diversity of values in society at large has forced schools to reflect much more carefully on their underlying values, to articulate them more explicitly, and to bring to consciousness the indirect influences they may be having on children. This process of reflection may bring to light existing power structures within the school, for example, which teachers may wish to challenge. Such reflection may also encourage the school to become more caring (Best and Curran, 1995) and to put more emphasis on developing confident, responsible, active citizens in the future.

One final area where schools have become much more sensitive to their influence on children's development in recent years is the provision of opportunities for them to observe democracy in action in the school. If schools are to contribute to a healthy and just democracy in society at large, children need to learn the value of democracy not just in their head, but in their heart. This probably means that schools need to be run more like democracies. This does not mean that the children need to be involved directly in every decision made in the school. But it does mean that they need opportunities to observe democracy in action (for example, seeing parents and other interested parties participating in debates about school policies, and key decisions being made by the whole staff rather than just the headteacher), and this 'implies a review of power relationships within schools' (Osler and Starkey, 2004, p. 153). The actions of an autocratic headteacher can easily undermine anything students are taught about the value of participatory democracy in Citizenship lessons. As Claire points out, 'Schools in which children are bullied by autocratic adults, herded, ordered about, shouted at and shown no respect are unlikely to achieve their goals of instilling democratic ideas, and cannot claim to be providing opportunities for experiencing citizenship' (2001, p. 107). A genuinely democratic ethos in schools probably means that students will have 'some say in the organisation and running of their schools' (Kerr et al., 2004, p. 3), and this may include involvement in decisions about school rules, perhaps even in interview panels for new staff. But it would be a mistake to assume that schools can ever be full democracies 'where everyone has an equal say and an equal vote'

(Claire, 2004, p. 93): schools are subject to tight central control, managers are accountable for decisions that are made, and students sometimes lack the under-standing and experience needed for wise decision-making. Nevertheless, if Dewey is right that 'democracy is more than a form of government; it is primarily a mode of associated living' (1916/2002, p. 101), observing democracy in action may not be enough; engaging in some forms of democratic action may be needed to help children to understand the privileges and responsibilities of citizenship.

Learning through participation and guided action

If people learn to swim by swimming and to ride a bike by riding a bike (in each case under the critical supervision of someone who can already do it), then there are good grounds for believing that they will learn active citizenship in a similar way, i.e. by being given opportunities to act like citizens and being guided as they do so. Similarly, perhaps the best way to learn to behave morally is to be given opportunities to behave morally. Arthur and Wright call this 'experiential learning', and argue that if students are to develop the dispositions and skills required by citizens in a democratic society, they need 'to develop active, collaborative and cooperative working patterns in their lives focused on real problems in a real community' (2001, p. 85). Such activities benefit students in many ways, develop-ing their confidence and initiative, giving them a sense of being part of a community, and contributing to the development of positive values like independence and a sense of purpose. Experiential learning falls into three main categories: simulations; involvement in school activities; and extra-curricular involvement in activities outside the school.

Since they are not allowed to stand for election or vote in local or national elections before the age of eighteen, students have to engage in simulations if they are to gain practical experience of these procedures. Mock elections (and indeed other forms of simulation such as mock trials) are becoming increasingly common in schools (Davies *et al.*, 1999, pp. 98–9), and may be an effective way of increas-ing both students' understanding of political campaigns, debates, manifestos and elections, and their commitment to democratic procedures. In any case, simulations are a well-established way of increasing students' understanding in many areas of life (think of the contribution that playing Monopoly can make to children's economic understanding), and Halstead (2001) argues that collective worship in many state schools may best be viewed as 'simulated worship' since it lacks several of the conditions (such as voluntariness and shared belief) that are necessary for 'real worship'.

However, students also have increasing opportunities to participate at different levels in the life of the school. The involvement of students, including disruptive students, in the development of school and classroom rules (Lickona, 1991, ch. 7; Garner, 1992) or playground rules (Evans, 1990) may help to develop their under-standing of the rights and responsibilities of citizenship in several ways. It may help them to understand the nature of rules, the role of law in society and the broad moral principles and shared values that are part of life in society. It may also empower students to make informed, rational decisions regarding their rights and duties, to be proactive in the face of injustice or wrongdoing, to understand the need for collective responsibility and self-discipline, and to be more motivated to obey rules when these have been negotiated with them. The forum for discussing rules is likely to be the School Council, where elected representatives have opportunities to engage more directly with democratic procedures through debating (and influencing) many areas of school policy (Taylor and Johnson, 2002). Through School Councils, students not only develop communication and other skills like how to conduct meetings, but also learn to take the views of others into account, and they may learn that their actions can make a difference. However, some students become disillusioned with the elitism of their representatives, the poor levels of consultation, and the feeling that the school management expects the council to be more concerned with service than empowerment (Rowe, 1996; Cunningham, 2000, pp. 136–8). Peer mediation is another way of actively involving students in the life of the school community: they are trained to address student conflict situations such as bullying, indiscipline and communication problems within schools. It is claimed that peer mediation can defuse tension, hostility and violence, and transform schools into more co-operative environments, with the students involved learning a wide range of skills (Trevaskis, 1994). This is just one of a number of initiatives that give children the opportunity to develop more caring attitudes (Lickona, 1991, ch. 16; Noddings, 1992, 1995), which can have longterm effects (Chaskin and Rauner, 1995, p. 671). Evidence suggests that children are less likely to develop a genuine concern for others as a result of exhortation, instruction or concrete rewards and praise, and more likely when they are encouraged as a result of their own behaviour to think of themselves as caring and helpful individuals (Grusec and Dix, 1986, p. 220).

Community service projects outside the school are equally likely to help children to become more caring and responsible by encouraging the internalization of pro-social norms and values (Battistich *et al.*, 1989). The National Curriculum for Citizenship expects students at Key Stages 3 and 4 to 'continue to be actively involved in the life of their school, neighbourhood and wider communities' and to 'take part responsibly in community activities' (QCA/DfEE, 1999a, pp. 14–15). For some students, the actual experience of confronting moral issues in a real-life structured setting (as in community service), or of resolving conflicting values and priorities in an intensive residential experience, may be significant for their development as citizens. Extra-curricular activities, including sport, can provide opportunities to explore new roles, work in a team, and develop leadership, interpersonal skills and skills of conflict resolution. Community service projects not only provide students with 'concrete opportunities to participate with others in serving the public' (Arthur and Wright, 2001, p. 96), but also contribute to community cohesion by helping them to learn networking skills, civic virtues, and the norms of reciprocity, co-operation and trust (Print and Coleman, 2003, pp. 134–6). However, as Claire (2001, pp. 137–52) points out, community awareness

the level of visiting old people's homes, donating pocket money
'ablishing e-mail links with a school in India. Projects involving
_ ike Oxfam and Save the Children can also raise awareness of
_anty, poverty and discrimination on a global scale, as well as the need for
grassroots participation, individual empowerment and sustainable development.

Learning through reflection

There is widespread agreement that learning through participation and action
is most effective when it is combined with critical reflection and discussion. One
reason may be that purely experiential activity may be associated in students' eyes
with low-status learning (Taylor, 1994, p. 52). Indeed, the National Curriculum
for Citizenship stresses the importance of developing skills of enquiry and communication and of 'reflecting on the process of participating' (QCA/DfEE, 1999a,
pp. 14–15). The affective experience of extra-curricular activities and community
service work may in itself contribute to the development of moral and civic values
among students, but lasting effects are most likely when accompanied by cognitive
strategies such as reflective journals, the discussion of moral dilemmas arising
within the activities, and opportunities to reflect on the personal meaning and
relevance of the experiences and activities (Boss, 1994; Rest, 1988; Walker, 1986).
Schools are ideally placed to provide such opportunities. At primary level, Circle
Time and Philosophy for Children can develop children's critical reasoning skills,
while less formal questions, conversations and discussions may also be part
of children's everyday experience. At secondary level, students learn to detect bias,
to engage in rational decision-making and to use a wide range of strategies to
analyse and reflect on their own experiences.

Circle Time is an increasingly popular method, particularly in primary schools,
for giving children a chance to reflect on their experiences and feelings, to clarify
their own values, to develop skills of speaking and listening, questioning and
hypothesizing, and to develop self-knowledge (Mosley, 1993; Taylor, 2003). It is
a carefully structured activity with clear ground rules, preferably negotiated directly
with the children, like not interrupting and not making fun of others. The children
sit in a circle with the teacher and share ideas, experiences and feelings from
a position of equality. Typically, an object is passed around the circle, and only
the person holding the object can speak. The teacher may offer a starter phrase
such as 'I felt very proud of myself when . . .' or may invite the children to suggest
ways of resolving specific problems which have arisen in the class. Each speaker
has the right to express personal views and opinions, and to be listened to with
interest and respect. Circle Time may help to create shared rules and encourage
acceptance of these, and may also help children to develop empathy, co-operation,
caring behaviour, respect for the feelings of others, and a strong sense of belonging
to a group or community. It may also help children's developing emotional
literacy. Housego and Burns (1994) advise that Circle Time is most effective if its
underlying values are in harmony with the general ethos of the classroom. They

also point out that if the quality of Circle Time is to be maintained, children must be discouraged from offering superficial contributions and must be encouraged to think carefully and build on what has been said before.

Philosophy for Children is an aid to critical reflection that aims to strengthen children's powers of reasoning and moral judgement through Socratic dialogue (Ross, 1996). It is a child-friendly way to help children understand discussion techniques, deductive reasoning, conceptual analysis, formulation of definitions, the use of examples and so on (Lipman, 1984, 1987). Pupils identify the issues they want to discuss from novels, picture books, poems or their own experience – in effect creating their own lesson plan – and then analyse, synthesize and evaluate, thereby engaging in higher order critical thinking. There is some debate about the transferability of such skills, but supporters of the approach claim that thinking and reasoning skills are improved across a wide range of subjects. The approach was boosted by the popular success of Jostein Gaarder's *Sophie's World* (1994).

Another approach which encourages reflection on the meaning of personal experiences and activities is the use of personal narratives (Vitz, 1990). Tappan and Brown (1989) argue that (1) individuals give meaning to their life experiences by representing them in narrative form; (2) individuals represent their lived experience of moral decision-making and moral action primarily through narrative; (3) individuals develop morally by 'authoring' their moral stories and by learning the moral lessons in the stories they tell about their own experiences. In contrast to a Kohlbergian approach to moral education (see Chapter 1), personal narratives imply that cognition, emotion and action are 'three interrelated and fundamentally indissociable dimensions of moral experience' (Tappan and Brown, 1989, p. 187). Papers in a Special Issue of the *Journal of Moral Education* (20, 3) explore narrative in relation to: autobiography and relationships (Pagano, 1991); racial conflict (Ward, 1991); cheating (Johnston, 1991); moral conflict and change (Day, 1991); and trust (Attanucci, 1991). A narrative approach depends on the relationship between the author and the audience (i.e. the student and the teacher) and the co-construction of meaning from the stories. The approach has some similarities with Values Clarification (see Chapter 1), but although questions of privacy may arise it can fire the moral imagination (Coles, 1989). It is particularly influenced by Vygotsky's view that children use inner speech to formulate their own problem-solving and to move from regulation by others to self-constructed rules, and by Bakhtin's (1981) description of the dialogic nature of speech, which explains how children construct a shared understanding of words, activities and moral principles through dialogue with adults.

Many other kinds of conversation and discussion, debating and arguing can contribute to the sharpening of students' critical thinking. Controversial issues in particular, which are discussed in some detail in the Final Report of the Advisory Group on Citizenship (1998, pp. 8–9, 27, 56–61), provide students with opportunities to wrestle with alternative viewpoints, to understand the difference between fact and opinion, to apply principles, to develop reasoning skills, to detect bias and loaded or emotive vocabulary, to evaluate evidence and to provide rational justifications for their own opinions and decisions (cf. Arthur and Wright, 2001, pp. 73–80). Discussion has been described as the best way of handling controversial issues, since it encourages active participation, helps students to appreciate both sides of an argument, and, with careful planning by the teacher, can challenge students to aim for greater clarity of thought and expression (ibid., p. 75). Discussion of dilemmas was used by Kohlberg and his colleagues to promote moral reasoning (Blatt and Kohlberg, 1975); discussion was particularly directed at modelling and eliciting reasoning at the next stage of moral development so that, by exposure to different moral points of view, cognitive conflict would be stimulated in the individual pupil's awareness of problematic situations, and their movement to a higher stage would be facilitated.

Finally, critical thinking skills are essential if students are to reflect effectively on the lessons learned through participation in community service and other action-based approaches to citizenship. Critical thinking has been defined as 'reasonable, reflective thinking that is focused on deciding what to believe or do' (Ennis, 1995, p. xvii). It includes the ability to interpret, analyse and evaluate ideas and arguments, to recognize false assumptions and conclusions, to assess the validity of generalizations, to distinguish between relevant and irrelevant information, to see through bias and propaganda, to use evidence impartially, to assess the strengths and weaknesses of an argument, and to draw justifiable conclusions. Such skills can be developed throughout a child's schooling through a range of teaching methods, but they can also be formally assessed in examinations like the OCR Board's AS-Level examination in Critical Thinking. Claire (2001, pp. 112–14) argues that the goal of critical thinking is usually problem-solving or decision-making, and that these lie at the heart of both responsible citizenship and personal moral development. Without these skills, the transmission of information within Citizenship lessons is of limited value.

Chapter 10

The morality of assessing Citizenship

The issue of assessing Citizenship raises important moral and practical questions and this chapter considers some of their implications. According to Ofsted and a number of researchers in the field, assessment is one of the least satisfactory elements of Citizenship in schools. The difficulties surrounding the assessment of Citizenship derive, in part, from the complexity and breadth of the subject, the ways in which it is taught and the differing models for its implementation in schools. Moral Education is a vital aspect of Citizenship because dispositions and values, as well as knowledge and skills, are to be inculcated. Moral ambiguity also surrounds the assessment of active Citizenship whereby specific behaviours and forms of participation in the community are evaluated. Given that Citizenship teaching entails the promotion of values as well as certain forms of activity, the issue of assessment of the subject is far from straightforward.

The morality of assessing Citizenship

We might recall the scenes accompanying the fall of the Berlin Wall where a young woman standing on the wall led the chanting of the crowd; features of life in the former communist East Germany were denounced and each one was repeated by the crowd. The list was a public 'naming and shaming' of restrictions on freedom experienced in the DDR. The list included, as one might expect, such features of a coercive state as the secret police but it also included 'Citizenship'. Any suggestion that Citizenship is, in some sense, 'policed' by the State once it is monitored and assessed warrants careful consideration. State control of 'Citizenship' and influence upon the behaviour of citizens is a momentous act and begs some important questions: Is this assessment by the people *of* the people or assessment by the people *for* the people? What right does the State have to promote and assess the inculcation of certain values or dispositions if these are different from those of the child's family? Is there moral justification for the values related to the perpetuation of democracy being promoted and assessed in schools? Are children encouraged to be critical of the values of our democracy? Are learners aware of the agenda promoted in Citizenship lessons and encouraged to perform their own assessment of mandatory Citizenship Education? In short, do assessment practices treat children as if they are *citizens* or *subjects*?

Assessment can be seen as a part of the learning process which is valuable to pupils and teachers or, as we have seen, it can be perceived as a device designed to exert control in a hierarchical system which perpetuates inequality and alienation. There are, evidently, dangers associated with an assessment-driven curriculum; assessment should support teaching and not be the reason for it. Formative assessment is entirely justified as it can enable the teacher to monitor a child's progress and attainment. The most compelling moral justification for assessment is that it can help the teacher learn about his or her teaching by gaining an understanding of pupils' learning. In this case the assessment is an aspect of 'responsive teaching' (Pike, 2004a), is relational and represents open communication between teachers and learners which in itself can be a lesson in Citizenship.

Moral justification for summative assessment that is geared towards reporting and accountability is more ambiguous. The argument for such assessment is that teachers and schools are paid for by taxpayers and need to be publicly accountable. Judgements can be made on the basis of assessments about a teacher's performance and effectiveness. If children of similar ability and socioeconomic backgrounds attain better results in one class or school than in another, judgements can be made about the abilities and skills of managers, administrators, LEAs and teachers. On this view, assessment is intimately connected with the exercise of power for the worth of teachers to society is judged on the basis of the assessment of children. This summative, external, government-controlled assessment of Citizenship, used to wield power over children and teachers, may not be entirely congruent with many of the aims and principles of the Citizenship curriculum.

The morality of assessing citizens

One of the best questions that can be asked about any assessment is 'What's the point?' and it is a particularly good question to ask when Citizenship is to be assessed. There is a pressing need to understand what the purpose of the assessment is and why it is being carried out. Given the resources of time and energy that teachers and curriculum managers devote to assessment as well as the cost of external assessment provided by examination boards and the impact that such assessment can have on pupils, we need to be especially clear about the purpose that it purports to serve. Schooling is an ideological intervention in children's lives and when aspects of that intervention are assessed a similarly ideological task is being undertaken. Children can be shaped by the values of the dominant power structure, value system and worldview which produces the assessment. Ironically, Citizenship that is concerned to teach children about differentials of power in society exemplifies inequality when the child is subjected to an assessment which can have an impact upon his or her present identity and future life. Questions need to be asked so that the moral implications of assessing Citizenship can be considered. Given the inequalities in the relationship between assessor and assessed, and the power wielded by the former over the latter, does our model of assessment undermine the values of equality promoted by our teaching? In short, is there a sharp contrast between what our lessons and our tests teach children about Citizenship?

In Citizenship lessons students learn about living in a 'free' society but we might reflect upon the 'freedom' children in compulsory education actually experience. We need to consider whether a citizen's freedom can be infringed by the assessment of Citizenship if there is an inherent tension between the individual's right to liberty and the practice of assessment which limits the individual's liberty by pronouncing judgements about him or her. Assessment in Citizenship that marks out success and failure and discriminates between them may be inappropriate for a subject which seeks to promote inclusion. Issues such as these must be touched upon if the ethics of assessment are to be examined for what can appear innocuous and is defined as 'any activity used to appraise pupils' performance' (Kyriacou, 1998, p. 102) often judges children on a scale common to all in relation to areas of learning that others, in power, have chosen. The guiding principle of the assessment is to place people in relation to a supposed 'norm' and this itself is a powerful message to send young citizens. For some children assessment and testing appeals to a competitive nature and can foster morally suspect extrinsic motivation (unlike intrinsic motivation where the work is valued apart from its reward). Fostering competition and relying too heavily on extrinsic motivation within an area such as Citizenship, which seeks to promote voluntary service and places an emphasis on the intrinsic worth of certain actions, would appear somewhat contradictory. Comparison with one's peers according to a predetermined standard of attainment which bears little relation to individual progress may be entirely inappropriate in an education *for* citizens which places emphasis upon their equal moral worth.

Of particular relevance to the present discussion of the assessment of Citizenship in schools is Foucault's *Discipline and Punish* (1977a) which provides an analysis of the examination in relation to the individual's freedom in western democracies. Since the 1990s the influence of the late Michel Foucault has been growing, especially in the US, and Foucault's theory about the role of schooling in general and the examination in particular in our society punctures our complacency and casts doubt upon the conventional and widely accepted notion that over the past two centuries those in the West have gained greater freedom. A brief outline of Foucault's intellectual project, so far as the role of schooling in society is concerned, will be helpful as the relation of assessment in schools to capitalist economies warrants careful analysis.

For Foucault power is 'among the best hidden things in the social body' (Foucault, 1988, p. 118) and the effects of power are everywhere. In a 'disciplinary' society 'power produces; it produces reality; it produces domains of objects and rituals of truth' (1977a, p. 194). In schools, examinations and assessments wield power over students and for Foucault the examination provides an example of disciplinary power. In the case of students, teachers can readily appreciate what Foucault means when he asserts that disciplinary power *produces* subjects: 'Without power over students, examinations could not yield "truths" about them and these "truths" could not be used for purposes of "placing" them in social hierarchies and shaping their expectations of themselves and others' (Schrag, 1999, p. 377). Foucault's account of the social transformation that has occurred over the last two hundred years in the West challenges the commonly held view that greater freedom has been gained during this period:

> Whereas, in earlier times, the masses of people remained invisible, now each of us becomes visible as an individual, but only along dimensions that apply to all. Thanks to the exam, each of us can be put in his or her place on a finely graded hierarchy – one that is organized around the concept of the norm.
>
> (Schrag, 1999, p. 377)

Citizenship educators need to consider Foucault's theorizing about the examination as the assessment of their subject is so closely related to the freedom citizens experience in a democracy. If apathy towards the voting process is endemic among 18- to 24-year-olds and this is related to their perception of power within society then the introduction of a mandatory assessment of Citizenship in schools, an instance of 'disciplinary power', may not be the best way to convince young people to vote. Given the events of the start of the twenty-first century there is a pressing need within Western democracies to consider the validity of Foucault's arguments.

The morality of assessing values

The assessment of children's learning in Citizenship is directly related to the values of a specific form of government for 'a democratic society is one in which certain moral and interpersonal values prevail' (Wringe, 1992, p. 32). A curriculum which promotes active involvement in democratic processes and seeks to foster tolerance and pluralism may be less hospitable to ways of living that do not subscribe to democratic values. Indeed,

> Democratic education, whether it admits it or not, wants and needs to produce men and women who have the tastes, knowledge, and character supportive of a democratic regime.
>
> (Bloom, 1987, p. 26)

The political regime seeks to perpetuate and legitimate itself by fostering 'citizens who are in accord with its fundamental principle' (Bloom, 1987, p. 26). In Citizenship lessons children 'are to be brought to understand the benefits of living in a "democratic" or, as it is sometimes termed, a "free" society' but teachers should ensure they 'understand what these benefits are and how to use them, rather than that they are to understand how jolly lucky they are to be living in a democratic society and be less critical' (Wringe, 1992, p. 31).

Assessing children's understanding of the values of a liberal democracy and its distinctive features is essential. Children may be taught that shoplifting is wrong but, as Wringe points out, such behaviour is also considered to be wrong in a monarchy or a military dictatorship. It is necessary to ensure that pupils understand that the rule of law is important 'not as an alternative to petty larceny, but as an alternative to arbitrary arrest, unjust imprisonment, forced entry, unauthorised searches and the abuse of power generally' (Wringe, 1992, p. 32). Within British democracy the emphasis has been upon restraining government and limiting its authority to intervene in our lives and pupils should appreciate 'the duty of government to establish a framework of law which enshrines and protects these liberties while government itself remains impartial between parties who disagree about what is good in life' (Beck, 1998, p. 75). Previous research (Halstead, 1995a, 1999a; Pike, 2005a, 2005b) has shown that a democracy which considers itself to be liberal and tolerant can all too easily discriminate against those who do not share the views and values of the majority. Students' appreciation of the 'principle of toleration' and 'the right of others to choose their own version of the good life (including versions with which we may ourselves profoundly disagree) so long as they are not injurious to others' (Beck, 1998, p. 75) can be usefully assessed within Citizenship.

When students' understanding of democracy is evaluated it is vital that the appreciation of dissent is valued; their understanding of a liberal democracy should include a 'strong valuation of individual freedom and the right of individuals to choose their own conception of the good life' (Beck, 1998, p. 75). Assessing children's values and, by implication, those of the families and communities to which they belong, is therefore something which many teachers and educationalists in a liberal democracy may be decidedly uneasy about. Indeed it has been argued that

> poor quality assessment that focuses on judging a pupil's attitudes and beliefs or those of their family, community and cultural group, rather than assessing their progress in awareness of and understanding of values would distort the aims of citizenship education and could discriminate against particular groups of learners on the grounds of race, gender, disability or sexual orientation.
>
> (Arthur and Wright, 2001, p. 127)

Here it is asserted that 'progress', 'awareness' and 'understanding' are legitimate areas for assessment within Citizenship but that 'judging a pupil's attitudes and beliefs' is inappropriate as such judgement does not sit well with the values of 'multicultural, liberal society'. On the other hand, others have asked if there is 'no instance where aspects of other cultures attract opprobrium, and that the majority of people would reject or at least criticize?' (Cairns and Gardner, 2003, p. 186). It should be pointed out that there are many aspects of our own culture that will attract the opprobrium of some citizens and whether or not the 'majority' rejects or criticizes these aspects is not the end of the matter for in a liberal democracy the objections of minorities must be sufficiently regarded.

In assessing children's understanding of democratic values it is important that their ability to be critical of their own society should be assessed so that it can inform teaching. Teachers should monitor understanding to ascertain whether children realize that 'a democratic society may perfectly well be one in which major inequalities of both life conditions and political influence exist' (Wringe, 1992, p. 31). When assessing children's understanding of the values of their own society one finds they are all too often aware that

> neither government nor powerful groups or persons may have much regard for the wishes of the less influential and most people may spend most of their time in institutions over which they have little control and therefore, in real terms, most of their lives are subject to regimes which are not in any sense democratic at all.
>
> (Wringe, 1992, p. 31)

Citizens can be exploited in democracies and it is possible that citizens of a democracy can experience less 'freedom' as they go about their daily affairs than subjects under the rule of a benevolent monarch. It is important that learners consider how citizens can have their freedom restricted by economic forces; those who are poor, illiterate or lacking in skills often find they do not experience the freedom they would wish in 'free' countries.

If Citizenship is to be assessed in our schools we must ensure that it encourages citizens to critically evaluate democratic values and to reflect upon the extent to which these are congruent with their own. Teachers can assess children's understanding of the concept of freedom which should 'be interpreted liberally to include freedom from want, fear and insecurity as well as freedom from constraint' (Wringe, 1992, p. 32). Whether the values a society or a person claims to espouse are evident in the community's activities or the individual's deeds should be the subject of sustained reflection in any course of Citizenship and Moral Education. Children seem to have an innate capacity to detect hypocrisy and this is an entirely legitimate faculty to assess in Citizenship lessons where the link between values and actions is reflected upon.

The morality of assessing active Citizenship

The radical nature of Citizenship Education is summed up in *Education for Citizenship and the Teaching of Democracy in Schools* (AGC, 1998) which is quite explicit about the aim of such education being a 'change in the political culture of this country' where people 'think of themselves as active citizens' and become 'confident in finding new forms of involvement and acting among themselves' (ibid.). It has been argued that the Crick Report's emphasis upon 'the responsibilities and rights of citizens, and the value of community activity' (ibid., p. 4) is very much of its time and is congruent with the post-1979 Thatcherite agenda taken up by New Labour where duties as well as the rights of citizens are emphasized. New Labour sees a much greater role for voluntary organizations and groups and it might be pointed out that promoting public services can mean there is less for the state to do and less to pay for; when voluntary organizations such as churches and charities do more the state may do less. If the emphasis on active citizenship is part of such an agenda the consequences of increasing voluntary sector activity need to be carefully considered. If the provision of voluntary aid increases there is the possibility that 'it may inhibit the provision of more reliable forms of relief' (Wringe, 1992, p. 35) so that vulnerable members of society will suffer as a result. On the other hand, neighbourliness and unalloyed acts of kindness and charity must be among the duties of all citizens regardless of governmental provision and few would argue that they should not be promoted in schools.

The politics of promoting participation aside, whether it is appropriate to encourage active citizenship and voluntary service by ensuring that it is assessed in schools is debatable. Whether it is ethical or not, the assessment of such activity will now happen across the nation's schools and it is essential that this should be implemented ethically and engaged in by participants who are empowered to assess the impact of their activity in their own communities. Democratizing assessment processes is especially necessary with regard to Citizenship and as community involvement is assessed it is only fitting that members of the community, in addition to teachers and students, should be involved in the assessment process:

> Pupils will need skills in assessing their own progress in order to improve their performance in citizenship education and in gathering evidence of their progress and achievements throughout the key stages. Teachers will need to share ownership of the assessment process with pupils. They may also need to involve others including community partners, learning mentors, other colleagues – as assessors.
>
> (Arthur and Wright, 2001, p. 127)

Communication is at the heart of the Citizenship curriculum and to a greater extent than in many subjects Citizenship will involve much group discussion. Consequently Citizenship teachers and students need to know how to assess understanding and reflection in and through group talk. Involving pupils in reflection on action through group discussion sits well with the aims of Citizenship as students are required to evaluate their own activities.

Teachers have been advised not to wait for aspects of a learner's performance to be unavoidably obvious for 'monitoring should be investigative and active, in the sense that you actively probe pupils' current understanding and difficulties' (Kyriacou, 1998, p. 108) but in Citizenship it should be the students as well as the teachers who are engaged in such probing. Such an approach to assessment in Citizenship is also in keeping with the messages found in the professional standards document *Qualifying to Teach* (Teacher Training Agency, 2002) which is quite explicit in Section 3.2 ('Monitoring and Assessment') about pupil involvement in assessment. Indeed, in order to be awarded Qualified Teacher Status (QTS) trainee teachers of Citizenship must have clear evidence that they 'involve pupils in reflecting on, evaluating and improving their own performance' (ibid., p. 10, 3.2.2).

Those training to teach Citizenship face a particular challenge in this respect because most schools have yet to put in place adequate arrangements for assessing the progress and attainment of their pupils in Citizenship. There is considerable opportunity to influence policy in schools that are striving to implement new models of assessment which actively involve young citizens in the monitoring and evaluation of their own progress. The recent initiative Assessment for Learning (AfL) shows that it is especially valuable if children are involved in this assessment of their own progress and thereby take responsibility for their learning. When learners are included in the evaluation of their activity and participation rather than receiving pronouncements about the level they have attained from those in authority (and, in the case of external assessment, from those who are removed from the learning situation) this represents a democratization of the assessment process.

Recently, a distinguished researcher of children's reading claimed there was 'a chasm between the liberal positions of our pedagogy and the coercive positions of our assessment' (Harrison, 2004, p. 18) and advocated the use of portfolios in assessment. Asking questions as a way of assessing children's knowledge is fraught with difficulty and it is fitting that work is assessed through a portfolio at the end of Key Stage 3. This would seem ideally suited to providing evidence of reflection on active citizenship as well as the development of the learner's thinking about values. The portfolio would appear to be a better place for such assessment than an exam room where children write about their community involvement while being isolated and segregated from the community they are describing – in order to engage in what may be perceived as 'school' work which in many minds is divorced from anything that takes place outside of the school.

Our assessment methods should be appropriate to what is being assessed and while a portfolio assessment system offers significant possibilities a great deal of care and imagination is needed if the work included in a portfolio is to demonstrate appropriate attention to learning objectives as well as the specific subject knowledge of National Curriculum Citizenship without resorting to traditional and inappropriate tasks. Being innovative is a requirement when Citizenship is assessed and suitable as well as unsuitable assessments for a portfolio will be considered shortly. Imagination is needed so that inclusion is at the heart of the portfolio. Work such as video diaries or interviews with community members can be included as well as other evidence of community projects. An exclusive reliance on traditional academic forms of assessment, such as writing, may very often fail to reflect the quality of a child's active citizenship. A subject as innovative as Citizenship should be innovatively assessed and this requires time and resources as well as imagination on the part of the teacher.

The state of Citizenship assessment

Although pockets of good practice exist the present state of much assessment in Citizenship is far from innovative or imaginative. Given the reservations expressed about external assessment there is a case for promoting teacher assessment. There are, however, problems associated with the current teacher assessment of Citizenship undertaken in schools. When assessment happens at all there are concerns about the accuracy of assessment, its usefulness to pupils and whether appropriate subject knowledge is being assessed. There are also concerns about recording progression and the assessment of active citizenship.

Although from 2003, there has been 'a requirement to assess pupils' progress and report on their achievement at the end of Year 9' many schools are still failing to comply and only a 'minority of schools have made a good start at this, using assessed tasks and pupils' own assessment of their work to underpin progress' (Ofsted, 2005a, p. 5). It is clear that for many schools 'assessment is as yet at an early stage so that they are not in a position to meet the requirement' (ibid.). Even when assessment is undertaken it is often unsatisfactory:

> In some schools, pupils produce very little written work in citizenship, and some files contain work that is low level, including much completion of worksheets. The work is too often well below the pupils' achievement in other subjects, and higher attainers tend to be the group least well served by these activities. The subject has a written requirement and pupils should have opportunities for enquiry and communication that allow them to pursue topics in depth.
>
> (Ofsted, 2005a, p. 5)

As so many schools are not complying, as yet, with the requirement for teacher assessment of a portfolio of Citizenship work at the end of KS3 the danger is that pupils' learning and achievement in the subject will suffer because they will be unaware of how they are progressing and of what they need to do to improve.

In other schools, although students retain their work in files teachers have yet to establish reliable, systematic assessment procedures, and teachers' marking is of insufficient quality either to help pupils develop or to measure accurately attainment and progress made. That this is the case in schools means that students following PGCE courses in Citizenship rarely have models of good practice to emulate. Indeed the Ofsted report *HMI 2299 Initial Teacher Training for Teachers of Citizenship 03/04* states that: 'It is particularly difficult for trainees to demonstrate that they meet the Standards in monitoring and assessment of pupil progress, in part because most schools have not yet established ways of assessing pupils' progress and attainment in citizenship' (Ofsted, 2004a, p. 10). Student teachers following PGCE Citizenship courses often find it impossible to 'use their records' of progress and attainment to 'help pupils review their own progress' (Teacher Training Agency, 2002, p. 10, 3.2.6) because learning objectives are not defined with sufficient clarity. If pupils are to have democratic co-ownership of the learning process with their teachers then they will need to be able to evaluate and assess their own progress; current arrangements in schools often militate against such democratic assessment. Pupils can only be involved in the assessment process and evaluate 'progress towards planned learning objectives' (3.2.1) if learning objectives are clearly defined and measurable. If they are not then no one, least of all the pupil, will know when improvement is occurring.

Assessing and providing good-quality feedback to pupils is essential and further research is still required into what good assessment of Citizenship looks like. A particular challenge is apparent when form tutors or teachers of different subjects teach Citizenship or when it is embedded in other subjects. Although the integration of citizenship is advocated throughout this book it places added demands upon schools and teachers as far as assessment is concerned. Teachers need to see more examples of assessed tasks and should experience further moderation of work in Citizenship. It would appear to be rare for the Citizenship coordinator in a school to be released to participate in the assessment of pupils with the classroom teacher. Teachers need to employ clearly defined and measurable assessment objectives where the subject-specific knowledge for Citizenship is assessed, rather than focusing on the literacy skills required to write a letter (even if it is to a local councillor or MP). The subject knowledge specific to Citizenship seems to become easily obscured by the assessment demands of the 'host' subject if the same assignment is assessed for two entirely different disciplines.

Equally, when skills of enquiry and responsible action are assessed this does not necessarily qualify as 'National Curriculum Citizenship' where distinct subject knowledge is assessed. If teachers are to employ key stage descriptors as criteria in reaching judgements about attainment it would appear that further investment in training is necessary. Evidently, assessment is a weak aspect of Citizenship provision in schools and few schools have made much progress in this area. Principled, formative, AfL-type assessment should be implemented so that schools do not experience such difficulty achieving consistent and meaningful assessment of Citizenship. The variety of models of Citizenship provision in schools make assessment a very real challenge and a continuing lack of clarity in schools about definitions of Citizenship (see Chapter 9) has not helped to achieve the emergence of clear assessment policies.

Progression in Citizenship

A problem facing Citizenship teachers responsible for assessment is the absence of well-developed models of progression in their subject. These will necessarily develop over time as pupils' learning in the subject is studied. An example here of progression will give an indication of the development one might expect to see in pupils' understanding across a range of Citizenship topics. An awareness of progression can help teachers bring an appropriate challenge so that Citizenship is enjoyable and stimulating and is seen to require critical reflection rather than a regurgitation of facts. The teacher needs to be clear about the knowledge and understanding that is expected at different stages.

If the topic of 'Laws and Rules' is taken one might expect most children within Key Stage 1 (up to the age of seven) to understand what rules are, to be able to comply with them and to understand why we need rules. At a very simple level the message is being communicated that chaos results when we do not have rules or do not follow them. Simple playground rules can be used as examples and one might assess a child's ability to know what rules are, to understand what happens when they are not followed and then to be able to explain why we all need rules. By Key Stage 2 (ages seven to eleven) most children might be aware that rules can provide safety and security for both people and their property. Although from a very early age (at Key Stage 1 or before) one hears the familiar phrase 'It's not fair', it is more likely to be at Key Stage 2 that most children are ready to contemplate the notion of fairness in relation to rules. At this age children can also be prompted to consider rules that are applicable in wider society rather than just in their own immediate context. At Key Stage 2 the results of breaking certain of society's laws can be discussed and the ways in which crime is punished can be discussed. This might be kept to a discussion of fines and imprisonment with attention being devoted to the suffering of the victims of crime. The involvement of the police, courts, juries and judges can be explored at this stage.

When assessing children's knowledge and understanding of this topic at Key Stage 3 one might reasonably expect to be able to assess their understanding of the legal process and the criminal justice system. Most children at this level are capable of a more sophisticated analysis of how laws are made, including the influence of voluntary groups and the function of parliament, than they were during Key Stage 2. Children are usually introduced to the progress of a bill and the process of royal assent in the secondary school. They can consider topical initiatives such as ASBOs (Anti-Social Behaviour Orders) and curfews for teenagers in certain areas. Children can be assessed on their ability to describe what happens after a crime is committed, such as the way an offender is treated and the process he or she goes through. Learners at Key Stage 3 can also be assessed on the knowledge of legislation relevant to young people. They should be aware of how old they must be to work certain hours, what they are entitled to earn as well as the conditions to which they are entitled. They can be assessed on their knowledge of the ages at which certain forms of sexual activity are legal and the law concerning different classifications of drugs. Their knowledge and understanding, in relation to becoming informed citizens, should encompass the 'legal and human rights and responsibilities underpinning society, basic aspects of the criminal justice system, and how both relate to young people' (QCA/DfEE, 1999a, 1a).

At Key Stage 4 children can be assessed on their knowledge of 'legal and human rights and responsibilities underpinning society and how they relate to citizens, including the role and operation of the criminal and civil justice systems' (KS4 1a, Programme of Study for Citizenship). The understanding young people have of the concept of freedom in a democratic society can be assessed, as can their comprehension of concepts such as the rule of law. The applicability of laws globally, nationally and locally and the role of the UN in achieving human rights can be assessed. Topical areas such as the laws relating to the sale of alcohol, sexual involvement, racism, drugs, truancy and so on can be the knowledge that is assessed at Key Stage 4. In Years 10 and 11, a more developed understanding and appreciation of the reasons for and consequences of having laws can be analysed. In addition, Natural Law can be discussed and the extent to which morality and legality relate to each other can be analysed.

Assessment of subject knowledge at Key Stage 3

All too often when Citizenship work is assessed the knowledge one would expect to find submitted as evidence of attainment in what might be called 'National Curriculum Citizenship' is scarce. This is especially likely to be the case where the specific subject knowledge of Citizenship becomes obscured by another subject. For instance, when Citizenship is timetabled with PSHE political literacy can easily be marginalized. The introductory section of the Citizenship Programme of Study clearly states that 'teaching should ensure that knowledge and understanding about becoming informed citizens are acquired and applied when developing skills of enquiry and communication and participation and responsible action' (QCA/ DfEE, 1999a) and an approach many schools have adopted is to audit, across the curriculum, the prevalence and development of skills of 'enquiry and communication'. The risk of marginalizing the subject knowledge specific to Citizenship becomes apparent if these skills are not set within the context of children becoming 'informed citizens'.

If Citizenship is taught in time also allocated for English then, as we have seen, the skills of literacy can end up being assessed more than those of Citizenship. One example will suffice. As part of their Year 9 (end of Key Stage 3) portfolio in Citizenship teenagers are often required to write a letter on the topic of Law and Order. All may seem well at first especially as they are researching information to form an opinion on a Citizenship issue (such as binge drinking, a curfew or a shopping centre that bars teenagers wearing hooded tops). If the assessment is to write a letter to someone in authority in order to persuade the recipient to take a particular course of action, it is especially important to focus on the assessment objectives of Citizenship rather than those of En3 Writing, within English. This task can easily turn into an exercise in letter writing rather than an opportunity to display one's knowledge of legislation and how it is modified. At Year 9 such an assessment might be graded broadly within one of three levels. At level 4 or 5 an opinion may be stated, at level 5 or 6 evidence could be given and at level 7 suggestions for modification of a law could be made. Making children aware at the start of simple assessment objectives such as these can help them see what is being required of them. A host of imaginative possibilities exist for assessing Citizenship in non-traditional and less academic ways especially when the freedom to use a portfolio exists. Video diaries, radio interviews, posters for pressure groups or political parties accompanied by oral explanation, photographs, drama sketches, and animation using an Apple eMac are all possible ways of ensuring children enjoy the assessment process at the end of Year 9.

Assessing Citizenship or Citizenship Studies at Key Stage 4

At the end of KS4 assessment applies particularly to those opting to take the short course GCSE in Citizenship Studies. It is important to note that GCSE Citizenship Studies does not reflect the full statutory programme of study in Citizenship for Key Stage 4. Consequently, the 'choice of title is significant and sends a clear message that it is not assessment of citizenship but of a particular and partial aspect of it' (Arthur and Wright, 2001, p. 135). Evidently Citizenship Studies is not a GCSE in 'Citizenship' and one supposes that this is meant to avoid the possibility of someone failing in 'Citizenship' or their quality as a citizen being graded. For many, though, this is unconvincing and as soon as 'accrediting citizenship' is undertaken 'there is a tension between citizenship as an entitlement of *all* and the nature of qualifications, such as GCSE, which differentiate between candidates using grade criteria' (Arthur and Wright, 2001, p. 128). Foucault's views about the examination have been explored in this chapter and it is essential that students are not 'put in the position of "failing" citizenship' or denied 'the opportunity to enter a qualification in the first place' (ibid.).

Whether Citizenship should be certificated at all, on moral grounds, is highly questionable but the influence of performance league tables on a school automatically ensures that those subjects which might contribute to a school's position in the league are accorded greater value. The introduction of GCSE Citizenship Studies can mean a move away from the original ethos and spirit of Citizenship where the emphasis was upon it being an entitlement for all. There are advantages as well as disadvantages to a school providing such a GCSE course for its students. On the one hand providing an examination may give the subject status and lead to the employment of specialist teachers. On the other hand it can shift the emphasis away from participation and action and towards knowledge and understanding. Schools that attach a great deal of importance to Citizenship often resist the pressure to introduce GCSE because teachers believe the emphasis upon summative assessment of Citizenship is not in keeping with the aims and nature of the subject. Whether GCSE is taken or not, feedback to students should focus on their own progress rather than comparing them to others.

Students should be familiar with the requirements of the GCSE if they are to be examination candidates. Retention of subject knowledge tends to be tested in early parts of the GCSE paper. In 2004 the OCR paper in GCSE Citizenship Studies began with multiple choice questions. Children were given four possible answers to the following questions: 'Choose one example of a pressure group'; 'Choose one example of local taxation'; 'What is meant by the term global interdependence?'; and, 'What is meant by the term Local Agenda 21?'. They were also asked:

4. When deciding whether someone is guilty of a criminal offence, which one of the following questions should a jury consider?

   (i)   Has the accused person done something like this before?
   (ii) Has the prosecution proved that the accused person is guilty?

(iii) Has the defence shown that the accused person had a good reason for his/her actions?
(iv) Is the accused person sorry for what he/she has done?

What is significant here is that the substantive subject knowledge as specified by the National Curriculum for Citizenship is being assessed. In GCSE Citizenship Studies (OCR 2004) candidates were asked to show that they knew a source of legal advice that could be trusted and one legal power that the police have. Such information is directly relevant to their lives and should be possessed by all citizens.

The final question of the GCSE OCR (2004) examination paper required an essay to be written 'to show how far individual, group and government action can bring about change and development locally and nationally'. Three 'documents' were provided; the first being a quote from Nelson Mandela ('It's not kings and generals that make history, but the masses of the people') accompanied by his photograph; the second was a quotation from Margaret Mead, 'Never doubt that a small group of people can change the world. Indeed, it is the only thing that ever has'; the third contained the following information: 'In 1992, the nations of the world discussed global warming at the Earth Summit. The conference at Rio produced a number of important international agreements. One was to manage the environment in a way that met present needs without damaging our ability to meet those of the future. Government action can bring real change and development'.

Candidates gaining a Level 2 (four to six marks out of a possible fifteen) show a clear understanding of 'the benefits of active citizenship for the school or local area and give relevant examples' whereas those gaining a Level 3 (seven to nine marks out of a possible fifteen) provide examples that 'demonstrate the ability to reflect on their own experience OR the experiences of others'. Those gaining Level 4 (ten to twelve marks out of a possible fifteen), in addition, provide 'a detailed case' that 'demonstrates the benefits of the different levels of action on local and global scales', and those gaining Level 5 (thirteen to fifteen marks out of a possible fifteen) are aware that 'action at all levels can be important in bringing about change' or indeed 'make a convincing case that one level of action can stimulate action at the other levels'. Understanding the benefits of active citizenship is integral to all these answers and reflection upon action is clearly central.

The limitations of assessing active Citizenship in a written examination have been noted already but it is the view of Ofsted that 'reflections on participation can produce very good work' (2005a). Section C of the 2004 OCR examination in GCSE Citizenship Studies informs candidates that 'you should use examples from any school, college, workplace or community action that you have taken part in' (OCR, 2004, p. 12). Within Section C, question 21 requires that candidates 'State three things you could do to increase people's knowledge and understanding about an issue such as fair trade, human rights or sustainable development' and they are reminded to use 'examples from your studies and from any personal, school, college or workplace action'. Reflecting on participation gains candidates marks in a GCSE examination but whether it is an adequate means of assessing active citizenship is another matter. Promoting active citizenship through the introduction of GCSE Citizenship Studies may exclude and marginalize some members of the student body whose activity does not count towards a GCSE grade. It is clear that: 'Participation and responsible action remain an issue in many schools. Most schools create opportunities for some pupils, but in National Curriculum citizenship this should be an entitlement for all' (Ofsted, 2005a, p. 7). Assessing the 'more complex participatory elements' (Arthur and Wright, 2001, p. 127) of Citizenship is a particular challenge, and we should be aware that far more is at stake than is often realized when governments officially recognize and reward the actions of some of its citizens but not the efforts of all.

Chapter 11

Reflections on professional practice in Citizenship and Moral Education

In this volume, we have paid equal attention to the theory and practice of Citizenship and Moral Education. We argued in Part One that citizenship is the unifying force that enables people from different beliefs and backgrounds to live together co-operatively in spite of differing allegiances, opinions, priorities and tastes. The purpose of Citizenship Education therefore is to help children to understand their role as citizens, to develop a commitment to this role in practice, and ultimately to engage in critical reflection on the rights and responsibilities associated with this role. Living together as citizens requires a framework of shared political and civic values, and we argued that political liberalism provides this framework without impinging unduly on the freedom of citizens to pursue their own vision of the good. However, we believe that values education would be unbalanced if it focused only on political and civic values. Children also need opportunities to learn personal moral values if they are to become mature, informed, committed, critically reflective moral agents, capable of meeting the moral challenges they face in their ordinary lives. Moral Education is therefore a necessary counterbalance to Citizenship Education, and indeed it provides a basis from which the ethical appropriateness of laws and political decisions can be judged.

In Part Two, the focus of our attention turned to the practice of Citizenship and Moral Education, and we argued that there are good reasons why these subjects are most closely linked in schools with the Arts and Humanities. In Chapter 4 we looked at the contribution of critical literacy to Citizenship, including the development of the skills of communication and discernment, and also examined the relationship between language, identity and values. In Chapters 5 to 7 we examined the relationship of Citizenship and Moral Education to the Arts, the Humanities and Religious Education/PSHE. We argue that it is in the Arts and the Humanities that students are most likely to encounter issues relating to their own role as citizens and moral agents, and also that these two domains develop empathy, imagination, social engagement and a broad understanding of moral and civic issues. Citizenship and PSHE have much in common in both content and approach, but we argue that it is justifiable to keep a form of Moral Education outside these subjects (perhaps within Religious Education) since Moral Education provides the resources for identifying and critiquing unjust laws or oppressive political action.

In Part Three, we sketched out seven models of Citizenship provision in schools and argued that a combination of discrete and integrated provision is most likely to be successful, so long as decisions about integration are based not on convenience but on which subjects have the greatest capacity to provide good citizenship lessons. We also looked at communication skills and ICT skills in Citizenship, and the teaching of controversial issues. The different ways that children learn values are explored, including direct instruction, observation, participation and guided action, and reflection; the part played by teacher example, the hidden curriculum, the ethos of the school, school rituals and the school environment must not be underestimated. Finally, we considered the morality of assessing citizenship, and warned of the danger that assessment might lead to an overemphasis on the aim of producing informed citizens at the expense of the aim of producing committed, autonomous citizens who play an active part in their communities.

It seems appropriate in view of the emphasis throughout the book on critical reflection as an essential component of both Citizenship and Moral Education that we should conclude with a reflective glance back at the underlying principles and practices that are central to these subjects. Why has Citizenship in particular been introduced as a new National Curriculum subject in England in recent years? What purposes is it intended to achieve? What new knowledge, skills, attitudes and values will children and young people learn as a result of it? What conditions are needed for such learning to be successful? Will it increase their personal well-being or the contribution they are able to make to society? Will society itself be changed as a result of it, and if so, how? What will society be like in the future?

A crisis in values?

In the last ten years, both Moral Education and Citizenship Education have been presented as appropriate responses to a perceived crisis in the values of young people. The National Forum for Values in Education and the Community (SCAA, 1996a, 1996b) was set up in response to a popular view that many children and young people have little or no sense of right or wrong and that there is rampant indiscipline in some schools, with verbal and physical harassment and violence between students and sometimes assaults on teachers affecting the learning environment and educational experience and leading to a rise in exclusions from school. This sense of moral panic was exacerbated by a number of horrific events including murders and rapes by children and young people. Similarly, as we noted in Chapter 3, the Advisory Group on Citizenship links the political 'alienation and cynicism' of young people (as evidenced in their suspicion of institutionalized authority, their boredom with politics and their sense of disempowerment) to other indicators of youth alienation such as 'truancy, vandalism, random violence, premeditated crime and habitual drug-taking' (1998, p. 15).

In other words, underlying contemporary provision of Citizenship and Moral Education in schools is the assumption that moral and political apathy on the part of young people is a major threat to democracy and to the civilized values of our society. It is further assumed that the problem can only be resolved by a systematic programme of political education designed to transform young people's attitudes and behaviour and to make them into conscientious, committed (and perhaps compliant) citizens. The Advisory Group on Citizenship quotes the British Youth Council with enthusiasm: 'citizenship education must clearly enable children to understand their duties as citizens' (1998, p. 20). Yet for many people, this analysis of problem and solution is too simplistic. Skinner and McCollum, for example, claim that

> many commentators believe that the political attitudes and behaviour of young people in Britain today are representative of deeper problems in our democratic society in relation to major structural changes and cultural changes which have produced new patterns of social and economic exclusion and which have profound implications for how we conceptualise identity and culture. These changes also undermine traditional forms of citizenship, and alter our understanding of what it means to live in democratic culturally diverse societies. They therefore require a fundamental reappraisal of the theoretical and pedagogical assumptions that underlie our educational practices.
>
> (2004, pp. 149–50)

Taking this as its starting point, this final chapter sets out three core principles which we believe are not sufficiently emphasized in the recent initiatives in Citizenship and Moral Education, but without which any such initiative is likely to enjoy only limited success. They are: respecting young people as individuals with their own values, opinions and decision-making capacities, rather than as future adults who need shaping to fit a predetermined model of citizenship; promoting social justice in a society which is becoming increasingly culturally diverse; and planning for the challenges of a future in which traditional forms of citizenship may be outdated. We shall now look at each of these points in more detail.

Respecting young people

The first problem with justifying the decision to provide Citizenship and Moral Education on assumptions of young people's moral and political alienation is that it conflicts with research findings. Research suggests that children's moral development begins as early as the second year of life, when children begin to use standards in evaluating their own behaviour and the behaviour of others (Buzzelli, 1992). These standards may arise initially from an emotional response to adult approval and disapproval of children's behaviour, but by the age of four children are likely to abide by parental standards not out of fear of punishment but out of a desire to imitate parents who have established a warm and loving relationship with them (Kagan, 1984). This growing awareness of standards (see, for example, Woolfson, 1995, on lying and truth-telling) may also be linked to children's developing cognitive, linguistic and affective abilities. Smetana and Braeges (1990) suggest that by the age of three-and-a-half children are able to judge for themselves the comparative seriousness of moral and social–conventional transgressions, and Iakobson and Moreva (1992) claim that by the age of six children begin to comply consciously with the norms and rules of interaction and behaviour when they find themselves in situations of moral choice. In research into the developing sexual values and attitudes of nine- to ten-year-olds, children were found discussing the need for honesty and openness in relationships, debating whether love could transform people to the extent of helping them overcome addiction, and exploring some of the complex moral dilemmas in television soap operas (Halstead and Waite, 2001a, 2001b). A qualitative study of the values of thirteen- to fourteen-year-olds in four ethnically diverse secondary schools showed that students were generally well able to voice their own values and articulate and reflect on their moral and cultural experiences in school in relationships with teachers and peers (Taylor, 1996). A Mori poll of 196 eleven- to sixteen-year-olds found that four-fifths of them thought that 'people don't care enough about the environment' (SCAA, 1996a, p. 22), and the British Social Attitudes Survey of 580 young people aged twelve to nineteen found that eighty-eight per cent considered British society to be prejudiced against Asians and black people (Sachdev, 1996).

This evidence of children's moral sophistication and concern for social and political issues does not sit easily with claims about a crisis in the moral and civic values of young people. Perhaps children are being blamed for what is effectively an adult problem. In Chapter 9 we noted how influential the example of adults can be on the developing values of children and young people. It would not be surprising therefore if they were to be influenced by the low standards of ethics in many areas of public life, and by the questionable example set by some leading figures in politics, business, sport and the entertainment industry, especially when the media feel obliged to expose every last detail of the private lives of these public figures. The media are another source of children's developing values, and yet by prioritizing entertainment over moral purpose, the media inevitably shape 'facts' and feelings about situations in a particular way and may unintentionally and without their realizing it influence children's perceptions, actions and whole value framework.

But it is likely that children are more influenced by adults with whom they come into contact personally. If they lose confidence in adult authority, it may be because they find themselves on the receiving end of sustained disrespect, insensitivity and lack of trust. These negative attitudes towards children are unfortunately still widespread among representatives of institutional authority, from police to school teachers. There is still a common assumption that children should always do what teachers tell them, however disrespectful the teacher's attitude towards them may be. In one school visited recently, pride of place on the list of school rules was given to the requirement to 'follow the instructions of the teacher or support staff without question'. The same school had recently installed a six-foot-high metal fence around the whole perimeter of its grounds, with razor-sharp spikes on top, as if in conscious imitation of the Foucauldian asylum or prison. Both school rules and school environment seemed to be used as a means of disciplining children and making the body 'docile' (Foucault, 1977a, p. 156) through a system of constant supervision and total control. However, disrespectful behaviour on the part of teachers can also take many other, more personal forms: domineering behaviour, hurtful sarcasm, bullying, shouting, swearing (even under one's breath), condescension, impatience, the imposition of petty rules, inappropriate discipline such as punishing a whole class for the misdemeanours of a few students, and failure to listen to students' explanations or to respond to their legitimate requests. A similar lack of respect is present in the title of Susan Cowley's book, *Getting the Buggers to Behave* (2001), however much it may be claimed that this is simply a light-hearted approach to issues of discipline.

At a less extreme level, it is disrespectful to students to ignore the skills, values or opinions they bring with them to school, or to assume that maintaining the school's structures is more important than meeting the needs of individual students. It is disrespectful if the students' voice is ignored when real decisions are being made within the school. Skinner and McCollum (2004, p. 155) tell the story of a school that in response to the Muslim requirement that girls should be allowed to cover their legs changed its dress code to allow Muslim girls to wear trousers. This created ill-feeling on the part of non-Muslim girls who also wanted the freedom to wear trousers, and the situation was only resolved when a working party was set up that included pupils as well as staff and parents (cf. Verma *et al.*, 1994). It was the initial assumption that the voice of pupils was not needed in the decision-making process that caused the problem in the first place; indeed, one way of showing children respect is to take their participation in decision-making for granted.

However, if children are shown scant respect in schools, it is not surprising that some of them develop negative attitudes to authority. In a survey of over 13,000 students aged thirteen to fifteen from sixty-five maintained schools in England and Wales, Francis and Kay (1995) found that over one-quarter did not think teachers were doing a good job, almost half would be reluctant to discuss their problems with a teacher, and about one-third thought school was not preparing them for life. About two-fifths were unpersuaded that the police did a good job either. Negative attitudes to institutional authority may not be indicative of either a failure in moral development or ineffective socialization into the values of citizenship (cf. Emler and Reicher, 1987), but may simply be a response to negative experiences at the hands of adults. In our view, this runs counter to everything that Citizenship and Moral Education should stand for in schools: young people will not feel respected as citizens if they do not experience respect in schools, and some may come to perceive themselves as outside the structures that bind citizens together in a common purpose.

Respect comes high on most lists of what pupils want from teachers (Rhodes, 1990), for respect underpins children's self-esteem and positive self-concepts. As we noted in Chapter 9, children are most likely to be influenced by teachers whose qualities they admire – qualities such as gentleness and courtesy (Haberman, 1994), sensitivity and responsiveness to the needs of pupils (Kutnik and Jules, 1993) and tolerance, fairness, acting in a reasonable manner and a willingness to explain things (Hayes, 1993). All of these can be viewed as amplifications of the concept of respect. If a young child has a warm, positive and secure relationship with a teacher, this can make it more likely that the child will grow up to be well adjusted and self-sufficient in adolescence and adulthood (Werner and Smith, 1992). Children not only respond better to teachers who show them respect, but also learn to show respect to others. If children are taught Citizenship in an environment where they do not feel respected themselves, it will roll off them like water off a duck's back.

Promoting social justice within an open framework of Citizenship

Skinner and McCollum argue that the final report of the Advisory Group on Citizenship (1998) is flawed in two ways. First, they claim, it pays inadequate attention to complex and controversial questions about the nature of citizenship (how to balance individual and community rights, for example, or how to define common values or British identity). Secondly, it pays inadequate attention to social and economic inequalities and institutional racism in schools and in society at large, and fails to engage adequately with issues such as diversity and equality (Skinner and McCollum, 2004, p. 146). If these criticisms are valid, they go a long way towards undermining the superstructure of legislation and official guidance which has been built on the foundation of that final report. It is therefore important to look at these criticisms more closely.

With regard to the complexities in the concept of citizenship, Miller identifies four types of 'cultural subject' (or citizen) which the state seeks to train and develop through education:

- the ethically incomplete subject in need of training into humanness;
- the national public in need of a dramatological mirror in which to recognize itself;
- the politically incomplete public subject in need of democratic training in citizenship;
- the rational consuming subject in need of alignment with this public citizen.

(1993, pp. xi–xii)

These four elements (which we may relabel the moral, the cultural, the political and the economic) interact in many different ways. For example, rock music has been described as 'a cry of revolt underwritten by major corporations' (Miller, 1988, p. 180), in other words, an example of unexpected interaction between the moral and the economic. Another interesting interaction is that between the political and the economic, because they make conflicting demands on the citizen: democracy requires citizens who put the needs of the state and the community before themselves, whereas capitalism requires consumers who put their own self-centred desires first. It is partly the task of Citizenship Education to reconcile the conflicting goals of the political and economic systems. However, Citizenship Education as it is defined by the Advisory Group on Citizenship is primarily concerned with another set of interactions, between the political and the cultural. The good citizen, or 'virtuous political participant' (to use Miller's words: 1993, p. xxi) is defined as someone who sees his or her cultural identity primarily in terms of loyalty to the nation-state of which he or she is a member. This creates difficulties for those who have divided loyalties (for example, those who were born, or who have ancestral links, outside the UK) or who take their primary identity from some other source (for example, Muslims or evangelical Christians who may consider their faith more important than their nationality). Perhaps it is inevitable that those who do not conform to the dominant definitions of national identity are in danger of becoming targets of prejudice and discrimination. In relation to culture and national identity, Foucault claims that there is 'only a single drama . . . , the endlessly repeated play of dominations' (1977b, p. 149). This relationship of domination, he says, is fixed 'in rituals, in meticulous procedures that impose rights and obligations . . . [and in] the universe of rules' (ibid.).

So the question now arises as to how far this 'drama of domination' relates to contemporary understandings of citizenship and to the experiences of young people being prepared for citizenship in schools. If Foucault is right in his discussion of history when he suggests that traditional history is a justifying mechanism for the values that maintain the privileges of the dominant group in our society, then we need to be aware of the possibility that Citizenship has been planned with the same underlying if unstated aims. Is Citizenship a means of further marginalizing those without power, or is it a way of promoting social justice?

The growing number of articles devoted to Special Educational Needs and Citizenship (for example, Hartas, 2003; Lawson, 2003) is an encouraging sign and suggests an awareness that principles like social justice, human rights and inclusion should inform the practice of Citizenship Education. As Hartas points out, children and young people with emotional/behavioural difficulties or difficulties with language and learning may become disaffected, and teaching citizenship and issues of personal and social responsibility to disaffected young people 'can be particularly challenging unless it is delivered in a way that is relevant to their lives' (2003, p. 138). Effective teaching depends on both a caring and inclusive school ethos and on the willingness of teachers to pay attention to factors like social skills, motivation, self esteem and belonging. Only in such a context are children with special needs likely to develop the trust and confidence necessary to express their views and engage in problem solving. But it is clear that when schools create such a context they are at the same time making a significant contribution to children's learning about values like social justice and inclusion that are central to citizenship.

Nevertheless, there are other areas where citizenship can operate as a mechanism of exclusion as well as of inclusion (Lister, 1997, p. 4). Let us take the example of Muslims in the UK, since they are a group suffering from multiple socio-economic disadvantages, racial and religious prejudice, low achievement levels in school and low employment levels in the community (Halstead, 2005b). What can Citizenship Education do to improve community cohesion and the fuller integration of Muslims into the broader society? It is clear that social cohesion will not be achieved without social justice and respect for minority communities. Muslim children (and indeed children from any faith group) must not be put in a position where they are expected to act against their core beliefs and values. School policies against Islamophobia and other forms of prejudice and discrimination must be developed and implemented. The linguistic and cultural skills of minorities must be celebrated, not problematized. Learning about (and respecting) other cultures must be seen as enriching to everyone, not as a 'concession' to minority groups. The 'us-and-them' mentality (whether this is black versus white, child versus adult, Muslim versus non-Muslim) must be broken down, within the hidden curriculum as well as the formal curriculum, so that children do not pick up unintended negative messages. We were shocked (and so were many of the children) in a school visited recently when a teacher spoke to the children of the fear she felt if she found herself sitting in front of a person of Arab/Muslim appearance on public transport. Some schools have a long way to go in helping children to understand and appreciate multicultural citizenship.

Gender is another area where it has been claimed that Citizenship is more about domination than social justice. Yuval-Davies says that 'the liberal definition of citizenship constructs all citizens as basically the same and considers the differences of class, ethnicity and gender and so on as irrelevant to their status as citizens' (quoted in Dillabough and Arnot, 2004, p. 158). The formal equality of men and women as citizens does not do away with differences of power and dominance, and the way that citizenship is defined (largely by men) tends inevitably to privilege men and marginalize women. The gulf that exists between men's and women's values has been well researched and documented (Gilligan, 1982), and appears to develop early in life (Halstead and Waite, 2001a). In relation to citizenship, the problem is that the rhetoric is based on gender-neutrality, but the reality is gender differentiation, with more emphasis placed on 'masculine' concepts like justice and rights, and less on 'feminine' concepts like caring and interdependence. Lister (1997, ch. 4) argues that such binary oppositions are themselves unhelpful, and that a more 'woman-friendly' understanding of citizenship is needed which at the same time recognizes the differences that exist between women.

Preparing citizens for an uncertain future

We should not be satisfied with teaching Citizenship as if the future is going to be pretty much the same as the present. Developments in recent years in communication and even in language itself since the advent of the mobile phone, e-mail communication and the Internet suggest that some aspects of life are in the process of very rapid change. In view of increasing globalization, we need to consider how long schools will be able to continue to define citizenship primarily in terms of membership of a nation-state. How long will current economic patterns survive? What will be the impact of the expanding world population? What new political alliances will emerge, what new wars, what new exploitations? By how much will life expectancy increase? What new technologies will develop as non-renewable resources are used up?

If contemporary society is increasingly marked out by rapid social and cultural transformations, including the globalization of information and economic enterprise, the emphasis on consumption, the privatization of public enterprises, job insecurity, the arrival of the digital age, the decline in state provision of welfare, the dominance of the electronic media and the breakdown of old certainties, we need to ask what impact all of these will have on our understanding of citizenship. Postmodern critics such as Baudrillard (1983) claim that society is being replaced by the hyper-reality of virtual cities and imagined communities and that politics is being reduced to a television spectacle, a set of sound-bites and a series of manipulations by spin-doctors (cf. Bauman, 1992, p. 151). Poster suggests that individuals are no longer citizens of a rationally ordered state, eager to maximize their civil rights, nor yet proletarians anticipating the onset of communism, but merely passive consumers faced with a myriad of advertising images and self-referential signs (1995, p. 112). In such a world, it is easy to see modernist conceptions of citizenship and individual moral autonomy being 'lost in the face of the media's fragmented rendition of the world' (Gilbert, 1997, p. 71).

Or is it? Bauman argues persuasively that we *can* regain truly human forms of moral agency in the postmodern age, not by giving children 'the learnable knowledge of rules' (1993, p. 11) based on rational, law-oriented ethics, but by looking for alternative conceptions of moral responsibility based on human spontaneity, ambiguity and wonder. Wilson argues that both perspectives on morality are equally important – the interpersonal dimension which emphasizes social norms and rules which operate for our mutual benefit in society (1990, pp. 47–9), and the personal (and often religious) dimension concerned with 'the basic ecology . . . of human desires, emotions and deeds' and 'the state of our soul' (ibid., pp. 82–8; cf. McLaughlin and Halstead, 2000). Perhaps the distinctiveness of morality as a form of thought lies in the fusion of these two dimensions. However, it is clear that the skills of critical reflection and the creative use of the imagination that have been emphasized throughout the present volume are central to the process of both moral development and the preparation of citizens for an unknown future. We have also argued that there are lasting, universal values that lie at the heart of morality; that morality paves the way for both an enriched understanding and a critique of Citizenship in schools; and that Citizenship and Moral Education of the kind we have described will together help children to face with confidence the moral and civic challenges they will undoubtedly face in the future.

Bibliography

Abrams, M., Gerard, D. and Timms, N. (1985) *Values and Social Change in Britain*, London: Macmillan.

Achebe, C. (1971) *Beware Soul Brother*, London: Heinemann African Writers Series.

Advisory Group for Education (2000) *Citizenship for 16–19-year-olds in Education and Training. Report of the Advisory Group to the Secretary of State for Education and Employment*, Coventry: Further Education Funding Council.

Advisory Group on Citizenship (1998) *Education for Citizenship and the Teaching of Democracy in Schools: final report of the advisory group on citizenship*, London: QCA.

Andrews, G. (1991) 'Introduction', in G. Andrews (ed.) *Citizenship*, London: Lawrence and Wishart.

Applebaum, B. (1995) 'Creating a trusting atmosphere in the classroom', *Educational Theory*, 45, 4: 443–52.

Aristotle (1953) *Nicomachean Ethics*, Harmondsworth: Penguin.

Aristotle (1962) *Nichomachean Ethics*, tr. M. Ostwald, Indianapolis: Liberal Arts Press.

Arnold, M. (1879/1988) 'Preface to Wordsworth's poems', in R. Selden (ed.) *The Theory of Criticism – From Plato to the Present*, London and New York: Longman.

Arthur, J. (1994) 'The ambiguities of Catholic schooling', *Westminster Studies in Education*, 17: 65–77.

Arthur, J. and Wright, D. (2001) *Teaching Citizenship in the Secondary School*, London: David Fulton.

Attanucci, J. (1991) 'Changing subjects: growing up and growing older', *Journal of Moral Education*, 20, 3: 317–28.

Auden, W. H. (1968) *Secondary Worlds*, New York: Random House.

Augustine (1958) *The City of God*, tr. G. G. Walsh, Garden City, New York: Image Books.

Ayer, A. J. (1936) *Language, Truth and Logic*, London: Gollancz.

Bakhtin, M. M. (1981) *The Dialogic Imagination*, ed. M. Holquist, Austin: University of Texas Press.

Barker, D., Halman, L. and Vloet, A. (1992) *The European Values Study 1981–1990*, Aberdeen: Gordon Cook Foundation for European Values Group.

Batho, G. (1990) 'The history of the teaching of civics and citizenship in English schools', *The Curriculum Journal*, 1, 1: 91–100.

Battistich, V., Watson, M., Solomon, D., Schaps, E. and Soloman, J. (1989) 'The Child Development Project: a comprehensive programme for the development of prosocial character', in W. M. Kurtines and J. L. Gewirtz (eds) *Moral Behaviour and Development: Advances in Research, Theory and Applications*, Hillsdale, NJ: Erlbaum.

Baudrillard, J. (1983) *Simulations*, New York: Semiotext(e).

Baudrillard, J. (1992) *The Transparency of Evil*, London: Verso.

Bauman, Z. (1992) *Intimations of Postmodernity*, London: Routledge.

Bauman, Z. (1993) *Post-modern Ethics*, Oxford: Blackwell.

Bauman, Z. (1994) *Alone Again: ethics after certainty*, London: Demos.

Baumfield, V. (2003) 'Democratic RE: preparing young people for citizenship', *British Journal of Religious Education*, 25, 3: 173–84.

Beck, C. (1990) *Better Schools: A Values Perspective*, London: Falmer Press.

Beck, J. (1998) *Morality and Citizenship in Education*, London: Cassell.

Beiner, R. (1995) *Theorizing Citizenship*, Albany, NY: State University of New York Press.

Bell, D. 'Citizenship', paper presented at Hansard Society Conference, Ofsted lecture, January 2005. Available at http://www.ofsted.gov.uk/publications (accessed 30 August 2005).

Bennett, W. J. (1993) *The Book of Virtues: a Treasury of Great Moral Stories*, New York: Simon and Schuster.

Bentham, J. (1799/1948) *Introduction to Principles of Morals and Legislation*, New York: Hafner.

Benton, M. (1995) 'From "A Rake's Progress" to "Rosie's Walk": lessons in aesthetic reading', *Journal of Aesthetic Education*, 29, 1: 33–46.

Berlin, I. (1969) *Four Essays on Liberty*, London: Oxford University Press.

Berlin, I. (1991) *The Crooked Timber of Humanity*, New York: Alfred Knopf.

Best, R. and Curran, C. (1995) *The Caring Teacher in the Junior School: a Case Study and Discussion*, London: Roehampton Institute.

Blackman, S. and France, A. (2001) 'Youth Marginality under "Postmodernism"', in N. Stevenson (ed.) *Culture and Citizenship*, London: Sage.

Blatt, M. M. and Kohlberg, L. (1975) 'The effects of classroom moral discussion upon children's level of moral judgement', *Journal of Moral Education*, 4, 2: 129–61.

Blaycock, L. (ed.) (2002) *Secondary RE and Citizenship: towards an open frontier*, Birmingham: Christian Education Publications.

Bloom, A. (1987) *The Closing of the American Mind*, London: Penguin.

Bloom, H. (1994) *The Western Canon: The Books and School of the Ages*, New York: Harcourt and Brace.

Boss, J. (1994) 'The effect of community service work on the moral development of college ethics students', *Journal of Moral Education*, 23, 2: 183–98.

Bottery, M. (2003) 'The end of citizenship? The nation state, threats to its legitimacy and Citizenship Education in the twenty-first century', *Cambridge Journal of Education*, 33, 1: 101–22.

Bourn, D. (2004) 'Development education and science education', *School Science Review*, 86, 314: 87–92.

Broadbent, L. (2004) 'Values education, citizenship and the contribution of RE', in R. Bailey (ed.) *Teaching Values and Citizenship Across the Curriculum: educating children for the world*, London: RoutledgeFalmer.

Brown, A. and E. (1999) 'Religious Education', in S. Bigger and E. Brown (eds) *Spiritual, Moral, Social and Cultural Education: exploring values in the curriculum*, London: David Fulton.

Brown, G. (2004) British Council Annual Lecture, 7 July. Available at http://politics.guardian.co.uk/labour/story/0,9061,125655000.html (accessed 18 August 2005).

Buckingham, D. (2000) *The Making of Citizens – Young People, News and Politics*, London: Routledge.

Bulmer, M. and Rees, A. M. (eds) (1996) *Citizenship Today: the contemporary relevance of T. H. Marshall*, London: University College London Press.

Burns, G. (1992) *The Frontiers of Catholicism: the Politics of Ideology in a Liberal World*, Berkeley: University of California Press.

Burtonwood, N. (1995) 'Beyond local cultures: towards a cosmopolitan art education', *Journal of Art and Design Education*, 14: 205–12.

Burtonwood, N. (2000) 'Must liberal support for separate schools be subject to a condition of individual autonomy?' *British Journal of Educational Studies*, 48, 3: 269–84.

Burtonwood, N. (2003) 'Isaiah Berlin, diversity liberalism, and education', *Educational Review*, 55, 3: 323–31.

Buzzelli, C. A. (1992) 'Young children's moral understanding: learning about right and wrong', *Young Children*, 47, 6: 47–53.

Byatt, A. S. (1998) 'Hauntings', in B. Cox (ed.) *Literacy is not enough*, Manchester: Manchester University Press.

Cairns, J. and Gardner, R. (2003) 'Assessment in Citizenship', in L. Gearon (ed.) *Learning to Teach Citizenship in the Secondary School*, London: RoutledgeFalmer.

Callan, E. (1997) *Creating Citizens: Political Education and Liberal Democracy*, Oxford: Clarendon Press.

Cameron, L. (2003) *Writing in English as an additional language at Key Stage 4 and post-16*, London: Ofsted.

Carr, D. (1991) *Educating the Virtues: an essay on the philosophical psychology of moral development and education*, London: Routledge.

Carr, D. (1993) 'Moral values and the teacher: beyond the paternal and the permissive', *Journal of Philosophy of Education*, 27, 2: 193–207.

Carr, D. and Steutel, J. (eds) (1999) *Virtue Ethics and Moral Education*, London: Routledge.

Carrington, V. (2002) *New Times: New Families*, Dordrecht: Kluwer Academic Press.

Chaskin, R. J. and Rauner, D. M. (1995) 'Youth and caring: an introduction', *Phi Delta Kappan*, 76, 9: 667–74.

Claire, H. (2001) *Not Aliens: primary school children and the Citizenship/PSHE curriculum*, Stoke on Trent: Trentham.

Claire, H. (2004) *Teaching Citizenship in Primary Schools*, Exeter: Learning Matters.

Clark, N. (2004) 'Citizenship and ecological obligations', in J. Demaine (ed.) *Citizenship and Political Education Today*, New York: Palgrave Macmillan.

Coady, C. A. J. (ed.) (2005) Special Issue: Moralism, *Journal of Applied Philosophy*, 22: 2.

Colby, A. and Kohlberg, L. (1987) *The Measurement of Moral Judgement, Volume 1: Theoretical Foundations and Research Validation*, Cambridge: Cambridge University Press.

Coles, R. (1989) *The Call of Stories: Teaching and the Moral Imagination*, Boston: Houghton Mifflin Co.

Conover, P. J., Crewe, I. M. and Searing, D. D. (1999) 'The nature of citizenship in the United States and Great Britain: empirical comments on theoretical themes', *Journal of Politics*, 53: 801–27.

Cooper, D. E. (1999) *Existentialism: a reconstruction*, Oxford: Blackwell.

Costa, M. V. (2004) 'Rawlsian civic education: political not minimal', *Journal of Applied Philosophy*, 21, 1: 1–14.

Cottingham, M. (2005) 'Developing spirituality through the use of literature in history education', *International Journal of Children's Spirituality*, 10, 1: 45–60.

Cowley, S. (2001) *Getting the Buggers to Behave*, London: Continuum.

Cox, C. and Scruton, R. (1984) *Peace Studies: a critical survey*, London: Institute for European Defence and Strategic Studies.

Cox, W. (1997) 'Lessons about education that Christianity can learn from a defector', *Journal of Education and Christian Belief*, 1, 2: 111–18.

Cox, W. F. (2000) 'Relationship of enlightenment to the cultural mandate for a Biblical view of education', *Journal of Research on Christian Education*, 9: 1.

Crick, B. (1998a) 'Values education for democracy and citizenship', in D. Christie, H. Maitles and J. Halliday (eds) *Values Education for Democracy and Citizenship*, Aberdeen: Gordon Cook Foundation.

Crick, B. (ed.) (1998b) *Education for Citizenship and the Teaching of Democracy in Schools*, London: QCA.

Crick, B. (2000a) *Essays on Citizenship*, London: Continuum.

Crick, B. (2000b) 'The Citizenship Order for schools', in N. Pearce and J. Hallgarten (eds) *Tomorrow's Citizens: critical debates in citizenship and education*, London: Institute for Public Policy Research.

Crick, B. (ed.) (2001) 'Citizens: towards a citizenship culture', *The Political Quarterly*, Oxford: Blackwell.

Crick, B. and Porter, A. (eds) (1978) *Political Education and Political Literacy*, London: Longman.

Cross, M. (2000) 'Key assessment issues', in N. Pearce and J. Hallgarten (eds) *Tomorrow's Citizens: critical debates in citizenship and education*, London: Institute for Public Policy Research.

Crystal, D. (1995) *The Cambridge Encyclopaedia of the English Language*, Cambridge: Cambridge University Press.

Csikszentmihalyi, M. and McCormack, J. (1986) 'The influence of teachers', *Phi Delta Kappan*, February, 415–19.

Cunningham, J. (2000) 'Democratic practice in a secondary school', in A. Osler (ed.) *Citizenship and democracy in schools: diversity, identity, equality*, Stoke on Trent: Trentham Books.

Davies, C. (1996) *What is English Teaching?* Buckingham: Open University Press.

Davies, I. (2004) 'Science and Citizenship Education', *International Journal of Science Education*, 26, 14: 1751–63.

Davies, I. and Sobisch, A. (1997) *Developing European Citizens*, Sheffield: Sheffield Hallam University Press.

Davies, I., Gregory, I. and Riley, S. C. (1999) *Good Citizenship and Educational Provision*, London: Falmer Press.

Day, J. M. (1991) 'Role-taking reconsidered: narrative and cognitive-developmental interpretations of moral growth', *Journal of Moral Education*, 20, 3: 305–15.

Day, J. M. (2002) '"Putting yourself in other people's shoes": the use of Forum theatre to explore refugee and homeless issues in schools', *Journal of Moral Education*, 31, 1: 21–34.

Deakin Crick, R., Coates, M., Taylor, M. and Ritchie, S. (2004) 'A systematic review of the impact of citizenship education on the provision of schooling', in *Research Evidence in Education Library*, London: EPPI-Centre, Social Science Research Unit, Institute of Education.

Deakin Crick, R., Taylor, M., Tew, M., Samuel, E., Durant, K. and Ritchie, S. (2005) 'A systematic review of the impact of citizenship education on student learning and achievement', in *Research Evidence in Education Library*, London: EPPI-Centre, Social Science Research Unit, Institute of Education.

Demaine, J. (2004) 'Citizenship education and globalization', in J. Demaine (ed.) *Citizenship and Political Education Today*, New York: Palgrave Macmillan.

Department for Education and Employment (1999) *Preparing Young People for Adult Life: a report of the National Advisory Group on Personal, Social and Health Education*, London: DfES.

Department for Education and Employment/Qualifications and Curriculum Authority (1999b) *The National Curriculum: a handbook for primary teachers in England – key stages 1 and 2*, London: DfEE/QCA.

Department for Education and Employment/Qualifications and Curriculum Authority (1999c) *The National Curriculum: a handbook for secondary teachers in England – key stages 3 and 4*, London: DfEE/QCA.

Department for Education and Employment/Qualifications and Curriculum Authority (2001) *Key Stage 3 National Strategy: Framework for Teaching English: years 7, 8 and 9*, DfEE 0019/2001, London: HMSO.

Department of Education and Science (1967) *Towards World History*, pamphlet no. 52, London: HMSO.

Department for Education and Skills (2002a) *Access and Engagement in English: Teaching Pupils for whom English is an Additional Language (Key Stage 3 National Strategy)*, (Ref 0609/2002), London: HMSO.

Department for Education and Skills (2002b) *Unlocking Potential – raising ethnic minority achievement at Key Stage 3*, London: HMSO.

Department for Education and Skills (2003) *Aiming High: Raising the Achievement of Minority Ethnic Pupils*, (Ref 0183/2003), London: HMSO.

Department for Education and Skills (2004a) *Aiming High: Understanding the educational needs of minority ethnic pupils in mainly white schools*, (Ref 0416/2004), London: HMSO.

Department for Education and Skills (2004b) *Key Stage 3 National Strategy ICT across the curriculum – ICT in Citizenship*, (Ref 0197/2004 G), London: HMSO.

Department for Education and Skills (2004c) *Literacy in Citizenship*, (Ref 0258/2004), London: HMSO.

Devlin, P. (1965) *The Enforcement of Morals*, Oxford: Oxford University Press.

Devon County Council (2001) *The Devon, Plymouth and Torbay Agreed Syllabus for Religious Education*, Exeter: Devon County Council.

Dewey, J. (1916/2002) *Democracy and Education*, New York: Free Press.

Dillabough, J.-A. and Arnot, M. (2004) 'A magnified image of female citizenship in education: illusions of democracy or liberal challenges to symbolic domination?' in J. Demaine (ed.) *Citizenship and Political Education Today*, New York: Palgrave Macmillan.

Donnelly, J. (2004) 'Humanizing Science Education', available at www.interscience.wiley.com (accessed 30 August 2005).

Draycott, P. (ed.) (2002) *Primary RE and Citizenship*, Birmingham: Christian Education.

Dunn, J. (1987) 'The beginnings of moral understanding: development in the second year', in J. Kagan and S. Lamb (eds) *The Emergence of Morality in Young Children*, London: University of Chicago Press.

Dunn, J. (1988) *The Beginnings of Social Understanding*, Oxford: Blackwell.

Dworkin, R. (1978) 'Liberalism', in S. Hampshire (ed.) *Public and Private Morality*, Cambridge: Cambridge University Press.

Edmonds, M. (2005) 'Science and the citizen', *Teaching Citizenship*, 10: 30–33.

Edwards, D. and Mercer, N. (1987) *Common Knowledge*, London: Routledge.

Elias, J. L. (1989) *Moral Education: Secular and Religious*, Malabar: Robert E. Krieger.

Elicker, J. and Fortner-Wood, C. (1995) 'Adult-child relationships in early childhood programmes', *Young Children*, 51, 2: 69–78.

Eliot, T. S. (1935) 'Religion and literature', *Selected Essays*, London: Faber.

Elliott, J. (2000) 'Revising the National Curriculum: a comment on the Secretary of State's proposals', *Journal of Educational Policy*, 15, 2: 247–55.

Emler, N. and Reicher, S. (1987) 'Orientations to institutional authority in adolescence', *Journal of Moral Education*, 16, 2: 108–16

Engle, S. H. and Ochoa, A. S. (1988) *Education for Democratic Citizenship*, New York: Teachers College Press.

Ennis, R. H. (1995) *Critical Thinking*, Upper Saddle River, NJ: Prentice Hall.

Evans, J. (1990) 'Teacher-child interaction during yard duty: the Australian experience', *Education 3–13*, 18, 2: 48–54.

Fahim Khan, M. (1995) *Essays in Islamic Economics*, Leicester: Islamic Foundation.

Farrer, F. (2000) *A Quiet Revolution: encouraging practice values in our children*, London: Rider Books.

Finnis, J. (1980) *Natural Law and Natural Rights*, Oxford: Clarendon Press.

Fishkin, J. S. (1984) *Beyond Subjective Morality*, New Haven, CT: Yale University Press.

Foster, V. (1997) 'Feminist theory and the construction of citizenship education', in K. Kennedy (ed.) *Citizenship Education and the Modern State*, London: Falmer Press.

Foucault, M. (1977a) *Discipline and Punish*, London: Allen Lane.

Foucault, M. (1977b) 'Nietzsche, genealogy, history', in D. Bouchard (ed.) *Language, Counter-memory, Practise*, Ithaca, NY: Cornell University Press.

Foucault, M. (1988) *Politics, Philosophy, Culture: Interviews and Other Writings, 1977–1984*, tr. A. Sheridan and others, New York and London: Routledge.

Francis, L. J. and Kay, W. K. (1995) *Teenage Religion and Values*, Leominster: Gracewing/Fowler Wright.

Franks, A. (1999) 'Where the action is: how drama contributes to the art of the teaching and learning of English', *English in Education*, 33, 2: 39–49.

Frazer, E. (2000) 'Citizenship Education: anti-political culture and political education in Britain', *Political Studies*, 48: 88–103.

Freathy, R. (2004) 'Religious Education and education for citizenship: religious traditionalism versus secular progressivism', paper presented at the University of Exeter, September.

Freeden, M. (1978) *The New Liberalism*, Oxford: Clarendon Press.

Friere, P. and Macedo, S. (1987) *Literacy: Reading the Word and World*, South Hadley, MA: Bergin and Garvey.

Gaarder, J. (1994) *Sophie's World*, London: Phoenix House.

Gallagher, S. V. and Lundin, R. (1989) *Literature through the Eyes of Faith*, San Francisco: HarperCollins.

Galston, W. (1989) 'Civic education and the liberal state', in N. L. Rosenblum (ed.) *Liberalism and the Moral Life*, Cambridge, MA: Harvard University Press.

Gardner, H. (1949) *The Art of T. S. Eliot*, London: Faber.

Garner, P. (1992) 'Involving "disruptive" pupils in school discipline structures', *Pastoral Care*, 10, 3: 13–19.

Giddens, A. (2000) 'Citizenship in the global era', in N. Pearce and J. Hallgarten (eds) *Tomorrow's Citizens: critical debates in citizenship and education*, London: Institute for Public Policy Research.

Gilbert, R. (1992) 'Citizenship, education and postmodernity', *British Journal of Sociology of Education*, 13, 1: 51–68.

Gilbert, R. (1997) 'Issues for citizenship in a post-modern world', in K. Kennedy (ed.) *Citizenship Education and the Modern State*, London: Falmer Press.

Gilligan, C. (1982) *In a Different Voice: Psychological Theory and Women's Moral Development*, Cambridge, MA: Harvard University Press.

Grainger, T. (1998) 'Drama and reading: illuminating their interaction', *English in Education*, 32, 1: 29–36.

Great Britain. Statutes (1988) *Education Reform Act 1988*. Chapter 40. (Part 1. 2 (b)) London: HMSO.

Graham, G. (1994) 'Liberal vs radical feminism revisited', *Journal of Applied Philosophy* 11, 2: 155–70.

Grimmitt, M. (1987) *Religious Education and Human Development*, Great Wakering: McCrimmon.

Grimmitt, M. (2000) *Pedagogies of Religious Education*, Great Wakering: McCrimmon.

Grusec, J. E. and Dix, T. (1986) 'The socialisation of pro-social behaviour: theory and reality', in C. Zahn-Waxler, E. M. Cummings and R. Iannotti (eds) *Altruism and Aggression: Biological and Social Origins*, Cambridge: Cambridge University Press.

Gutmann, A. (1980) *Liberal Equality*, Cambridge: Cambridge University Press.

Gutmann, A. (1987) *Democratic Education*, Princeton, NJ: Princeton University Press.

Haberman, M. (1994) 'Gentle teaching in a violent society', *Educational Horizons*, 72, 3: 131–5.

Hahn, C. L. (1998) *Becoming Political: comparative perspectives on citizenship education*, Albany, NY: State University of New York Press.

Hall, K. (2003) *Listening to Stephen Read – multiple perspectives on literacy*, Buckingham: Open University Press.

Hall, S. (2000) 'Multicultural citizens, monocultural citizenship?' in N. Pearce and J. Hallgarten (eds) *Tomorrow's Citizens: critical debates in citizenship and education*, London: Institute for Public Policy Research.

Halstead, J. M. (1995a) 'Voluntary apartheid? Problems of schooling for religious and other minorities in democratic societies', *Journal of Philosophy of Education*, 29, 2: 257–72.

Halstead, J. M. (1995b) 'Should schools reinforce children's religious identity?' *Religious Education*, 90, 3–4: 360–76.

Halstead, J. M. (1996) 'Values and values education in schools', in J. M. Halstead and M. J. Taylor (eds) *Values in Education and Education in Values*, London: Falmer Press.

Halstead, J. M. (1998) 'Should homosexuality be taught as an acceptable alternative lifestyle? A Muslim perspective', *Cambridge Journal of Education*, 28, 1: 49–64.

Halstead, J. M. (1999a) 'Moral education in family life: the effects of diversity', *Journal of Moral Education*, 28, 3: 265–81.

Halstead, J. M. (1999b) 'Teaching about homosexuality: a response to John Beck', *Cambridge Journal of Education*, 29, 1: 131–6.

Halstead, J. M. (2001) 'Baudrillard, simulation and the debate about worship in schools', in L. J. Francis, J. Astley and M. Robbins (eds) *The Fourth R for the Third Millennium: education in religion and values for the global future*, Dublin: Lindisfarne Books.

Halstead, J. M. (2003) 'Schooling and cultural maintenance for religious minorities in the liberal state', in K. McDonough and W. Feinberg (eds) *Collective Identities and Cosmopolitan Values: group rights and public education in liberal democratic societies*, New York: Oxford University Press.

Halstead, J. M. (2004) 'An Islamic concept of education', *Comparative Education*, 40, 4: 517–29.

Halstead J. M. (2005a) 'Liberal values and liberal education', in W. Carr (ed.) *The RoutledgeFalmer Reader in Philosophy of Education*, London: Routledge.

Halstead, J. M. (2005b) 'Muslims in the UK and education', in T. Choudhury (ed.) *Muslims in the UK: Policies for Engaged Citizens*, Budapest and New York: Open Society Institute.

Halstead, J. M. (2005c) 'Teaching about love', *British Journal of Educational Studies*, 53, 3: 290–305.

Halstead, J. M. (2006) 'Does Citizenship Education make moral education redundant?' in L. Lo, J. Lee and R. Cheng (eds) *Values Education for Citizens in the New Century*, Hong Kong: Hong Kong Institute for Educational Research.

Halstead, J. M. and McLaughlin, T. H. (2005) 'Are faith schools divisive?' in R. Gardner, J. Cairns and D. Lawton (eds) *Faith Schools: consensus or conflict?* London: RoutledgeFalmer.

Halstead, J. M. and Outram Halstead, A. (2004) 'Awe, tragedy and the human condition', *International Journal of Children's Spirituality*, 9, 2: 163–77.

Halstead, J. M. and Reiss, M. J. (2003) *Values in Sex Education: from principles to practice*, London: RoutledgeFalmer.

Halstead, J. M. and Taylor, M. J. (2000a) *The Development of Values, Attitudes and Personal Qualities: a review of recent research*, Slough: National Foundation for Educational Research.

Halstead, J. M. and Taylor, M. J. (2000b) 'Learning and teaching about values: a review of recent research', *Cambridge Journal of Education*, 30, 2: 169–202.

Halstead, J. M and Waite, S. (2001a) '"Living in different worlds": gender differences in the developing sexual values and attitudes of primary school children', *Sex Education*, 1: 59–76.

Halstead, J. M and Waite, S. (2001b) 'Nurturing the spiritual in children's sexual development', *International Journal of Children's Spirituality*, 6: 185–206.

Hansen, D. T. (1992) 'From role to person: the moral layeredness of classroom teaching', *American Educational Research Journal*, 30, 4: 651–74.

Hansen, D. T. (1993a) 'The emergence of a shared morality in a classroom', *Curriculum Inquiry*, 22, 4: 345–61.

Hansen, D. T. (1993b) 'The moral importance of the teacher's style', *Journal of Curriculum Studies*, 25, 5: 397–421.

Hare, R. M. (1979) 'Language and moral education', in D. B. Cochrane, C. M. Hamm and A. C. Kazeides (eds) *The Domain of Moral Education*, New York: Paulist Press.

Hargreaves, D. H. (1994) *The Mosaic of Learning: schools and teachers for the next century*, London: Demos.

Harman, G. and Jarvis-Thomson, J. (1996) *Moral Relativism and Moral Objectivity*, Oxford: Blackwell.

Harris, K. (1979) *Education and Knowledge*, London: Routledge and Kegan Paul.

Harris, P. L. (1989) *Children and Emotion. The Development of Psychological Understanding*, Oxford: Blackwell.

Harrison, C. (2004) *Understanding Reading Development*, London: Sage/Paul Chapman.

Hart, A. (2001) 'Awkward practice: teaching media', *Changing English – studies in reading and culture*, 8, 1: 65–81.

Hart, H. L. A. (1963) *Law, Liberty and Morality*, Oxford: Oxford University Press.

Hart, H. L. A. (1984) 'Are there any natural rights?' in J. Waldron (ed.) *Theories of Rights*, Oxford: Oxford University Press.

Hartas, D. (2003) 'Special Educational Needs in Citizenship', in L. Gearon (ed.) *Learning to Teach Citizenship in the Secondary School*, London: RoutledgeFalmer.

Hawkes, N. (2001) *Being a School of Excellence: Values-based Education*, Oxford: Oxfordshire County Council Education Service.

Haydon, D. (1999) *What is Citizenship?*, Cambridge: Polity Press.

Haydon, G. (2000a) 'The moral agenda of Citizenship Education', in R. Gardner (ed.) *Citizenship and Education*, London: Kogan Page.

Haydon, G. (2000b) 'John Wilson and the place of morality in education', *Journal of Moral Education*, 29, 3: 355–65.

Hayek, F. A. (1960) *The Constitution of Liberty*, London: Routledge and Kegan Paul.

Hayes, D. (1993) 'The good, the bad, the ugly and the memorable: a retrospective view of teacher-pupil relationships', *Education 3–13*, 21, 1: 53–9.

Heater, D. (1980) *World Studies: education for international understanding in Britain*, London: Harrap.

Heater, D. (1990) *Citizenship: the civic ideal in world history, politics and education*, London: Longman.

Heater, D. (2001) 'The history of citizenship education in England', *The Curriculum Journal*, 12, 1: 103–23.

Hicks, D. (1988) *Education for Peace: Issues, principles and action in the classroom*, London: Routledge.

Hills-Potter, P. (2004) 'The art of citizenship', *Teaching Citizenship*, Issue 9, Summer: 39–43.

Hilton, M. (2003) 'Mary Hilton's observations, suggestions and theoretical perspectives', in K. Hall (ed.) *Listening to Stephen Read – multiple perspectives on literacy*, Buckingham: Open University Press.

Hirsch, E. D. (1987) *Cultural Literacy: what every American needs to know*, Boston, MA: Houghton Mifflin.

Hirst, P. H. (1974) *Moral Education in a Secular Society*, London: Hodder and Stoughton.

Hobbes, T. (1651/1996) *Leviathan*, Oxford: Oxford University Press.

Hoekema, A. (1986) *Created in God's Image*, Grand Rapids: Eerdmans.

Hoffmeister, F. (2004) 'European rights: citizen rights or human rights?' in J. Demaine (ed.) *Citizenship and Political Education Today*, New York: Palgrave Macmillan.

Houghton, B. (1998) *The Good Child: how to instil a sense of right and wrong in your child*, London: Headline.

Housego, E. and Burns, C. (1994) 'Are you sitting too comfortably? A critical look at circle time in primary classrooms', *English in Education*, 28, 2: 23–9.

Hull, J. M. (2001) *Religious Education in Schools: Ideas and Experiences from around the world*, Oxford: International Association for Religious Freedom.

Hume, D. (1739/2000) *A Treatise of Human Nature*, Oxford: Oxford University Press.

Husbands, C. (1996) *What is History Teaching? Language, ideas and meaning in learning about the past*, Birmingham: Open University Press.

Hutcheon, L. (2003) *The Politics of Postmodernism*, London: Routledge.

Iakobson, S. G. and Moreva, G. I. (1992) 'Preschoolers' self-image and moral behaviour', *Russian Education and Society*, 34, 2: 5–21.

Ibrahim, T. (2005) 'Global citizenship education: mainstreaming the curriculum', *Cambridge Journal of Education*, 35, 2: 177–94.

Ichilov, O. (ed.) (1998) *Citizenship and Citizenship Education in a Changing World*, London: Woburn Press.

Ignatieff, M. (1991) 'Citizenship and moral narcissism', in G. Andrews (ed.) *Citizenship*, London: Lawrence and Wishart.

Iser, W. (1971) 'Indeterminacy and the reader's response in prose fiction', in J. Hillis Miller (ed.) *Aspects of Narrative: Selected Papers from the English Institute*, New York: Columbia University Press.

Isin, E. F. and Wood, P. K. (1999) *Citizenship and Identity*, London: Sage.

Jackson, P. W. (1992) 'The enactment of the moral in what teachers do', *Curriculum Inquiry*, 22, 4: 401–7.

Jackson, P. W., Boostrom, R. E. and Hansen, D. T. (1993) *The Moral Life of Schools*, San Francisco: Jossey-Bass.

Jackson, R. (2002) 'Editorial: Religious education and education for citizenship', *British Journal of Religious Education*, 24, 3: 162–9.

Jackson, R. (ed.) (2003) *International Perspectives on Citizenship, Education and Religious Diversity*, London: RoutledgeFalmer.

Jassat, A. (2003) 'British citizenship tests', *Khilafah Magazine*, October issue.

Jauss, H. R. (1982) *Toward an Aesthetic of Reception*, trans. T. Bahti, Minneapolis, MN: University of Minnesota Press.

John, P. D. and Osborne, A. (1992) 'The influence of school ethos on pupils' citizenship attitudes', *Educational Review*, 44, 2: 153–65.

Johnston, D. K. (1991) 'Cheating: reflections on a moral dilemma', *Journal of Moral Education*, 20, 3: 283–91.

Jones, A. (ed.) (1998) *Science in Faith: A Christian Perspective on Teaching Science*, Romford, Essex: Christian Schools Trust (CST).

Kagan, J. (1984) *The Nature of the Child*, New York: Basic Books.

Kagan, J. and Lamb, S. (1987) *The Emergence of Morality in Young Children*, London: University of Chicago Press.

Kant, I. (1784) 'Idee zu einer allgemeinen Geschichte in weltburgerlicher Absicht' (The idea of a general history of world citizenship aims), *Philosophische Bibliothek*, Vol. 24, Leipzig: Felix Meiner.

Kant, I. (1785/1948) *The Moral Law*, London: Hutchinson.

Kekes, J. (1999) 'Pluralism, moral imagination and moral education', in J. M. Halstead and T. H. McLaughlin (eds) *Education in Morality*, London: Routledge.

Kerr, D. (1999) 'Re-examining citizenship education in England', in J. Torney-Purta, J. Schwille and J.-A. Amadeo (eds) *Civic Education across Countries: 24 Case Studies from the IEA Civic Education Project*, Amsterdam: Eburon Publishers for IEA.

Kerr, D. (2003) 'Citizenship: local, national and international', in L. Gearon (ed.) *Learning to Teach Citizenship in the Secondary School*, London: RoutledgeFalmer.

Kerr, D., Cleaver, E., Ireland, E. and Blenkinsop, S. (2003) *Citizenship Education Longitudinal Study. First cross-sectional survey 2001–2003*, London: DfES.

Kerr, D., Ireland, E., Lopes, J. and Craig, R. with Cleaver, E. (2004) *Making Citizenship Education Real – Citizenship Education Longitudinal Study: Second Annual Report: First Longitudinal Survey, DfES Research Report 531*, London: DfES.

Kilpatrick, W. (1992) *Why Johnny Can't Tell Right from Wrong: Moral Illiteracy and the Case for Character Education*, New York: Simon and Schuster.

King, A. (2005) 'Fair play and tolerance stand out', *Daily Telegraph*, 27 July: 12.

Kirk, P. (2004) 'Mapping the contours of faith in the land of separation: spiritual geographies for children', *International Journal of Children's Spirituality*, 9, 2: 189–202.

Kohlberg, L. (1969) 'Stage and sequence: the cognitive developmental approach to socialisation', in D. Gosling (ed.) *Handbook of Socialisation, Theory and Research*, Chicago: Rand McNally.

Kohlberg, L. (1971) 'From is to ought: how to commit the naturalistic fallacy and get away with it in the study of moral development', in T. Mischel (ed.) *Cognitive Development and Epistemology*, New York: Academic Press.

Kristjansson, K. (2004) 'Beyond democratic justice: a further misgiving about Citizenship Education', *Journal of Philosophy of Education*, 38, 2: 207–19.

Kutnik, P. and Jules, V. (1993) 'Pupils' perceptions of a good teacher: a developmental perspective from Trinidad and Tobago', *British Journal of Educational Psychology*, 63, 3: 400–13.

Kymlicka, W. (1999) 'Education for Citizenship', in J. M. Halstead and T. H. McLaughlin (eds) *Education in Morality*, London: Routledge.

Kyriacou, C. (1998) *Essential Teaching Skills*, Cheltenham: Nelson Thornes.

Langer, S. (1957) *Problems of Art – Ten Philosophical Lectures*, London: Routledge & Kegan Paul.

Lawson, H. (2003) 'Citizenship education for pupils with learning difficulties: towards participation?' *Support for Learning*, 18, 3: 117–22.

Leavis, F. R. (1948) *The Great Tradition*, London: Chatto and Windus.

Leavis, F. R. (1975) *The Living Principle: 'English' as a Discipline of Thought*, London: Chatto and Windus.

Lees, J. and Plant, S. (2000) *PASSPORT: a framework for personal and social development*, London: Calouste Gulbenkian Foundation.

Leighton, R. (2004) 'The nature of citizenship education provision: an initial study', *The Curriculum Journal*, 15: 2.

Lewis, C. S. (1943/1978) *The Abolition of Man or Reflections on education with special reference to the teaching of English in the upper forms of schools*, Glasgow: Collins/ Fount Paperbacks.

Lewis, C. S. (1955/1970) *The Magician's Nephew*, New York: Macmillan, Collier Books.

Lickona, T. (1991) *Educating for Character: How our Schools can Teach Respect and Responsibility*, New York: Bantam.

Lickona, T. (1996) 'Eleven principles of effective character education', *Journal of Moral Education*, 25, 1: 93–100.

Life in the UK Advisory Group (2004) *Life in the UK: a journey to citizenship*, London: The Stationery Office.

Linsley, B. and Rayment, E. (eds) (2004) *Beyond the Classroom: exploring active citizenship in 11–16 education*, London: New Politics Network.

Lipman, M. (1984) 'The cultivation of reasoning through philosophy', *Educational Leadership*, 42, 2: 51–6.

Lipman, M. (1987) 'Ethical reasoning and the craft of moral practice', *Journal of Moral Education*, 16, 2: 139–47.

Lister, R. (1997) *Citizenship: Feminist Perspectives*, Basingstoke: Macmillan.

Lovat, T. J. (1995) *Teaching and Learning Religion: a phenomenological approach*, Wentworth Falls, NSW: Social Science Press.

Luke, A., Carrington, V. and Kapitzke, C. (2003) 'Textbooks and early childhood literacy', in J. Marsh (ed.) *Handbook of Early Childhood Literacy*, London: Falmer.

Lynch, J. (1992) *Education for Citizenship in a Multi-cultural Society*, London and New York: Cassell.

Macedo, S. (1990) *Liberal Virtues: Citizenship, Virtues and Community in Liberal Constitutionalism*, Oxford: Clarendon Press.

Macedo, S. (2000) *Diversity and Distrust: civic education in a multicultural democracy*, Cambridge, MA: Harvard University Press.

MacIntyre, A. (1984) *After Virtue. A Study in Moral Theory*, London: Duckworth.

Mannan, M. A. (1986) *Islamic Economics: theory and practice*, Cambridge: Islamic Academy.

Marks, D. (2001) 'Disability and cultural citizenship: exclusion, "integration" and resistance', in N. Stevenson (ed.) *Culture and Citizenship*, London: Sage.

Marks, J. (1984) *Peace Studies in our Schools: propaganda for defencelessness*, London: Women and Families for Defence.

Matthews, M. (1980) *The Marxist Theory of Schooling*, London: Routledge and Kegan Paul.

Maybin, J. (1996) 'An English canon', in N. Mercer and J. Maybin (eds) *Using English: From Conversation to Canon?* London: Routledge.

McCulloch, R. and Mathieson, M. (1995) *Moral Education through English 11–16*, London: David Fulton.

McLaughlin, T. H. (1992) 'Citizenship, diversity and education: a philosophical perspective', *Journal of Moral Education*, 21, 3: 235–50.

McLaughlin, T. H. (1995) 'Public values, private values and educational responsibility', in E. Pybus and T. H. McLaughlin (eds) *Values, Education and Responsibility*, St Andrews: University of St Andrews Centre for Philosophy and Public Affairs.

McLaughlin, T. H. (1999) 'Beyond the reflective practitioner', *Educational Philosophy and Theory*, 31, 1: 9–25.

McLaughlin, T. H. (2000) 'Citizenship education in England: the Crick Report and beyond', *Journal of Philosophy of Education*, 34, 4: 541–70.

McLaughlin, T. H. and Halstead, J. M. (1999) 'Education in character and virtue', in J. M. Halstead and T. H. McLaughlin (eds) *Education in Morality*, London: Routledge.

McLaughlin, T. H and Halstead, J. M. (2000) 'John Wilson on moral education', *Journal of Moral Education*, 29: 3.

McPhail, P., Ungoed-Thomas, J. R. and Chapman, H. (1972) *Moral Education in the Secondary School*, London: Longman Group Limited.

Mead, N. (2000) 'Researching skills common to Religious Education and Citizenship', in S. Clipson-Boyles (ed.) *Putting Research into Practice in Primary Teaching and Learning*, London: Fulton.

Mead, N. (2001) 'Identifying pedagogic skills common to primary Religious Education and PSHE/Citizenship and the implications for continuing professional development', *Curriculum*, 22, 2: 43–51.

Mead, N. (2004) 'The provision for Personal, Social, Health Education (PSHE) and

Citizenship in school-based elements of primary initial teacher education', *Pastoral Care*, 22, 2: 19–26.

Mellor, S. and Elliott, M. (1996) *School Ethos and Citizenship*, Melbourne: Australian Council for Educational Research.

Mill, J. S. (1863/1970) *Utilitarianism*, London: Everyman.

Miller, D. (2000a) 'Citizenship: what does it mean and why is it important?' in N. Pearce and J. Hallgarten (eds) *Tomorrow's Citizens: critical debates in citizenship and education*, London: Institute for Public Policy Research.

Miller, D. (2000b) *Citizenship and National Identity*, Cambridge: Polity Press in association with Blackwell Publishers.

Miller, M. C. (1988) *Boxed In: the culture of TV*, Evanston, Ill.: North-western University Press.

Miller, T. (1993) *The Well-tempered Self: citizenship, culture and the postmodern subject*, Baltimore: Johns Hopkins University Press.

Ministry of Education (1949) *Citizens Growing Up: at home, in school and after*, (pamphlet no. 16), London: HMSO.

Modood, T. (1992) *Not Easy Being British: colour, culture and citizenship*, Stoke-on-Trent: Runnymede Trust and Trentham Books.

Molnar, A. (1997) *The Construction of Children's Character*, Chicago: National Society for the Study of Education.

Moore, G. E. (1903) *Principia Ethica*, Cambridge: Cambridge University Press.

Morris, J. G. (1998) *Get the Picture – A Personal History of Photojournalism*, New York: Random House.

Mosley, J. (1993) *Turn Your School Round*, Wisbech: LDA.

Murray, L. (1998) 'Research into the social purposes of schooling: Personal and Social Education in secondary schools in England and Wales', *Pastoral Care*, 16, 3: 28–35.

Nash, R. J. (1997) *Answering the 'Virtuecrats'. A Moral Conversation on Character Education*, New York and London: Teachers College Press.

National Curriculum Council (1990a) *The Whole Curriculum*, (Curriculum Guidance 3), York: NCC.

National Curriculum Council (1990b) *Education for Citizenship*, (Curriculum Guidance 8), York: NCC.

Naugle, D. K. (2002) *Worldview – The History of a Concept*, Cambridge and Grand Rapids, Michigan: Eerdmans.

Newbolt Committee (1921) *The Teaching of English in England*, London: HMSO.

Noddings, N. (1984) *Caring: a Feminine Approach to Ethics and Moral Education*, Berkeley: University of California Press.

Noddings, N. (1992) *The Challenge to Care in Schools: an Alternative Approach to Education*, New York: Teachers College Press.

Noddings, N. (1995) 'Teaching themes of care', *Phi Delta Kappan*, 76, 9: 675–9.

Oakeshott, M. (1956) 'Political education', in P. Laslett (ed.) *Philosophy, Politics and Society*, Oxford: Blackwell.

Oakeshott, M. (1989) *The Voice of Liberal Learning*, ed. T. Fuller, New Haven, CT: Yale University Press.

OCR (Oxford, Cambridge and the Royal Society of Arts Examination Board) (2004) *GCSE Citizenship Studies Examination Paper*, Foundation Tier, Summer.

Office for Standards in Education (2004a) *Initial teacher training for teachers of citizenship 2003/4: overview*, HMI report 2299, London: Ofsted.

Office for Standards in Education (2004b) *Promoting and Evaluating Pupils' Spiritual, Moral, Social and Cultural Development*, London: Ofsted.

Office for Standards in Education (2005a) *Citizenship in secondary schools: evidence from Ofsted inspections (2003/2004)*, HMI report 2335, London: Ofsted.

Office for Standards in Education (2005b) *Personal, Social and Health Education in Secondary Schools*, HMI report 2311, London, Ofsted.

Okin, S. M. (1992) *Women in Western Political Thought*, (revised edition), Princeton: Princeton University Press.

Osler, A. (ed.) (2000) *Citizenship and Democracy in Schools: diversity, identity, equality*, Stoke-on-Trent: Trentham Books.

Osler, A. and Starkey, H. (2000) 'Intercultural education and foreign language learning: issues of racism, identity and modernity', *Race, Ethnicity and Education*, 3: 2.

Osler, A. and Starkey, H. (2004) *Changing Citizenship – Democracy and Inclusion in Education*, Buckingham: Open University Press.

Osler, A. and Starkey, H. (2005) *Citizenship and Language Learning: international perspectives*, Stoke-on-Trent: Trentham.

Oxfam (1997) *A Curriculum for Global Citizenship*, Oxfam: London.

Pagano, J. (1991) 'Relating to one's students: identity, morality, stories and questions', *Journal of Moral Education*, 20, 3: 257–66.

Palmer, P. (1983) *To Know As We Are Known*, London: HarperCollins.

Parekh, B. (1991) 'British citizenship and cultural difference', in G. Andrews (ed.) *Citizenship*, London: Lawrence and Wishart.

Parker, W. (2001) 'Towards enlightened political engagement', in W. Stanley (ed.) *Critical Issues in Social Studies Research*, Greenwich: Information Age Press.

Passy, R. A. (2003) 'Children and family values: a critical appraisal of "family" in schools', unpublished PhD thesis, University of Plymouth.

Pateman, C. (1989) 'Feminist critiques of the public/private dichotomy', in C. Pateman (ed.) *The Disorder of Women: democracy, feminism and political theory*, Cambridge: Polity Press.

Pearce, N. and Hallgarten, J. (2000) 'Introduction', in N. Pearce and J. Hallgarten (eds) *Tomorrow's Citizens: critical debates in citizenship and education*, London: Institute for Public Policy Research.

Pestridge, J. (ed.) (2002) *Citizens of faith: making a difference*, Birmingham: Christian Education Publications.

Peters, R. S. (1974) *Psychology and Ethical Development*, London: George Allen and Unwin.

Phillips, A. (1991) 'Citizenship and feminist politics', in G. Andrews (ed.) *Citizenship*, London: Lawrence and Wishart.

Phillips, A. (2000) 'Second-class citizenship', in N. Pearce and J. Hallgarten (eds), *Tomorrow's Citizens: critical debates in citizenship and education*, London: Institute for Public Policy Research.

Pike, G. and Selby, D. (1988) *Global Teacher, Global Learner*, London: Hodder and Stoughton.

Pike, M. A. (2000a) 'Pupils' poetics', *Changing English – studies in reading and culture*, 7, 1: 45–54.

Pike, M. A. (2000b) 'Spirituality, morality, poetry', *International Journal of Children's Spirituality*, 5, 2: 177–91.

Pike, M.A. (2000c) 'Keen readers: adolescents and pre-twentieth century poetry', *Educational Review*, 52, 1: 13–28.

Pike, M. A. (2002) 'Aesthetic distance and the spiritual journey: educating for morally and spiritually significant events across the art and literature curriculum', *International Journal of Children's Spirituality*, 7, 1: 9–21.

Pike, M. A. (2003a) 'From personal to social transaction: a model of aesthetic reading', *Journal of Aesthetic Education*, 37, 2: 61–72.

Pike, M. A. (2003b) 'From the picture to the diagram? Literacy and the art of English teaching', *The Use of English*, 54, 3: 211–16.

Pike, M. A. (2003c) 'The canon in the classroom: students' experiences of texts from other times', *Journal of Curriculum Studies*, 35, 3: 355–70.

Pike, M. A. (2003d) 'The Bible and the reader's response', *Journal of Education and Christian Belief*, 7, 1: 37–52.

Pike, M. A. (2003e) 'Belief as an obstacle to reading? The case of the Bible', *Journal of Beliefs and Values*, 24, 2: 155–63.

Pike, M. A. (2003f) 'On being in English teaching: a time for Heidegger?', *Changing English – studies in reading and culture*, 10, 1: 91–9.

Pike, M. A. (2004a) *Teaching Secondary English*, London: Paul Chapman.

Pike, M. A. (2004b) 'Aesthetic teaching', *Journal of Aesthetic Education*, 38, 2: 20–37.

Pike, M. A. (2004c) 'Well-being through reading: drawing upon literature and literacy in spiritual education', *International Journal of Children's Spirituality*, 9, 2: 155–62.

Pike, M. A. (2004d) 'The challenge of Christian schooling in a liberal democracy', *Journal of Research on Christian Education*, 13, 2: 149–66.

Pike, M. A. (2005a) 'Citizenship Education and Faith Schools: What should children in Christian schools understand and appreciate about a liberal and secular society?' *Journal of Education and Christian Belief*, 9, 1: 35–46.

Pike, M. A. (2005b) 'Reading and responding to Biblical texts: aesthetic distance and the spiritual journey', in C. Ota and C. Erricker (eds) *Spiritual Education – Literary, Empirical and Pedagogical Approaches*, Brighton: Sussex Academic Press.

Poster, M. (1995) *The Second Media Age*, Cambridge: Polity Press.

Postman, N. (1992) *Technopoly: The Surrender of Culture to Technology*, New York: Alfred A. Knopf.

Potter, J. (2002) *Active Citizenship in Schools: a good-practice guide to developing a whole-school policy*, London: Kogan Page.

Poulson, C. L, and Kymissis, E. (1988) 'Generalised imitation in infants', *Journal of Experimental Child Psychology*, 46, 3: 324–36.

Powell, R., Chambers Cantrell, S. and Adams, S. (2005) 'Saving Black Mountain: the promise of critical literacy in a multicultural society', in G. Moss (ed.) *Critical Reading in the Content Areas 2004/2005*, Dubuque, IA: McGraw Hill/Dishking.

Priestley, J. (1987) 'Comic role or cosmic vision? Religious Education and the teaching of values', in J. Thacker, R. Pring and D. Evans (eds) *Personal, Social and Moral Education in a Changing World*, Windsor: NFER-Nelson.

Pring, R. (1984) *Personal and Social Education in the Curriculum*, London: Hodder and Stoughton.

Print, M. and Coleman, D. (2003) 'Towards understanding of social capital and citizenship education', *Cambridge Journal of Education*, 33, 1: 123–49.

Pritchard, I. (1988) 'Character education: research, prospects and problems', *American Journal of Education*, 96, 4: 469–95.

Prosser, J. (ed.) (1998) *Image-based Research*, London: RoutledgeFalmer.

Purpel, D. E. (1997) 'The politics of character education', in A. Molnar (ed.) *The Construction of Children's Character*, Chicago: National Society for the Study of Education.

Qualifications and Curriculum Authority (2000a) *Personal, Social and Health Education at Key Stages 1 and 2: initial guidance for schools*, London: QCA.

Qualifications and Curriculum Authority (2000b) *Personal, Social and Health Education at Key Stages 3 and 4: initial guidance for schools*, London: QCA.

Qualifications and Curriculum Authority (2000c) *Religious Education: non-statutory guidance on RE 5–16*, London: DfEE.

Qualifications and Curriculum Authority (2000d) *Religious Education and Collective Worship, an analysis of 1999 SACRE reports*, London: QCA.

Qualifications and Curriculum Authority (2001a) *Citizenship at Key Stages 3 and 4. Initial guidance for schools*, London: QCA.

Qualifications and Curriculum Authority (2001b) *Citizenship: a scheme of work for Key Stage 3*, London: QCA.

Qualifications and Curriculum Authority (2001c) *Citizenship through Religious Education at Key Stage 3*, London: QCA.

Qualifications and Curriculum Authority (2001d) *Citizenship through Geography at Key Stage 3*, London: QCA.

Qualifications and Curriculum Authority (2002a) *Citizenship: a scheme for work for Key Stage 4*, London: QCA.

Qualifications and Curriculum Authority (2002b) *Citizenship at Key Stages 1–4: guidance on assessment, recording and reporting*, London: QCA.

Qualifications and Curriculum Authority (2004) *Personal, Social and Health Education: 2002–3 annual report on curriculum and assessment*, London: QCA.

Qualifications and Curriculum Authority/Department for Education and Employment (1998) *Teaching: high status, high standards: Circular 4/98*, London: HMSO.

Qualifications and Curriculum Authority/Department for Education and Employment (1999a) *Citizenship – The National Curriculum for England*, London: QCA.

Qualifications and Curriculum Authority/Department for Education and Employment (1999b) *Geography – The National Curriculum for England*, London: HMSO.

Qualifications and Curriculum Authority/Department for Education and Employment (1999c) *History – The National Curriculum for England*, London: HMSO.

Raths, L. E., Harmin, M. and Simon, S. B. (1966) *Values and Teaching: Working with Values in the Classroom*, Columbus, OH: Charles E. Merrill.

Rawls, J. (1993) *Political Liberalism*, New York: Columbia University Press.

Raz, J. (1986) *The Morality of Freedom*, Oxford: Clarendon.

Rest, J. (1988) 'Why does college promote development in moral judgement?' *Journal of Moral Education*, 17, 3: 183–94.

Rhodes, J. (1990) 'Telling off: methods and morality', *Pastoral Care*, 8, 4: 32–4.

Richardson, D. (2001) 'Extending Citizenship: cultural citizenships and sexuality', in N. Stevenson (ed.) *Culture and Citizenship*, London: Sage.

Rosenblatt, L. (1985) 'The transactional theory of the literary work: implications for research', in C. R. Cooper (ed.) *Researching Response to Literature and the Teaching of Literature*, London and New York: Ablex.

Ross, G. M. (1996) 'Socrates versus Plato: the origins and development of Socratic thinking', *Thinking: the Journal of Philosophy for Children*, 12, 4: 2–8.

Rotblat, J. (2002) 'Citizenship and Science', *Physics Education*, 37, 3: 186–90.

Rousseau, J.-J. (1762/1911) *Emile*, London: Dent.

Rowe, D. (1996) 'The business of school councils: a investigation into democracy in schools', unpublished report, available from Citizenship Foundation.

Rowe, D. and Newton, J. (1997) *Aims of Citizenship Education*, London: Citizenship Foundation.

Ryle, G. (1972) 'Can virtue be taught?' in R. F. Dearden, P. H. Hirst and R. S. Peters (eds) *Education and the Development of Reason*, London: Routledge and Kegan Paul.

Sachdev, D. (1996) 'Racial prejudice and racial discrimination: whither British youth?' in H. Roberts and D. Sachdev (eds) *Young People's Social Attitudes. Having Their Say – the views of 12–19 Year Olds*, Ilford: Barnardos.

Sartre, J.-P. (1948/1971) *Existentialism and Humanism*, London: Methuen.

School Curriculum and Assessment Authority (1995) *Spiritual and Moral Development*, SCAA Discussion Papers: No. 3, London: SCAA.

School Curriculum and Assessment Authority (1996a) *Education for Adult Life: the Spiritual and Moral Development of Young People*, SCAA Discussion Papers: No. 6, London: SCAA.

School Curriculum and Assessment Authority (1996b) *The National Forum for Values in Education and the Community. Final Report and Recommendations*, SCAA/96/43, London: SCAA.

Schools Council (1970) *The Humanities Project: an introduction*, London: Heinemann Educational.

Schrag, F. (1999) 'Why Foucault now?' *Journal of Curriculum Studies*, 31, 4: 375–83.

Scruton, R. (1984) *The Meaning of Conservatism*, 2nd edn, London: Macmillan.

Scruton, R. (1985) *World Studies: education as indoctrination*, London: Institute for European Defence and Strategic Studies.

Seerveld, C. (1995) *A Christian Critique of Art and Literature*, Sioux Centre, Iowa: Dordt College Press.

Selden, R. and Widdowsen, P. (1993) *A Reader's Guide to Contemporary Literary Theory*, 3rd edn, Lexington KN: University of Kentucky Press.

Sevenhuijsen, S. (1998) *Citizenship and the Ethics of Care: feminist considerations on justice, morality and politics*, London: Routledge.

Shaver, J. P. and Strong, W. (1976) *Facing Value Decisions: Rationale-building for Teachers*, Belmont, CA: Wadsworth.

Shortt, J. (1980) *Towards a Reformed Epistemology and its Significance for Education*, unpublished PhD thesis, University of London.

Simon, S. B., Howe, L. W. and Kirschenbaum, H. (1972) *Values Clarification: A Handbook of Practical Strategies for Teachers and Students*, New York: Hart.

Skinner, G. and McCollum, A. (2004) 'Values education, citizenship and the challenge of cultural diversity', in R. Bailey (ed.) *Teaching Values and Citizenship Across the Curriculum: educating children for the world*, London: RoutledgeFalmer.

Slater, J. (1993) 'Where there is dogma, let us sow doubt', in P. Lee, J. Slater, P. Walsh, and J. White, *The Aims of School History: The National Curriculum and Beyond*, London: Institute of Education, University of London.

Small, T. (2004) *Developing Citizenship in Schools*, Bristol: Doveton Press.

Smart, J. C. C. and Williams, B. (1973) *Utilitarianism: for and against*, Cambridge: Cambridge University Press.

Smetana, J. G. and Braeges, J. L. (1990) 'The development of toddlers' moral and conventional judgments', *Merrill-Palmer Quarterly*, 36: 329–46.

Smith, A. and Print, M. (eds) (2003) 'Special Issue: Citizenship Education in Divided Societies', *Cambridge Journal of Education*, 33: 1.

Smith, D. (2004) 'The poet, the child and the blackbird: aesthetic reading and spiritual development', *International Journal of Children's Spirituality*, 9, 2: 143–54.

Smith, D. and Shortt, J. (2005) 'Editorial: Technology, learning and the "Ephesian moment"', *Journal of Education and Christian Belief*, 9, 1: 3–6.

Smith, D. I. (2004) 'Technology and pedagogical meaning: lessons from the language classroom', *Christian Scholar's Review*, XXXIII, 4, Summer 2004.

Speaker's Commission in Citizenship (1990) *Encouraging Citizenship*, London: HMSO.

Stibbs, A. (1998) 'Language in art and art in language', *Journal of Art and Design Education*, 17, 2: 201–9.

Stibbs, A. (2000) 'Can you (almost) read a poem backwards and view a painting upside down? Restoring aesthetics to poetry teaching', *Journal of Aesthetic Education*, 34, 2: 37–47.

Stibbs, A. (2001) 'For how long, where, and with whom: narrative time, place and company as generic distinguishers and ideological indicators', *Changing English*, 8, 1: 35–42.

Stow, W. (2000) 'History: values in the diversity of human experience', in R. Bailey (ed.) *Teaching Values and Citizenship Across the Curriculum: Educating children for the world*, London: RoutledgeFalmer.

Straughan, R. (1982) *I Ought to But . . . A Philosophical Approach to the Problem of Weakness of Will in Education*, Windsor: NFER-Nelson.

Straughan, R. (1988) *Can We Teach Children to be Good? Basic Issues in Moral, Personal and Social Education*, Milton Keynes: Open University Press.

Straughan, R. (1999) 'Weakness, wants and the will', in J. M. Halstead and T. H. McLaughlin (eds) *Education in Morality*, London: Routledge.

Strike, K. A. (1982b) *Educational Policy and the Just Society*, Urbana, IL: University of Illinois Press.

Tappan, M. B. and Brown, L. M. (1989) 'Stories told and lessons learned: toward a narrative approach to moral development and education', *Harvard Educational Review*, 59, 2: 182–205.

Tate, N. (1995) 'Teach children to be British idea stirs up a storm', *The Guardian*, 19 July 1995.

Tattum, D. and Tattum, E. (1992) *Social Education and Personal Development*, London: David Fulton.

Taylor, M. J. (1989) *Religious Education, Values and Worship: LEA advisers' perspectives on the implementation of the Education Reform Act 1988*, Slough: NFER.

Taylor, M. J. (ed.) (1994) *Values Education in Europe: a Comparative Overview of a Survey of 26 Countries in 1993*, Dundee: SCCC for UNESCO/CIDREE.

Taylor, M. J. (1996) 'Voicing their values: pupils' moral and cultural experience', in J. M. Halstead and M. J. Taylor (eds) *Values in Education and Education in Values*, London: Falmer Press.

Taylor, M. J. (2003) *Going Round in Circles: implementing and learning from circle time*, Slough: NFER.

Taylor, M. J and Johnson, R. (2002) *School Councils: their role in Citizenship and Personal and Social Education*, Slough: NFER.

Teece, G. (1998) 'Citizenship education and religious education: threat or opportunity?' *Resource: Journal of the Professional Council for RE*, 21, 1: 7–10.

Thompson, P. (2004a) *Whatever Happened to Religious Education?* Cambridge: Lutterworth Press.

Thompson, P. (2004b) 'Whose confession? Which tradition?', *British Journal of Religious Education*, 26, 1: 61–72.

Tierno, M. J. (1996) 'Teaching as modeling: the impact of teacher behaviours upon student character formation', *The Educational Forum*, 60, 2: 174–80.

Tooley, J. (2000) *Reclaiming Education*, London: Cassell.

Torney-Purta, J. (1996) 'The connections of values education and civic education. The IEA Civic Education Study in twenty countries', paper presented at the *Journal of Moral Education* Conference, University College of St Martin, Lancaster.

Torney-Purta, J., Lehaman, R., Oswald, H. and Schulz, W. (2001) *Citizenship and Education in Twenty-Eight Countries: civic knowledge and engagement at age fourteen*, Amsterdam: International Association for the Evaluation of Educational Achievement.

Torney-Purta, J., Schwille, J. and Amadeo, J. A. (eds) (1999) *Civic Education Across Countries: Twenty-four National Case Studies from the IEA Civic Education Project*, Amsterdam: The International Association for the Evaluation of Educational Achievement.

Trevaskis, D. K. (1994) *Mediation in Schools*. Bloomington, in ERIC Clearinghouse for Social Studies and Social Science, ERIC Digest.

Trousdale, A. (2004) 'Black and white fire: the interplay of stories, imagination and children's spirituality', *International Journal of Children's Spirituality*, 9, 2: 177–88.

Teacher Training Agency (2002) *Qualifying to Teach: Standards for the Award of QTS*.

Twine, F. (1994) *Citizenship and Social Rights: The Interdependence of Self and Society*, London: Sage.

Ungoed-Thomas, J. (1996) 'Vision, values and virtues', in J. M. Halstead and M. J. Taylor (eds) *Values in Education and Education in Values*, London: Falmer Press.

Verma, G. K., Zec, P. and Skinner, G. D. (1994)*The Ethnic Crucible: harmony and hostility in multi-ethnic schools*, London: Falmer Press.

Veugelers, W. (2000) 'Different ways of teaching values', *Educational Review*, 52: 1.

Vitz, P. C. (1990) 'The use of stories in moral development: new psychological reasons for an old education method', *American Psychologist*, 45, 6: 709–20.

Vygotsky, L. S. (1986) *Thought and Language*, Cambridge, MA: MIT Press.

Vygotsky, L. S. (1971) *The Psychology of Art*, Cambridge, MA: MIT Press.

Walker, L. J. (1986) 'Experimental and cognitive sources of moral development in adulthood', *Human Development*, 29: 113–24.

Walkington, H. (2000) 'Geography, values education and citizenship', in R. Bailey (ed.) *Teaching Values and Citizenship Across the Curriculum: Educating children for the world*, London: RoutledgeFalmer.

Walzer, M. (1980) *Radical Principles: reflections of an unreconstructed democrat*, New York: Basic Books.

Ward, J. V. (1991) '"Eyes in the back of your head": moral themes in African American narratives of racial conflict', *Journal of Moral Education*, 20, 3: 267–81.

Warnock, M. (1979) *Education: The Way Ahead*, Oxford: Blackwell.

Warnock, M. (1996) 'Moral values', in J. M. Halstead, and M. J. Taylor (eds) *Values in Education and Education in Values*, London: Falmer Press.

Watson, J. (2004) 'Educating for Citizenship – the emerging relationship between religious education and citizenship education', *British Journal of Religious Education*, 26, 3: 259–71.

Werner, E. E. and Smith, R. S. (1992) *Overcoming the Odds: High Risk Children from Birth to Adulthood*, Ithaca, NY: Cornell University Press.

Wexler, P. (1990) 'Citizenship in the semiotic society', in B. Turner (ed.) *Theories of Modernity and Postmodernity*, London: Sage.

White, J. (1989) 'The aims of personal and social education', in P. White (ed.) *Personal and Social Education: philosophical perspectives*, London: Kogan Page.

White, J. (1993) 'The purpose of school history: has the National Curriculum got it right?' in P. Lee, J. Slater, P. Walsh, and J. White, *The Aims of School History: The National Curriculum and Beyond*, London: Institute of Education, University of London.

White, P. (1996) *Civic Virtues and Public Schooling: educating citizens for a democratic society*, New York: Teachers College Press.

Whitty, G., Rowe, G. and Aggleton, P. (1994) 'Subjects and themes in the secondary school curriculum', *Research Papers in Education*, 9, 2: 159–81.

Wilson, J. (1973) *A Teacher's Guide to Moral Education*, London: Geoffrey Chapman.

Wilson, J. (1990) *A New Introduction to Moral Education*, London: Cassell.

Wilson, J. (1995) *Love Between Equals. A philosophical study of love and sexual relationships*, London: Macmillan.

Wilson, J. (1996) 'First steps in moral education', *Journal of Moral Education*, 25: 85–91.

Wilson, J. and Cowell, B. (1987) 'Method, content and motivation in moral education', *Journal of Moral Education*, 16: 31–6.

Wilson, J. B., Williams, N. and Sugarman, B. (1967) *Introduction to Moral Education*, Middlesex: Penguin Books.

Winston, J. (1999) 'Theorising drama as moral education', *Journal of Moral Education*, 28, 4: 459–71.

Witte-Townsend, D. and DiGiulo, E. (2004) 'Something from nothing: exploring dimensions of children's knowing through the repeated reading of favourite books', *International Journal of Children's Spirituality*, 9, 2: 127–42.

Woff, R. (1991) 'The scope of the humanities', in P. Gordon (ed.) *Teaching the Humanities*, London: Woburn Press.

Wolterstorff, N. (2002) *Educating for Life*, Grand Rapids, Michigan: Baker Academic.

Woolfson, R. (1995) 'True or false – do children mean to lie?' *Nursery World*, 95, 23.3.95: 12–13.

Wray, D. and Lewis, M. (1997) *Extending Literacy: Reading and Writing Non-fiction in the Primary School*, London: Routledge.

Wright, A. (1996) 'The child in relationship: towards a communal model of spirituality', in R. Best (ed.) *Education, Spirituality and the Whole Child*, London: Cassell.

Wright, A. (2000) *Spirituality and Education*, London: RoutledgeFalmer.

Wringe, C. (1992) 'The ambiguities of education for active citizenship', *Journal of Philosophy of Education*, 26, 1: 29–38.

Wynn, E. A. and Ryan, K. (1992) *Reclaiming our Schools: a Handbook on Teaching Character, Academics and Discipline*, New York: Merrill.

Yeatman, A. (2001) 'Feminism and citizenship', in N. Stevenson (ed.) *Culture and Citizenship*, London: Sage.

Young, I. M. (1989) 'Polity and group difference: a critique of the ideal of universal citizenship', *Ethics*, 99, 2: 250–74.

Young, I. M. (1990) *Justice and the Politics of Difference*, Princeton, NJ: Princeton University Press.

Index

absolutism 17
Achebe, C. 76
active citizenship 10, 35–40, 51–3, 55–6,
    64–6 , 92, 156–7; morality of assessing
    156–8, 164–5; through the arts 64, 79
adult example 169–70
Advisory Group on Citizenship (AGC) 12,
    14, 37, 156, 168, 171–2
aesthetic: distance 68, 70, 79–81; needs
    65–6; response 65, 79–81
AfL 160
aims of Citizenship Education 34–40
aims of Moral Education 40–3
Amazon rainforest 87–8
Arthur, J & Wright, D. 155, 157
art and design education 70–4
Arts 64–81; and citizenship 64–81; and
    cultural literacy 68–70; and social
    satire 73–4; as worship 67–8; canonical
    70; censorship of 74; Christian
    perspectives on 69, 76–7; English and
    the language arts 74–7; drama 77–9,
    126–7; for active citizenship 64, 79; for
    reflection upon values 65; for moral
    development 66–8, 79–81; for social
    engagement 66; graffiti artists 71–2;
    Islamic 69; taxes to fund 66; to foster
    empathy 66
ASBO 97, 161
assessing Citizenship 151–65;
    justifications for 152–3; methods of
    158–60; problems with 151–6
audit of Citizenship provision 125
autonomy 99–101

Bell, D. 123–5, 129, 130
bias 55–7, 60–2
Bible 61

Boccaccio's *Decameron* 62
British Empire 94

censorship 74, 89
change, preparing children for 173–4
character 16
character education 32, 44, 140–1
child protection 74
Christianity 8, 15–16, 61–2, 93, 100, 110,
    111–12, 118
circle time 148–9
citizenship: autonomous 38–40; British
    7–9; committed 35–8; concept of 7–11;
    definitions of 124–5; European 8;
    global 8, 87–8, 89–90; informed 34–5,
    86; multiple 8; national 8, 90–2; tests
    69; *see also* active citizenship
Citizenship Education 11–12, 34;
    definitions of 11–14, 124–5; history of
    11; purposes of 33; new subject 127;
    government control of 151–2
civic virtues 37, 39, 141
common schools 45,101
commonwealth 86
community cohesion 173
community involvement 35–6, 38, 39, 147
conflict resolution 68, 106, 129
conservative and radical critiques 14
controversial issues 137–8, 150
Crick, B. 10, 12, 38, 118, 156
crisis in values 167–8
critical distance 120
critical literacy 52–6, 132
critical reflection 27, 38–40, 43, 44, 65
critical thinking 150
cross-cultural understanding 56–7
cross-curricular approaches 125–7, 130–1
cultural difference 70